GENDER, HEALTH, AND ILLNESS

A **Health Care for Women International** Publication

Phyllis Noerager Stern, DNS, RN, FAAN, *Editor*

Women, Health, and Culture *Stern*
Culture, Society, and Menstruation *Olesen and Woods*
Women's Work, Families, and Health: The Balancing Act *Swanson-Kauffman*
Pregnancy and Parenting *Stern*
Gender, Health, and Illness: The Case of Nerves *Davis and Low*

GENDER, HEALTH, AND ILLNESS

The Case of Nerves

Edited by

Dona L. Davis, Ph.D.
Department of Social Behavior,
University of South Dakota,
Vermillion, South Dakota

and

Setha M. Low, Ph.D.
Ph.D. Programs in Environmental Psychology and Anthropology
Graduate School and University Center
City University of New York
New York, New York

HEMISPHERE PUBLISHING CORPORATION
A member of the Taylor & Francis Group

New York Washington Philadelphia London

NOTICE

Because this volume is appearing as an issue of *Health Care for Women International,* as well as a hardbound book, it was necessary to use a numbering system that would incorporate both the continuous journal page numbers and the book page numbers. The pages are double-numbered as follows: page 1 of the book is equivalent to page 93 of the journal. The numbers appear on the pages as journal page number followed by book page number in brackets.

GENDER, HEALTH, AND ILLNESS: The Case of Nerves

1 2 3 4 5 6 7 8 9 0 B R B R 8 9 8 7 6 5 4 3 2 1 0 9

This book was set in Times Roman by Hemisphere Publishing Corporation. The editors were Carolyn V. Ormes and Deborah Klenotic. The production supervisor was Peggy M. Rote, and the typesetter was Laurie E. Agee.

Library of Congress Cataloging-in-Publication Data

Gender, health, and illness: the case of nerves / edited by Dona L.
Davis and Setha Low.
p. cm.—(A Health care for women international publication)
Includes bibliographies and index.
1. Anxiety—Sex factors. 2. Depression, Mental—Sex factors.
3. Anxiety—Cross-cultural studies. 4. Depression, Mental—Cross
-cultural studies. 5. Psychiatry, Transcultural. I. Davis, Dona
Lee, 1948- . II. Low, Setha M. III. Series.
[DNLM: 1. Anxiety Disorders—ethnology. 2. Culture.
3. Depression—ethnology. 4. Identification (Psychology). Wm 171
G325].
RDC531.G46 1989
616.85'223—dc20

ISBN 0-89116-903-2

CONTENTS

CONTRIBUTORS

ELYSE ANN BARNETT, PhD
Department of Anthropology
Foothill College
Los Altos, California

LINDA A. CAMINO, PhD
International Counseling Center
Washington, DC

MARI H. CLARK, PhD
Office of Women in Development
Agency for International Development
Washington, DC

DONA L. DAVIS, PhD
Department of Social Behavior
University of South Dakota
Vermillion, South Dakota

RUTHBETH FINERMAN, PhD
Department of Anthropology
Memphis State University
Memphis, Tennessee

KAJA FINKLER, PhD
Department of Anthropology
University of North Carolina
Chapel Hill, North Carolina

MARGARITA KAY, PhD
College of Nursing
University of Arizona
Tucson, Arizona

JOAN D. KOSS-CHIOINO, PhD
Department of Psychiatry
University of New Mexico
School of Medicine
Albuquerque, New Mexico

LAURIE KRIEGER, PhD
Program for Appropriate Technology in Health (PATH)
Washington, DC

SETHA M. LOW, PhD
PhD Programs in Environmental Psychology and Anthropology
Graduate School and University Center
City University of New York
New York, New York

CARMEN PORTILLO, MS
College of Nursing
University of Arizona
Tucson, Arizona

JEFFREY A. SLUKA, PhD
Department of Social Anthropology
Massey University
Palmerston North
New Zealand

FOREWORD

THE WORLD CONNECTION

Dona Davis and Setha Low have collected a world view on a single syndrome that plagues us all: nerves. We frame having nerves differently, though, and that's what this volume is all about: accounts of how the cultural beliefs of individuals affect their perceptions of what having nerves means.

The concept of examining cultural beliefs around a single theme is exciting. The view of life held by exotic people is enormously interesting to us, because of its seeming strangeness. When we read about *nerfiza* or *nervios* or *nevra* they seem alien conditions that people far away might experience. We may even smile at the idea that people believe these conditions exist. Queer people who affirm queer words.

But when we read about people "living on their nerves" in Northern Ireland, or the meaning of "nerves" for lower class black women in the southern United States, the foreign begins to define the familiar. Suddenly we see nerves as a Western phenomenon too. Otherwise, why would words and phrases connected with nerves be an integral part of our language: "lost his nerve," "nerves are shot," "nervous breakdown," "you're getting on my nerves." Paul Shaffer, bandleader and musical director of NBC's "Late Night with David Letterman" told an interviewer recently that he doesn't do much composing because it makes him nervous—and that he "threw up" while he was writing the theme for the show.

Nerves as a metaphor for distress is detailed here. Those of us who are interested in the health care of women (and men too, as it turns out) may wonder what our response to this syndrome should be. Respectful attention, these authors seem to say, is an excellent beginning.

Phyllis Noerager Stern

PREFACE

Nerves[1] is a popular illness category and idiom for emotional and social distress that exhibits similar symptoms in a variety of cultural settings. In each culture, a complex set of meanings related to physical and mental health, interpersonal and family relationships, socioeconomic and political exploitation, and rapid culture change defines this pervasive health complaint. Nerves has attracted the attention of researchers in medical anthropology and psychiatry who have completed a series of baseline studies identifying its etiological and nosological characteristics and its sufferers, many of whom are women. However, even though researchers suggest that women are more likely to suffer from nerves than men, there has not been a systematic exploration of the relationship between gender and nerves. In this collection we offer a comprehensive examination of this relationship by bringing together cross-cultural and cross-disciplinary articles that address theoretical, methodological, and applied aspects of gender, illness, and nerves.

Contributors were invited to consider a number of themes—the biology and epidemiology of nerves; interpersonal and social relationships that affect nerves; the social construction of gender, symbolic, and affective dimensions of nerves; and clinical models and treatment of nerves—within the context of their fieldwork experience. The resulting articles reflect a variety of theoretical and methodological approaches to these themes within diverse cultural and institutional settings.

The collection begins with historical perspective on gender and illness provided by Davis's analysis of nerves and neurasthenia in late 19th century North America, followed by fieldwork studies organized by culture area. Section I on Latin America includes studies of *nervios* by Low on residents in a resettled urban neighborhood in Guatemala, by Finerman on rural women in Ecuador, by Barnett on women in a rapidly changing Peruvian town, and by Finkler, who draws on fieldwork in rural Mexico and the American South. Section II includes studies from the Mediterranean area by Krieger on *nerfiz* in urban Egypt and by Clark on *nevra* in rural Greece. A northern European study of nerves in Ireland is described by Sluka. Section III focuses on ethnic minorities in the United States and includes studies by Koss-Chioino on mental health and Spiritist patients in Puerto Rico, by Kay and Portillo on bereaved Mexican Americans, and by Camino on urban southern Blacks in America. The methodological, theoretical, and applied issues presented in these articles are outlined below.

---

[1]We use the term *nerves* to refer to the complex of nerves/*nervios*/*nevra*/*nerfiz*. When referring to the specific articles in this issue we use the terms appropriate to the cultural group.

METHODOLOGICAL ISSUES

The studies emphasize the description and analysis of the sociocultural context of nerves based on case histories of nerves sufferers and ethnographic observation of local community life. Although the majority of the projects were specifically designed to study nerves, some studies—Sluka's work on terrorism in Northern Ireland and Barnett's study of menopause on Peru—elicited these data indirectly.

A wide range of methods and research strategies were used, although the majority of the studies were fundamentally ethnographic in approach and research design. Davis drew on her previous field experience in Newfoundland and her earlier historical study on the English heritage of nerves to reveal the importance of Lydia Pinkham and George Beard in defining the condition of nerves in North American middle and lower classes. Clark, Finerman, Low, and Camino combined participant observation with formal and informal individual interviews to create detailed community-based descriptions of nerves sufferers. Sluka supplemented his ethnographic study with news reports and commentary from the Irish press. Using a biocultural approach, Barnett included physical assessments of women's hypertension in her community study, and Krieger's approach consists of life history analysis of a woman that she has known for more than 10 years.

For a number of the studies, community ethnography was only one part of the research methodology. Finkler and Koss-Chioino both observed healers—spiritualist healers in Mexico and spiritist healers and mental health professionals and doctors in Puerto Rico, respectively—thus adding a clinical dimension to their fieldwork. Kay and Portillo, Low, and Koss-Chioino were involved in large-scale health studies and participated as part of research teams. These studies, as well as the study by Barnett, employed standardized psychological, health, and socioeconomic assessments requiring structured interviewing techniques. In each study, the methods selected corresponded to the size of the research sample, which varied from a single case history presented by Krieger to samples of more than 100 individuals reported by Low, Kay and Portillo, Barnett, and Koss-Chioino.

Some of the methodological issues involved in the study of nerves, however, are not yet resolved. For example, a problem inherent in gender-based sampling is whether to study more women in order to obtain an adequate sample to describe the phenomenon among women, or, alternatively, to study an equal number of men and women in order to determine the incidence of the phenomenon in both groups. Each author attempts to address some aspect of this dilemma, but the lack of social epidemiological data on folk illness and the difficulties female researchers encounter working with men in some cultural settings confound other methodological concerns. Further, because the theoretically relevant samples of nerves sufferers are not the same in each culture, the studies are not strictly comparable. The findings can be interpreted only in the context of the specific cultural setting. Nonetheless, the diversity of methodological approaches and the context-dependent discussions of the meaning of nerves take us a long way toward understanding the phenomenon as embedded in each cultural setting.

THEORETICAL ISSUES: GENDER AND NERVES

One basic question that emerges in any discussion of nerves and gender is to what degree nerves is a gender-related illness. Barnett characterizes *nervios* as an exclusively female disease. Finerman, Camino, Low, Sluka, and Davis report that although nerves exists among both men and women, it is predominantly reported by and endemic to the women in their study populations. Koss-Chioino and Finkler are more hesitant to label nerves as a female complaint, and stress that *nervios* among women takes on different forms and meanings than among men. Clark, on the other hand, argues that in Methana, Greece, *nevra* is associated with age rather than gender so that older Greeks suffer more often regardless of gender.

A number of the studies found nerves to be a female expression of general social or emotional distress that men express in other symptomatic forms or with other kinds of behaviors. Camino and Sluka identify excessive alcohol consumption as the male counterpart to female nerves. Low's analysis of symptoms associated with nerves indicates that men report more somatic complaints and women more emotional ones, and Koss-Chioino found that contrasting sets of male and female symptoms were measured by standard anxiety scales. These findings suggest that although gender plays a role in modeling the expression of nerves, the experience of nerves is not necessarily gender specific.

Gender roles, however, do influence the way that nerves functions in women's daily lives. Finerman, Barnett, Krieger, and Kay and Portillo describe nerves as an important sick role for women that provides secondary gains in the form of access to new resources, social support, and a temporary escape from gender-bound definitions of culturally appropriate behavior. Krieger portrays *nerfiz* as an unstigmatized strategy for Egyptian women to jockey for power, emotional fulfillment, and sympathy. Barnett describes how middle-aged Peruvian women use their *nervios* to gain independence and distance themselves from the control of their husbands and family obligations. Finerman demonstrates how *ner-*

vios among Saraguro Indian women in Ecuador enhances their power and social status and helps them to cope with their responsibilities. And Kay and Portillo describe how *nervios* among Mexican American widows is part of a rich and highly differentiated vocabulary of sorrow related to these women's central role in the family.

In other cultural settings, however, nerves may reinforce negative aspects of cultural roles and work against social cohesion and support. Camino's study of nerves among southern Black women challenges assumptions about the communicative power of nerves as an idiom of distress. Nerves in this subculture is a female condition that does not activate helpful social support systems. And Clark argues that whereas younger rural Greek women retain their secure and respected place in village life, it is primarily elderly men and women, marginalized within their own culture by modernization and separated from traditional social contacts and modes of self-expression, who resort to *nevra* to express dissatisfaction with their lives.

Other dysfunctional aspects of the relationship between gender and nerves are reflected in the feminization and medicalization of female weakness documented in the studies of Davis and Low, and the relative powerlessness of women cross-culturally that Finkler argues contributes to women's low self-esteem and increased vulnerability to sickness. Nerves is often women's reaction to experiences with violence, poverty, and political oppression that are beyond the control of the individual or her family. Sluka's study of nerves in an Irish Catholic ghetto where there are daily killings and injuries of family members and Low's study of the high incidence of *nervios* and the unspoken fear of killings and accidents in Guatemala City both describe nerves as an indicator of unresolved social conflict. In addition, almost every contributor to this collection has commented on the relationship of gender and nerves as potentially dangerous when "nerves pills" are overprescribed for female sufferers thus promoting female drug abuse.

Nerves as a gender-linked phenomenon has both socially positive and negative consequences. It can release women from the constraints of their culturally defined roles and can activate social support. On the other hand, nerves also acts as a debilitating sick role, separating the sufferer from her family and friends. Finally, labeling emotional and social distress as nerves often sustains conflictual social relations by medicalizing political and socioeconomic problems, thereby placing the burden for the cure on the individual rather than on society.

APPLIED ISSUES: NERVES ETIOLOGY AND TREATMENT

The contributors to this collection describe nerves as an ambiguous and negotiable concept that serves as a metaphor for personal suffering and misfortune, interpersonal discord, social disorder, and social change. Each author then specifies the folk, and in some cases biomedical, explanatory model of nerves and describes how nerves is diagnosed and treated in the particular cultural setting. Explanations of nerves include emotional etiologies such as anger (Low), grief (Low, Kay and Portillo), "upsetness" (Krieger), worry (Clark, Sluka), and "worriation" (Camino); sociopolitical etiologies such as violence (Low, Sluka) and inequality (Krieger, Davis); and socioeconomic etiologies in which nerves is identified as an affliction of the poor (Low, Finkler, Finerman, Krieger, Koss-Chioino, Clark).

The articles herein contain important guidelines for the clinical assessment and treatment of nerves. Finkler and Koss-Chioino compare the treatment modalities of both traditional and medical healers. Barnett, Low, and Camino describe populations in which medical services are either unavailable or too costly, and discuss the choices that women make as they seek alternate treatment. Most of the studies describe women's self-treatment and the use of home and patent remedies and, where medical services were the dominant mode of treatment, the common use of tranquilizers and prescription drugs. Kay and Portillo's analysis of nerves in terms of *Diagnostic and Statistical Manual of Mental Disorders (Third Edition)* categories, Koss-Chioino's clinical model, and Camino's directive to physicians on how to communicate with, diagnose, and support a woman who suffers from nerves specifically address critical issues in the application of a sociocultural understanding of nerves in a medical setting. These studies contribute to our growing appreciation of the role that folk illness and local idioms of distress play both in communicating about physical and social discomfort and in facilitating the treatment of these complaints.

In sum, these studies provide insight into the multidimensional phenomenon of nerves and identify a broad range of characteristics—physical, moral, psychological, social, cultural, political, and economic—that define and describe this phenomenon. More specifically, the authors examine the interconnection of gender and nerves both as a cross-cultural experience and expression and in terms of its function in everyday life. Finally, these studies provide descriptive and prescriptive data for the treatment and interpretation of nerves in clinical settings.

Dona L. Davis
Setha M. Low

GEORGE BEARD AND LYDIA PINKHAM: GENDER, CLASS, AND NERVES IN LATE 19th CENTURY AMERICA

Dona L. Davis
Department of Social Behavior, University of South Dakota

A historical comparison of the careers of George Beard, medical doctor, and Lydia Pinkham, feminist and patent medicine maker, demonstrates the complex social nature of the experience of nerves among late 19th century women. Special attention is paid to the roles played by changing gender and class ideologies in Pinkham's and Beard's theories of nerves during the period from the 1870s to World War I. A comparison of contemporary anthropological and historical studies of gender and nerves leads to the conclusion that nerves, as a female complaint, takes hold of the popular and medical imagination during periods of dramatic social change which threaten women's traditional family roles and challenge their sense of self-identity.

Whereas the fashionable set of the 18th century centered ailments in the liver, elites of late 19th century focused on their nerves (Haller, 1971). Even though the nervous patient, easily fatigued, anxious, and complaining of vague physical ailments, was hardly a novelty to layfolk or medical practitioners of the day, and the complaint was not limited to the upper classes (Davis & Whitten, 1988), it was during this era that medical specialists, such as George Beard, and popular patent medicine makers, such as the Pinkhams, provided a new legitimacy for nervous complaints, especially for women, in the popular media of the day. Beard, a medical doctor, synthesized the symptoms of his urban, educated, upper class patients into a single disease with distinct somatic cause and pathology. This disease was known by several popular labels, including the American Disease, nervousness, nerve weakness, nervous exhaustion, or neurasthenia (Rosenberg, 1962). At the same time Lydia Pinkham, hailed as the most important businesswoman of her era, marketed her patent medicines as a cure for nerves and female complaints among the less educated, rural, and working classes (Stage, 1979).

Throughout history, nerves has had biological, physical, psychological, moral, and social meaning. The concept of nerves in the Victorian age is of interest to anthropologists because nerves in its various forms lies at the juncture of lay and professional health care beliefs (Davis & Whitten, 1988). During the Victorian era, although medicine was becoming a specialized profession with an ever-deepening claim to scientific knowledge, medical and popular views of health and illness overlapped. Health education was largely a matter of systematizing popular lore (Kleinman, 1983). Although today psychiatrists' concepts of anxiety, irritability, and depression are more differentiated than those of lay people (Leff, 1978), the concepts of melancholia, depression, neurasthenia, and hysteria were all intermingled in the popular and professional imagination of the late 19th century (Jackson, 1986). That neurasthenia could apply to almost any and all disease eventually led physicians to move away from the concept (Haller, 1970); however, it was precisely because of this amorphous character that nerves, the experience of nerves, and the theory of nerves flourished during the late 19th century. Today, as in the past, nerves is an excellent barometer of social concerns and emotional styles of the time and place in which it occurs.

An analysis of the lives and times of Beard and Pinkham and their views about gender, class, and the nature of nerves sheds light on the relationship of 19th century nerves to the nerves disorder extant today. Data for this analysis come from a combination of primary and secondary source materials. These include the biographies of Beard (Dana, 1923; Haller, 1971; Morton, 1883; Rockwell, 1883; Rosenberg, 1962) and Pinkham (Burton, 1949; Stage, 1979; Washburn, 1931), and popular books by Beard (*American Nervousness,* 1881, and *Sexual Neurasthenia,* 1884) and Pinkham (*Guide to Health,* 1893, and *Treatise on the Diseases of Women,* 1901). Copy from Pinkham health education pamphlets, testimonials, and advertising was also used.

BACKGROUND

Nervous Disorders of Women

Because women of the late 19th and early 20th centuries have been characterized as victims of a host of female complaints which were said to have originated in their pelvic organs, this period has been labeled the "Age of the Womb" and the women called "Angelic Invalids" (Drinka, 1985). Much of the literature about the period is dominated by reproductive events and disorders. Emotional or psychological facets of women's illness such as hysteria, anorexia, and neurasthenia, however, have also received scholarly attention (Cayleff, 1988; Davis & Whitten, 1988; Haller, 1971; Littlewood & Lipsedge, 1987; Skultans, 1979;

Turner, 1984; Veith, 1965). The salience and nature of these diseases have been attributed to gender conflict between women and their male physicians (Barker-Benfield, 1976; Daly, 1978; Ehrenreich & English, 1979; Wood, 1984) as well as conflict between male and female gender roles (Haller, 1971; Showalter, 1985; Stage, 1979). In this view, nervous disorders among turn-of-the-century women expressed conflict between their desire to act like individuals and achieve intellectual and financial success on the one hand, and their perceived obligations to conform to the self-sacrificing roles of mother and wife on the other. Neurasthenia and hysteria are seen as exaggerations of core social values of female economic and emotional dependency, which include concentration on marriage and family, reliance on a male provider, living vicariously through others, and lack of power (Littlewood & Lipsedge, 1987; Turner, 1984).

Given these perspectives, it is tempting to presume that (a) Beard, the male physician, medicalized nerves, sought to maintain the status quo of gender relations, and embodied a misogynic male model of women's nervous disorders; and (b) Pinkham, regarded as a feminist in her time, popularized nerves, rejected negative medical stereotypes of women, and embodied a battle of the sexes theme. Indeed, these distinctions have been made. Beard is often cited in a list of the misogynic thinkers of his time (Cayleff, 1988; Ehrenreich & English, 1979; Wood, 1984), and Pinkham is often heralded as a feminist (Stage, 1979; Washburn, 1931) and enlightened sex educator (Burton, 1949) whose ideas were progressive for her time. A closer look at Beard and Pinkham, however, clearly shows that, although they disagreed over the effectiveness of physicians, their perspectives on the nature of gender and illness were largely shared. Their most profound area of disagreement concerned the relationship of nerves to social class. A comparison of their perspectives on social class, however, is problematic since the Pinkham heirs, or the Lydia Pinkham Medical Company (LPMC), came to modify Pinkham's original rather socialistic perspectives on women's health during the 1890s. A brief background sets the scene for the analysis that follows.

The Times of Lydia Pinkham and George Beard

Although both Pinkham and Beard died in 1883, their ideas continued to reflect and influence American attitudes toward health and illness well into the next century. Beard's theories were eventually replaced by those of Freud and, later, modern psychiatry. Pinkham's Vegetable Compound eventually failed to compete with the new analgesic drugs. Despite a decline from popular favor, Pinkham's Vegetable Compound was sold until 1979 (Stage, 1979) and Beard's theories (in modified form) still appear in popular books on nerves (Asher, 1957; Weekes, 1981, 1987).

George Beard

Although he is credited with making neurasthenia a household commodity (Dana, 1923), not much is known about the life of George Beard. His biographers are mainly concerned with placing him in the history of psychiatry by pointing out his advocacy for the rights of the insane and his recognition of a relationship between social factors and mental illness. The "discovery" of neurasthenia, which became nationally and internationally recognized by physicians and laymen as the American Disease, is considered to be his most important contribution to medicine. Beard was born in Montville, Connecticut, in 1839. He graduated from Yale Medical School in 1866, specializing in electrotherapy and diseases of the nervous system. During his career, he wrote a standard treatise on "medical electricity," edited a popular medical encyclopedia, experimented with hypnosis, and carried on a very modest medical practice (Rosenberg, 1962). Beard was chronically in debt (Rockwell, 1883) and suffered from nervous exhaustion (Showalter, 1985).

Although he gained prominence as a nerves specialists, it was the familiarity of the concept rather than its novelty that made Beard's theory so acceptable (Rosenberg, 1962; Davis & Whitten, 1988). Beard was neither a profound nor critical thinker. He was criticized by his contemporaries for seeking notoriety and working selfishly for his own ends (Rockwell, 1883). He published what were essentially the same articles over and over again in different medical and popular scientific journals and then published them as popular books (Rosenberg, 1962). Beard's books *American Nervousness* (1881) and, to a more limited extent, *Sexual Neurasthenia* (1884), were addressed to an educated lay as well as medical public and enjoyed a wide circle of readers (Beard, 1881; Morton, 1883).

Lydia Ellis Pinkham

Lydia Pinkham has attracted the attention of biographers for more than 73 years (Burton, 1949; Hubbard, 1915; Stage, 1979; Washburn, 1931).[1] Early biographers eulogized her as a compassionate, but enter-

---

[1]Lydia's Pinkham's face, used to advertise the Compound, became so famous that it is regarded as a part of American folk culture. Lydia Pinkham and her Compound were commonly the subject of sexual jokes and dirty ditties (Stage, 1979; Washburn, 1931).

prising, feminist heroine. Stage (1979) continued to praise Lydia's radical proclivities, but provided a more critical analysis of her career. Although the biographies are titularly concerned with the life of Lydia Pinkham, they tend to focus on the importance of the LPMC in the history of advertising.

Lydia Ellis was born on a farm in Lynn, Massachusetts, in 1819. Like Beard, she taught school for 2 years. Before her marriage she was an active participant in abolition and social reform movements. She married Charles Pinkham in 1843 and had three sons. Her husband was a sort of ne'er do well and remained in the background as her sons founded and developed the patent medicine company. In 1874, one year after the Panic of 1873 when the Pinkhams lost all their capital in bad investments, the Pinkham family began to market Lydia's home remedy for female complaints—the Vegetable Compound. In 1876 the LPMC was officially formed and in 1879 newspaper advertising began to replace dodgers and door-to-door sales (Stage, 1979). These advertisements invited women to write to Lydia for advice about female complaints. She answered each letter personally and also sent her *Guide to Health* on request. After her death, the products were still advertised as though she were alive although her daughter-in-law and 30 professional correspondents had taken over the role of "Mrs. Pinkham."[2]

Social Change and 19th Century Nerves

The biographies of Pinkham and Beard show a substantial agreement over the major trends leading to the acceptance, popularity, and fluorescence of their respective ideas about nerves.

Pinkham's family began to sell her Vegetable Compound commercially in an era marked by medical controversy, public dissatisfaction with doctors, and concern over women's health and weakness (Stage, 1979). In addition, trends in late 19th century America toward self-medication, confused thinking about the nature of disease, expansion of American newspapers (daily, penny press, city and village papers, and weekly gazettes), opportunity for national advertising, and lack of governmental regulation greatly expanded the market for a wide variety of patent medicines (Young, 1961, 1967) and contributed to Pinkham's suc-

---

[2]Lydia Pinkham died long before the products reached their height of popularity. Original Pinkham copy was revised by James Wetherald, who became the company ad man during the late 1880s. In this article, *Pinkham* is used to refer to Lydia herself, and the *LMPC* [Lydia Pinkham Medical Company] is used to refer to the family business.

cess. Beard's popular books can also be viewed as a form of advertising to a curious, educated, and critical public, concerned and mystified about their health. Beard, rather than advertising a particular product or cure, was promoting himself as a modern man of science, who had discovered a new disease of civilization.

Themes of female weakness dominate Beard's books as well as Pinkham ad copy. During the late 1800s, women's roles were undergoing a rapid and profound change (Haller, 1971; Rosenberg & Smith-Rosenberg, 1981; Stage, 1979; Washburn, 1931). Social instability and urbanization created anxiety and confusion; much of this was mirrored in society's attitude toward women. The role of the female was changing from producer of goods to consumer of goods, and the genteel female and working-class female were to emerge as distinct social types. The women's question, or rights, duties, and privileges of women vis-à-vis those of men, was answered in part by the nature of nerves. Women's nerves were considered more vulnerable than men's nerves to misfortune, overwork, the hectic pace of urban life, and rapid social change (Haller, 1971; Stage, 1979).

No discussion of popular and medical notions of nerves in the late 19th century can take place without a discussion of the changing American class structure and the emergence of nationalism and urbanism during the late 19th century. Nervousness, according to Beard, was considered to be a product of the American climate and a way of life characterized by a growing spirit of nationalism and material prosperity (Haller, 1971). Americans were the first to suffer from "nervelessness" because of their country's lead in modernization and industrial development. As a counter to traditional rural values and stereotypes of the city as an evil place, explanations for neurasthenia became a rationalization for the superiority of urban life. Elitism and racism also marked the medical ideals of the neurasthenic woman. Among the neurasthenic set the very name of the disease connoted elite status. The neurasthenic was viewed as a cultured, sensitive genius, tortured by worry, and world wear—a brain worker. In contrast, the common man, the peasant, and inferior races were viewed as passive, mechanical workers—phlegmatic, easy-breeding, provincial laborers (Haller, 1971, p. 474). To the disdain of physicians, however, the complaint was far more democratic, as Haller (1971) indicates:

> The much larger class who prat of their nerves without due cause . . . advance them as a reason for holding back from the rough flight of everyday life. . . . Nine tenths of the nervous individuals in society who eagerly discuss their weak nerves ought never to have been conscious that they had any.

This two-tiered model of nerves, those who deserve their nerves and those who do not, marks the distinction between those who used physicians, such as Beard, to cope with their nerves and those who rejected the physician and relied on the Vegetable Compound to cope with theirs. These two populations of appeal underlie the major differences in the Beard and Pinkham nerves literature. An analysis of the areas of greatest overlap and their points of greatest difference leads one to argue that class, rather than gender, lies at the heart of the differences between these early nerves scholars.

SIMILARITIES OF BEARD AND PINKHAM'S VIEWS ON NERVES

Intellectual Traditions

Perfectionist rhetoric of the 1870s no longer expressed the belief that disease was God's retribution for immoral sins but was, instead, the result of violating nature's laws. In his attempt to build a comprehensive theory of nerves and establish neurasthenia as a distinct theory for the pathology of nervous exhaustion, Beard combined contemporary knowledge of the physical sciences (e.g., Helmholtz and Edison) with knowledge of the social sciences, notably the social Darwinism of Spencer, and showed a faith in technology and the triumph of scientific progress. Beard wrote that the physician had the duty to both heal and enlighten, to make himself a power in society (Rosenberg, 1962). Pinkham, too, believed in scientific progress and had a penchant for social reform. A life-long spiritualist, she was active in the antislavery, temperance, women's sufferage, and Greenback movements (Stage, 1979; Washburn, 1931).

Both Beard and Pinkham were influential in and influenced by the women's health and hygiene movement. The women's health movements of the 1830s provided an impetus for women to go into medicine and for women like Lydia Pinkham to develop their domestic medical skills. Health reformers promoted the assumption that men and women were responsible for their own health as well as the health of their families and society at large (Morantz-Sanchez, 1985). Whereas Pinkham's focus was on the individual and her family, Beard's focus was on a healthy society.

Styles of Public Education

Problems related to disease and thinking about disease were extremely complex in the late 19th century. Complexity, inconsistency, and confusion certainly characterize the writings of Beard and Pinkham. Despite their different populations of appeal, the educational styles of Pinkham and Beard are similar. For example, in the introduction to *American Nervousness,* Beard (1881) distinguishes between nerves as simple emotions and neurasthenia as an actual, physical lack of nerves force; this distinction is blurred in the remaining chapters. Pinkham copy recommends the efficiency of the Compound for dissolving "tumors" (as an abortificant), but also praises its power as a fertility enhancer. Throughout their literature, Beard and Pinkham are portrayed as the possessors of special credentials, experience, and knowledge; able to cure, and willing to guarantee cure; genuinely sympathetic and understanding—dedicated to improving the human condition. Pinkham copy reads, "Women should remember that a cure for all female diseases actually exists and the cure is Lydia E. Pinkham's Vegetable Compound. Take no substitute" (Stage, 1970, p. 125). Beard's preface (1881) reminds the reader of the depth of his scholarship: "The various subjects discussed in this work have occupied my mind from the time I first began to think. . . . They represent not far from a quarter of a century of research and toil."[3] Self-promotion and extravagant claims of cures were not unique to Beard and Pinkham, but characterized the medical treatises and promotions of patent medicines of the day.

Women's Weakness

The "Age of the Womb" clearly predominates the gender ideology of Pinkham and Beard. Both attributed female nervous complaints to the inherent weakness of women and their reproductive organs. According to Beard,

> The process of parturition is everywhere a measure of nerve strength. [To the civilized woman] the simple act of giving birth to a child opens the door to unnumbered woes; beginning with lacerations and relaxations, extending to displacements and ovarian imprisonments, and ending by setting the whole system on fire with neuralgias, tremors, etc., and com-

---

[3]**Beard and Pinkham styles of public education were not totally identical. Beard, in his book-length manuscripts, impressed readers with his expertise by juggling massive bodies of learned subject matter, including up-to-date thinking on the nature of savage society as well as the classic societies of ancient Greece and Rome. In contrast, the LPMC used short bits of common experience to advertise their products. In the typical Pinkham ad boldface headers such as "Women who Have the Blues," "I'm not Well Enough to Work," "Facts about Sick Women," "Painful Periods," and "I'm Simply Worn Out," were followed by brief testimonials of faith in the Pinkham cures.**

pelling a life-long slavery to sleeplessness, hysteria, or insanity. (Beard, 1881, pp. 76–77).

The following discussion of dysmenorrhea in *Treatise on the Diseases of Women* (LPMC, 1901, p. 116) also incorporates the nervous weakness of women theme.

> Congestion of the uterus almost invariably produces neuralgia of other parts of the body; while nervous exhaustion, nervous prostration, neuralgia and general nervousness often show themselves by increased pain at menstruation.

Although Pinkham was angered by women's lack of understanding of their basic reproductive processes and castigated men for their insensitivity toward their wives' suffering, neither Beard nor Pinkham questioned the basic tenets of the "Age of the Womb."[4]

Symptoms of Nerves

The list of symptoms attributed to nerves seems endless. Both Beard and Pinkham related the following symptoms to nervous disorders: weeping attacks, irritability, depression/melancholy, mental and physical weakness, general debility, fear, heart palpitations, headaches, feelings of profound exhaustion, fear of insanity, constant worry, itching, flying neuralgias, nervous dyspepsia, dizziness, chills, crises of puberty (cholorisis, masturbation), kidney complaints, nosebleeds, weight loss, and insomnia. To these Pinkham added the more traditional complaints of hot flashes, smothering spells, and inflammation of the women's organs and tumors. Among Beard's original and more exotic symptoms were susceptibility to stimulants and trance, writing cramps, magnificent oratory, beauty of women, and humor in speech and language. Exotic symptoms are not unique to Beard. For example, both LPMC copy of 1900 and Beard list occypodynia as a female distress which comes from riding a bicycle. Their language of nerves is also similar. For example, women in the Pinkham testimonials and Beard in his book (1881) use the terms *melancholia, nervous prostration, nervous exhaustion, hysteria, jittery nerves, overworked nerves,* and *nervous wrecks* interchangeably.

---

[4]Even though there was a large "man medicine" market for male weakness and male nervous debility remedies, such as a patent medicine called Sporty Days Invigorator (Young, 1967), and although the LPMC advertised the Vegetable Compound for male as well as female kidney and digestive complaints (Stage, 1979), the Pinkhams limited their weakness appeal to the female population.

DIFFERENCES BETWEEN PINKHAM AND BEARD

To a large extent Pinkham and Beard's theories shared the same intellectual traditions, commitments to social reform, styles of public education, and symptoms. Although Pinkham was an advocate of women's rights and female autonomy in health care, she did not refute or question contemporary medical models on the relationship between female reproductive organs and female weakness. As social class, however, enters the arena of analysis, more substantive differences between Pinkham and Beard's perspectives of nerves emerge.

The Nature of Nerves

Beard (1881) distinguished between the more traditional definitions of nervousness, as a mental quality (e.g., temper, unbalanced mental organization, or predominance of emotion over intellect), and the "new" American Nervousness as a physical disease. Nervousness was, according to Beard, literally a nervelessness or lack of nerve force, which manifested itself in functional debility and irritability of the nervous system. It was the challenge of brain work that depleted nerve force. The nervous system was described as a closed and continuous channel through which a fixed amount of energy, electrical in nature, coursed. This nervous force carried messages from one part of the body to another and served as the raw material of conscious thought (Rosenberg, 1962). The human body could produce only a limited amount of nervous force. If the nervous system was stressed or overloaded it would dim. There were three great reflex systems in the body—the brain, the stomach, and the reproductive system. An irritation in any one could cause symptoms anywhere in the body (Rosenberg, 1962).

Pinkham copy did not refer to the electrical nature of nerves or distinguish nervousness from simple excess of emotion or organic disease. Reflex theory, in early Pinkham copy, was vaguely stated, and the brain and stomach were of importance only in relation to the reproductive system. In Pinkham copy the theory of nerves originates in the reproductive system; the brain is relatively unimportant, although the digestive system as it impinges on the reproductive system can be of note. For example, in *Treatise on the Diseases of Women* (1901), the LPMC describe the problems of nerves as originating in abnormal conditions in the pelvis (tumors and swollen and congested organs) that can irritate the neighboring nerves. Although reproductive organs and processes may stress or irritate the nerves, the most suggested cause was the relationship between nervousness and constipation, for example, "A full colon presses on the generative organs and irritates the nerves" (p. 12).

This seemingly simple distinction between electrical (Beard) and congestion (Pinkham) versions of nerve irritation had important and socially complex ramifications. Beard distinguished between diseases of the nerves and diseases of the blood (also referred to as inflammatory or febrile diseases). Pinkham did not. According to Beard (1881), the subvarieties of nerves arise from cerebral, spinal, sexual, and digestive functions while the inflammatory diseases, such as gout and rheumatism, stem from the blood. Thus, the American urban brain worker suffers from nervous disease and the phlegmatic muscle worker, savage, barbarian, and European suffers from the inflammatory diseases.

Pinkham lumped nerve and blood diseases as well as types of workers and nationalities. The Pinkhams were not interested in distinguishing diseases but in listing, presenting, and discussing all the symptoms that the Vegetable Compound could cure. In early copy Lydia Pinkham's Blood Purifier (later renamed Lydia Pinkham's Herb Medicine) stood in equal stead with the Vegetable Compound. Blood flow and nervousness were symptomatically interrelated.

> To all women suffering from general debility, exhaustion and nervous prostration, I recommend Lydia Pinkham's Blood Purifier. If the female generative organs are involved use the Vegetable Compound and the Blood Purifier, if not, use only the Blood Purifier. . . . Blood Purifier builds up the system and purifies the blood. (LPMC, 1901, p. 31)

This appeared in testimonials as well:

> I . . . was thin, weak and nervous. When I would lie down it would seem as if I was going down out of sight in some dark hole. . . . My blood was poor, my circulation was so bad that I would be like a dead person at times. (Stage, 1979, p. 120)

Beard's distinctions between the muscle worker and the brain worker, and diseases of the nerves and blood reflect his elite patient population, while the Pinkhams, by lumping, attempted to appeal to the widest possible market. These classifications mark a change in the typology of chronic disease and must be viewed in terms of the classism, racism, and nationalism that informed Beard's theories. The different Pinkham and Beard perspectives on class emerge most clearly in the discussion of cause and treatment of nerves.

The Causes of Nerves

Social Darwinism pervades Beard's theory. American nervousness cannot be understood apart from modern civilization. Comparing nervous energy to steam power, Beard cited the recent invention of the telegraph and modern press (which enhance and spread information, thereby increasing competition in business), the development of the sciences (which begs for the constant discovery of new ideas and forces one to choose between religion and science), and the mental activity of women (which puts additional strain on their already delicate nervous systems) as forces that acted to siphon off the limited amount of power generated by the nerves, for example, "When the force is insufficient to keep all the lights burning, some go out and others burn faint and feebly" (Beard, 1881, p. 96). Clocks and watches, railway travel, specialization of work, increased education, city noise, politics of a free state, civil and religious freedom, personal habits of indulgence, combined with the dryness of the American air (which disturbs the electrical equilibrium of the body) and extremes of heat and cold (in adjusting to which nervous force must be expended) all came together to influence the greater prevalence of nerves in the United States. Although most Americans remained muscle workers, Beard argued that the new brain workers, who aspired to honor, eminence, and wealth, suffered from depletion of nervous force. The pressures of capitalism and the threat of financial failure also excited the nerves. Holding back, which was necessary for planning ahead and the sacrifice of the present for the future, and the repression of emotion also exhausted the nerve force of the new elite (in contrast to the peasant, who lives for the day and for whom laughter and tears are safety valves). Neurasthenia was limited to the wealthy and refined because, evolutionarily speaking, they had more sensitive, more highly evolved nerves. Nerves and modern civilization, Beard argued, went together. They were the growing pains of a better society. The American Indian, Negro, or immigrant may have shared the climate but did not suffer from nerves.

The Pinkhams advertised their cures to those who did not go to doctors. The market for Pinkham products consisted of uneducated, rural, working-class, middle-aged women (Stage, 1979). The hometown of the Pinkhams prided itself on being a working-class town, not a place for idlers and social parasites (Stage, 1979). Copy from a 1896 Vegetable Compound ad (Washburn, 1931, p. 198) reads, "No matter to what country she belongs, or whether she be black or white, as a women she desires to look well." By 1884, the compound was advertised in German, French, Spanish, Italian, Bohemian, Dutch, Swedish, Welsh, and Hebrew (Stage, 1979), and the *Treatise on the Diseases of Women* (LPMC, 1901) is dedicated to all the women in the world. The immense success of Lydia Pinkham's Vegetable Compound well illustrates the extent to which nonelite women identified with the complaint of nerves.

Treatment of Nerves

It is in the area of treatment that the greatest influence of gender and class may be seen. From the beginning Pinkham advertising copy both mirrored and magnified the population's dissatisfaction with physicians and medicine, especially the newly emerging subspeciality of women's doctors (Stage, 1979). "Write to Mrs. Pinkham" replaced the old cry of "Send for the doctor" (Washburn, 1931). The Thomasonians, homeopaths, botanic practitioner sects, and patent medicine manufacturers of the late 19th century emerged as a direct reaction against the heroic medical practice of the early 1800s and its dramatic cures of bloodletting, blistering, emetics and purgatives, and indiscriminate use of dangerous drugs (Stage, 1979). Thus, coupled with rising rates of surgery, led Pinkham to proclaim, "Let the doctors alone" (Stage, 1979). The very word *vegetable* connoted simple, safe, natural, and effective (Washburn, 1931), and the Compound was offered and advertised as more effective and less dangerous than the doctor (Stage, 1979).

There was a decidedly feminist slant to the early Pinkham literature. Pinkham copy proclaimed that only a woman could understand a woman. It was argued that not only were doctors dangerous, but male doctors made women suffering from female complaints uncomfortable. A Pinkham ad entitled "How Women Act When Consulting a Male Physician" explains:

> A woman is sick; some disease peculiar to her sex is fast developing in her system. She goes to her family physician and tells him a story, but not the whole story. She holds something back, loses her head, becomes agitated, forgets what she wants to say, and finally conceals what she ought to have told, and thus completely mystifies the doctor. Is it any wonder, therefore, that the doctor fails to cure the disease? Still, we cannot blame the woman, for it is very embarrassing to detail some of the symptoms. (Washburn, 1931, p. 185)

Pinkham offered herself as an alternative to male physicians. Women, who were assured that men never saw their letters, regularly wrote Mrs. Pinkham and she provided them with basic biological information on female reproductive processes. Pinkham copy and letters advised women to wash every night, eat starchy foods, and get exercise and fresh air as well as take the Vegetable Compound.

Although the Pinkhams did not question a physician's ability to diagnose the pathology-ridden nature of the female reproductive system, they did question the physician's ability to cure. Women were warned not to pass control of their health into the physician's hands and urged to become responsible for their own treatment by taking the Compound or other Pinkham products. The very appeal of the Vegetable Compound rested in its natural nature (vegetable), simplicity, and multipurpose effect. Promises of cures or success of treatment were dramatic. Pinkham copy promised to remove impurities, build up blood, dissolve tumors, and cure luccorhea, and other infections. The results were, according to Pinkham testimonials, radical. Women commonly testified to feeling like new women after completing the cure, and LPMC copy claimed to have absolutely and permanently cured millions of women. The texts of Pinkham's medical advice letters are filled with references to the effectiveness of the LPMC products—Sanitive Wash, Liver Pills, and Herb Medicine. In written testimonials cured women urged their peers to persevere in the use of the Vegetable Compound as a preventative and curative medicine.

The cost of the Vegetable Compound reflects its appeal to the less affluent classes. The Compound, in liquid, lozenge, and tablet form, commonly sold for one or two dollars per bottle. In its early days the Compound was not used by idle women, but by women who needed to build themselves up to get their work done.

In his more benign model, Beard (1881) maintained that the symptoms of nervousness would eventually correct themselves and that increasing wealth for all Americans along with modification of social customs would bring calm and repose. Beard's treatment for nerves was the same for men and women. The purpose of treatment should be to widen the margin of nervous force and teach the delicate, nervous brain-working patients how to keep from slipping over the edge. Unlike the widely appealing, multipurpose Vegetable Compound, Beard maintained that each patient and each case of nervousness might require a different cure. Despite the individualized attention, Beard's treatments seemed to justify Pinkham's advice to stay away from physicians. They are heroic and mortifying. Treatments advocated by Beard (1884) included drugs of his own formula (including belladonna, strychnine, ergot, and bromides), deep injections into the urethra, cold sounds, electrical sounds,[5] local (including anal and genital) electricalization, faradic baths, massage, and meat diets (Beard, 1881, 1884; Dana, 1923). Beard was skeptical about the effectiveness of the rest cure as advocated by his rival S. Weir Mitchell and concentrated his treatment strategies on the electrical

---

[5]Faradic bath refers to sitting in water through which an electric current is run. A sound is an instrument for exploring body cavities. Beard (1884) cautioned the novice practitioner not to put hot fluids through metal sounds since this can result in burning of the urethra or the body cavity being treated. Apparently Beard came to this conclusion through trial and error.

qualities of nerves. Beard seems to have preferred shocking his patients, both figuratively and literally.

Only the wealthy could afford Beard's treatments. Beard charged $100 to $300 for 3 to 6 months of treatment. He believed that muscle workers, unlike their brain-working counterparts, could better endure the effects of tobacco, coffee, and opium. This treatment strategy suggested that the muscle worker needed more violent and severe purging, bloodletting, and blistering than the higher orders could endure. Although Beard was widely read, it is no wonder that his theories were more popular than his cures.

PINKHAM AND BEARD AND THE FEMINIZATION OF NERVOUS DISORDERS

Although Pinkham had an avowedly feminist and populist bent, her heirs and the LPMC under the leadership of advertising strategist James Wetherald would eventually subsume issues of gender to issues of class in the Pinkham advertising copy of the late 1880s and 1890s. Nerves and nervousness began to rival reproductive complaints as the most popular topic of Pinkham advertisements as Wetherald drew his copy directly from popular medical books of the day, including the books of Beard (Stage, 1979).

Beard viewed the phenomenon of women's weakness in the late 19th century as new and temporary and attributed the problem to a small, elite segment of the American population. Modern women, Beard (1881) argued, with their constitutional tendency toward diseases of the nervous system, were characterized by a fine organization, superior intellect, and strong emotional nature, but because of a weakened nerve force "gestation among the upper classes has become a pathological sign of disease" (p. 78). For women in the savage state, however, "parturition was but a trifle more exhausting . . . than vomiting" (Beard, 1881, p. 76). The physique of savage women was not delicate or sensitive. They were strong and muscular with a capacity for enduring toil as well as childbearing, and they were even capable of beating their husbands.

Post-Beard LPMC copy began to show a considerable departure from Lydia Pinkham's original purposes of demystifying reproductive processes and putting women in control of their own health (Stage, 1979). Social forces such as social change, urbanization, and the development of civilization were linked to the experience of nerves. By the late 1890s, nerves had become a fashionable disease. The genteel woman and snob appeal were used to introduce nerves to a larger social spectrum. The physical explicitness of earlier ads was toned down. Women's emotional weakness received increased attention. Health and beauty, proper female comportment, and motherhood became important themes in the LPMC literature. Vegetable Compound ads were as concerned with legitimizing nervous complaints as with curing them.

Instead of claiming that the Vegetable Compound was a sure cure for prolapsed uterus, copy began to tout that the Vegetable Compound was the only positive cure and sure remedy for "those peculiar weakness and ailments of our best female population" (Stage, 1979, p. 122). By associating working-class women's problems with those of the rich, Pinkham copy attempted to sell the Compound through status emulation. The *Guide to Health* became a *Guide to Health and Etiquette.* Ads implied that both the seamstress who collapsed at her working table and the wealthy woman who suffered from the same female weakness, "one under the hot house culture, luxury and excitements, and the other through toil of necessity," could turn to the Vegetable Compound for help meeting "the demands of society" (Stage, 1979, p. 123). Although the best population did not buy the Vegetable Compound but went to physicians, Pinkham copy came to include the genteel, upper class woman of leisure in their advertising pictorials. Only 3 out of 26 of the 1890–1894 series of ads pictured working women, yet working women remained the major market for the Compound and other Pinkham products.

The women pictured in these ads were wasp waisted, passive-looking ideals of female gentility. Even when they are mentioned, ad copy freely ascribes elite characteristics to working-class women, for example, "Thousands of delicate young women are employed in fashionable dry goods" (Washburn, 1931, pp. 180–181). In another ad in which a begowned young lady is swooning toward the floor and held in the arms of a formally attired gentlemen, the copy describes her as a "Beautiful wreck [who felt] restless and nervous during the day, and is suddenly taken with that faint feeling so prevalent with our women" (Washburn, 1931, p. 181). This is a far cry from the early Pinkham copy, for example, "A FEARFUL TRAGEDY, A Clergyman of Stratford, Conn., KILLED BY HIS OWN WIFE, Insanity Brought on by 16 Years of Suffering With, FEMALE COMPLAINTS THE CAUSE" (Washburn, 1931, p. 134).

The weakness-of-women theme became more dramatic throughout the 1890s (Stage, 1979). Notions of the chronic illness of women were further enhanced by ads that equated normal with painless. Morning sickness, menstrual cramps, and pain during childbirth were characterized as unnatural and unnecessary (Stage, 1979).

Stage (1979) saw this as a big step backward and argued that the use of the themes of gentility, reflex theory, motherhood, and morbidity marked a decline in the position of women. Gentility revealed itself in the shift of ad style from a straightforward approach to more euphemistic descriptions of female complaints. Newspaper copy of the 1880s, which gave explicit references to menstrual pains, prolapsed uterus, and menopause, gave way by the 1890s to cryptic descriptions of "that all gone feeling," "that bearing down feeling," and "that nervous irritable feeling" (Stage, 1979). Motherhood and pronatalism also become important elements of Pinkham advertising, for example, "There's a baby in every bottle" (Stage, 1979), and "The crown jewel for delicate women comes with motherhood" (Washburn, 1931).

Reflex theories became further developed in Pinkham copy, expanding the biology of nerves and increasing the psychological sequelae. Digestive, nervous, and reproductive systems were further linked. Nervous disorders and, to a lesser degree, digestive disorders were brought into a more equal footing with reproductive disorders. One-third or more of the testimonials in Pinkham pamphlets (LPMC, 1928) described nervous problems. Pinkham copy came to sound more and more like Beard. The image of Pinkham women became both morbid and genteel; they were worn out, nervous, irritable, and so sickly they could not work or bear children (Stage, 1979).

Morality also entered the picture. The implied female revolt against male mistreatment and only-a-woman-can-understand-a-woman ads were replaced with ads admonishing a woman that it was her duty to stay healthy in order to fulfill her family obligations. Sickness became associated with sin (Washburn, 1931). Increasingly, women were portrayed less as hapless misinformed victims than as complicitors in their own suffering. An 1893 pamphlet entitled "Women's Beauty Peril and Duty" proclaimed that "sickness is often just an unnecessary as crime" and maintained that women must follow the laws of nature in order to preserve their own health and the health of the races (Stage, 1979, p. 124). Social and personal problems became equated with sickness—a concept that was extended to include dissatisfaction with women's lot. In their Dorothy Grey's advice columns the LMPC advised that a healthy woman was one who stuck to her traditional roles and the unhealthy woman was one who challenged them, for example, "I do wish that every woman who feels dissatisfied with her lot would realize that she is sick, and would take steps to make herself well. . . . Mrs. Pinkham's medicine will make her . . . more ready to meet the wishes of her husband" (Stage, 1979, p. 128). Ads began to suggest that a woman ought to take the Compound for her husband's sake. The Compound was also advertised as a way to keep a woman healthy and beautiful by ridding her of poisonous impurities, thus making and keeping her attractive to men.

According to Stage (1979), gentility, morbidity, and reflex theories began to decline after Word War I. Although it continued to be advertised as a treatment for jittery nerves, the Vegetable Compound was marketed as a general tonic, similar to today's Geritol. It is difficult, if not impossible, to actually assess the extent to which Beard's and Pinkham's theories created or captured popular lore. Their work did, however, focus attention on women's changing emotional styles and family roles. It is difficult to reconstruct women's experience of nerves in the late 19th century from limited historical source materials. The effects of changing roles on women's perceptions of self and health and illness during the late 19th century has certainly received the attention of many historical scholars (Cayleff, 1988; Rosenberg & Smith-Rosenberg, 1981; Turner, 1984). A consideration of the anthropological perspective and contemporary studies of nerves raises some additional issues about the relationship among class, gender, and the medical and popular nature of nerves.

CONCLUSION

Two salient features of late 19th century Beard and Pinkham nerves still dominate the nature of the nervous disorders of women today. They are the medicalization of nerves and the social/emotional elaboration of nerves.[6]

Current cures equivalent to Pinkham's all-purpose Vegetable Compound would include a wide variety of self-medications found in the medical cabinets of most Americans, for example, Geritol and daily vitamins; Midol and diuretics; sleeping pills and diet pills; Peptobismol, Tums, and antacids; and aspirin and Bufferin. The legacy of 19th century medical practice is less benign. Indiscriminate use of prescription drugs including Valium, Miltown, Librium, and amphetamines, along with hormone replacement and high rates of unnecessary surgery on women are still justified in the name of scientific medicine. This leds to the more negative side of nerves and the physician/patient relationship. Today, as in the past, women continue to be closely associated with psychotrophic medication and women outnumber men 15 to 1 in adver-

---

[6]It is important to note that nerves entails somatic as well as emotional complaints that could not be attributed to simple psychosomatic origin. Tuberculosis was widespread during the late 19th century. A variety of reproductive complaints, such as prolapsed uterus, incontinence, and chronic infections including gonorrhea were genuinely debilitating (Shorter, 1982; Stage, 1979). In addition to reproductive complaints, a wide variety of digestive complaints, including constipation, have been related to a 19th century urban diet deficient in fresh fruits and vegetables (Young, 1967), and a good number of health complaints have been attributed to the Victorian corset (Brain, 1979; Daves, 1982).

tisements for tranquilizers and antidepressants (Stimpson, 1975). Powerful, addictive drugs and unnecessary surgery are still being used to treat what are essentially social problems. The sexism, racism, and classism espoused by Beard have shown an amazing tenacity in medical practice (Ehrenreich & English, 1979).

The gender conflict perspective, however, can be misleading to the extent that it gives nerves on all-or-nothing, win-or-lose character. Late 19th century nerves, like nerves in the contemporary ethnographic record, is probably best viewed as a mixture of gains and losses. Recent studies (Davis, 1983; also articles by Barnett, Clark, Finerman, Krieger in this issue) show how the vocabulary of nerves can legitimize women's complaints and enhance rather than undermine women's status, both individually and collectively, or how nerves as a popular complaint can be a powerful tool among powerful women as well as a sign of weakness in women who lack status (Camino, in this issue; Clement, 1987; Lock & Dunk, 1987). First-hand observations of how the nervous sufferer interacts with others show how women can use their self-diagnosed cases of nerves to negotiate their way through a series of complex social networks in high-stress or rapidly changing social settings. Nerves is best viewed not as the product of status but as a tool for negotiating status.

It is also misleading to equate nerves with inversion reactions or simple secondary gain. Littlewood and Lipsedge (1987) suggested that *nervios*/nerves may qualify as a kind of inversion reaction that permits nondominant individuals (in this case women) to adjust to their situations by a limited contravention of society's core values. Although this concept may be arguable for cases of anorexia nervosa, 19th century institutionalized hysterics, and neurasthenics incapable of leaving their beds, the notion of inversion reaction does not apply to simple cases of nerves as described in Pinkham copy. When almost all women in a given population complain of nerves, nerves is best viewed not as a contravention of norms but as the norm. The legions of women who came to rely on Pinkham's Vegetable Compound were not the exception—they were the rule.

Nor should nerves be limited to or held distinct to a particular time, place, or class. Nerves has existed in the Western tradition since the beginning of written records (Davis & Whitten, 1988) and continues to flourish in a wide variety of social class and cultural contexts (Davis & Guarnaccia, 1988; Low, 1985). Nerves, past and present, is used universally by women to explain and link life events. To the extent that nerves focuses attention on the social and emotional problems of women, nerves may be viewed as a metaphor of discontent. This quality of nerves has been recognized for a long time, as Meyerson (1927, p. 34) stated:

> Nerves are caused by outward happenings rather than personality defects. The causes of nervousness are related to obvious facts of life. People get tired, apprehensive; they hate where they should love; . . . have their hopes, purposes, and desires frustrated and blocked.

Anthropological studies have described this individual, personal dimension of nerves, but they have also addressed the collective, more social character of nerves. Nervous complaints as expressed by peoples in marginal societies, rural immigrants to urban areas, and the poor are best seen as metaphors for social protest and social discontent that can be linked to ethnicity and class as well as gender (Davis & Guarnaccia, 1988). As such, nerves is a vehicle for the overt and covert expression of an individual's or group's ongoing relationships with others and the outside world.

Anthropological studies (Davis & Whitten, 1988; Guarnaccia & Farias, 1988) have also shown how cases of nerves become prevalent when traditional societies are exposed to dramatic and pervasive culture change. Nerves may be viewed as a barometer of changing life-styles and expectations. This is particularly true when (a) pervasive social change challenges one's traditional sense of self, self-identity, and core values; and (b) the direction of change is from a social world based on extensive intimate networks of primary, personalized relationships to a social world based on fragmented social networks, that are best characterized as utilitarian, secondary relationships.

The salience of nerves in late 19th century America may have arisen out of the transition from a society based on extended kin relationships, sociable neighbors, and primary relationships to a society based on secondary, utilitarian, and competitive relationships. The ever-present vocabulary of nerves expands and develops to give a legitimate voice to the expression of emotions and a sense of self that stems from the insecurity and discontent generated a combination of changing nature of social relations, questioning of old values and new sets of expectations. In this sense Beard's association of nerves with periods of dramatic and pervasive change is an appropriate as Pinkham's association of nerves with a wide range of emotional states.

REFERENCES

Asher, R. (1957). *Nerves explained.* Springfield, IL: Thomas.

Barker-Benfield, G. J. (1976). *The horrors of the half-known life.* New York: Harper and Row.

Beard, G. M. (1881). *American nervousness.* New York: G. P. Putnam's Sons.
Beard, G. M. (1884). *Sexual neurasthenia (nervous exhaustion).* New York: E. B. Treat.
Burton, J. (1949). *Lydia Pinkham is her name.* New York: Farrar, Strauss.
Brain, R. (1979). *The decorated body.* New York: Harper and Row.
Cayleff, S. E. (1988). "Prisoners of their own feebleness." *Social Science and Medicine, 26,* 1199–1208.
Clement, S. (1987). *Environmental stress and individual survival.* Unpublished manuscript.
Daly, M. (1978). *Gyn/ecology.* Boston: Beacon Press.
Dana, C. L. (1923). George M. Beard. *Archives of Neurology and Psychiatry, 10,* 427–435.
Daves, M. (1982). Corsets and conception. *Studies in Society and History, 24,* 611–641.
Davis, D. L. (1983). *Blood and nerves.* St. John's, Newfoundland: Memorial University of Newfoundland, Institute of Social and Economic Research.
Davis, D., & Guarnaccia, P. (1989). Health, culture and the nature of nerves. *Medical Anthropology, 11,* 1–7.
Davis, D., & Whitten, R. G. (1988). Medical and popular traditions of nerves. *Social Science and Medicine, 26,* 1209–1222.
Drinka, G. (1985). *The birth of neurosis.* New York: Simon & Schuster.
Ehrenreich, B., & English, D. (1979). *For her own good.* Garden City: Doubleday.
Guarnaccia, P., & Farias, P. (1988). The social meaning of nervios. *Social Science and Medicine, 26,* 1223–1231.
Haller, J. S. (1970). Neurasthenia. *New York State Journal of Medicine, 71,* 2489–2497.
Haller, J. S. (1971). Neurasthenia. *New York State Journal of Medicine, 71,* 473–482.
Hubbard, F. (1915). *Lydia Ellis Pinkham.* New York: The Roycrofters.
Jackson, S. W. (1986). *Melancholia and depression.* New Haven, CT: Yale University Press.
Kleinman, A. (1983). Neurasthenia and depression. *Culture, Medicine, and Psychiatry, 6,* 117–190.
Leff, J. P. (1978). Psychiatrists' versus patients' concepts of unpleasant emotions. *British Journal of Psychiatry, 133,* 306–313.
Littlewood, R., & Lipsedge, M. (1987). The butterfly and the serpent. *Culture, Medicine, and Psychiatry, 11,* 289–355.
Lock, M., & Dunk, P. (1987). My nerves are broken. In D. Coburn (Ed.), *Health in Canadian society: Sociological perspectives* (pp. 295–313). Toronto: Fitzhenry and Whiteside.
Low, S. M. (1985). Culturally interpreted symptoms of culture-bound syndromes. *Social Science and Medicine, 21,* 187–196.
Lydia Pinkham Medical Company. (1893). *Guide to health.* Lynn, MA: Author.
Lydia Pinkham Medical Company. (1901). *Treatise on the diseases of women.* Lynn, MA: Author.
Lydia Pinkham Medical Company. (1928). *On the trail of the sun.* Lynn, MA: Author.
Meyerson, A. (1927). *The nervous housewife.* Boston, MA: Little, Brown.
Morton, W. J. (1883). Obituary: George Miller Beard. *Journal of Nervous and Mental Disorders, 10,* 130–134.

Morantz-Sanchez, R. M. (1985). *Sympathy and science.* Oxford: Oxford University Press.

Rockwell, A. D. (1883). The late George M. Beard. *Medical Record, 24,* 399–401.

Rosenberg, C. E. (1962). The place of George M. Beard in nineteenth-century psychiatry. *Bulletin of the History of Medicine, 36,* 245–259.

Rosenberg, C., & Smith-Rosenberg, C. (1981). The female animal. In A. Caplin, H. Englehart, & J. McCartney (Eds.), *Concepts in health and disease.* Reading, MA: Addison-Wesley.

Shorter, E. (1982). *A history of women's bodies.* New York: Basic Books.

Showalter, E. (1985). *The female malady.* New York: Pantheon Books.

Stage, S. (1979). *Female complaints.* New York: W. W. Norton.

Skultans, V. (1979). *English madness.* Boston: Routledge & Kegan Paul.

Stimpson, G. (1975). Women in a doctored world. *New Society, 32,* 265–266.

Turner, B. (1984). *The body and society.* New York: Basil Blackwell.

Veith, I. (1965). *Hysteria.* Chicago: University of Chicago Press.

Washburn, R. C. (1931). *The life and times of Lydia E. Pinkham.* New York: G. P. Putnam's Sons.

Weekes, C. (1981). *Hope and help for your nerves.* New York: Bantam.

Weekes, C. (1987). *More help for your nerves.* New York: Bantam.

Wood, A. D. (1984). The fashionable diseases. In J. W. Leavitt (Ed.), *Women and health in America* (pp. 25–52). Madison: University of Wisconsin Press.

Young, J. H. (1961). *The toadstool millionaires.* Princeton, NJ: Princeton University Press.

Young, J. H. (1967). *The medical messiahs.* Princeton, NJ: Princeton University Press.

Section I

LATIN AMERICA

GENDER, EMOTION, AND *NERVIOS* IN URBAN GUATEMALA

Setha M. Low, PhD
PhD Programs in Environmental Psychology and Anthropology, Graduate School and University Center of the City University of New York

This study of *nervios* in a poor, resettled *colonia* (neighborhood) outside Guatemala City is part of an ongoing analysis of the cross-cultural significance and meaning of nerves. In the Guatemalan context, *nervios* is treated by sufferers as an illness, rather than a symptom, and is associated with experiencing strong emotions, particularly anger (*cólera, se enoja*) and grief or sorrow (*pena*), and with problems related to reproduction and child rearing. It is generally treated with "nerve pills" purchased at a local store or with home remedies. *Nervios* is predominantly reported by women, and the etiological explanations of emotion and childbearing problems suggest that at least part of the meaning of the Guatemalan version of *nervios* is linked to gender and gender-based concerns. The Guatemala data on *nervios* provide an excellent opportunity to explore the relationships between gender, emotion, and illness.

This study of *nervios* in a poor, resettled *colonia* (neighborhood) outside Guatemala City is part of an ongoing analysis of the cross-cultural significance and meaning of nerves. Nerves, or *nervios* among Spanish-speaking populations, is both a common, culturally acceptable distress symptom, that is, a sign of psychosocial discomfort, and a syndrome,

I thank the many dedicated interviewers of the El Progreso Project; the director of the project, Lic. Yetilu de Baessa of the Universidad del Valle; the interviewer for the case studies, Lic. Frances Porras; and my co-investigators, Dr. Francis Johnston of the University of Pennsylvania and Dr. Robert MacVean of the Universidad del Valle. Karen Hammer (Low & Hammer, 1983), Mindy Feller, and Meiskina Rowaan worked on analyses of the Guatemala *nervios* material while attending the University of Pennsylvania; their insights and hard work are greatly appreciated and contributed to this article. Lydia Greiner, a doctoral candidate at the University of Pennsylvania, also contributed to this project by working in the community, and by transcribing the in-depth interviews into usable computer files. I am grateful to her for completing this enormous task. This project was supported in part by the University Research Foundation of the University of Pennsylvania and a grant from the International Development Research Council of Canada.

that is, a local medical concept that identifies and gives meaning to a group of distress-related symptoms (Low, 1988a). It is a particularly interesting example of a popular illness that has no clear biomedical diagnosis or description but has developed culture-specific interpretations and meanings in a variety of cultural settings (Low, 1985a).

In the Guatemalan context, *nervios* is treated by sufferers as an illness, rather than a symptom, and is associated with experiencing strong emotions, particularly anger (*cólera, se enoja*) and grief or sorrow (*pena*), and with problems related to reproduction and child rearing. It is generally treated with "nerve pills" purchased at a local *tienda* (store) or with home remedies. *Nervios* is predominantly reported by women, and the etiological explanations of emotion and childbearing problems suggest that at least part of the meaning of the Guatemalan version of *nervios* is linked to gender and gender-based concerns. The Guatemala data on *nervios* provide an excellent opportunity to explore the relationships between gender, emotion, and illness.

The relationship between gender and nerves has emerged as an important theoretical focus in a series of recently published articles (Cayleff, 1988; Davis & Whitten, 1988; Guarnaccia & Farias, 1988). For many researchers, nerves is a "women's disease," and although I have argued that selective sampling has had considerable influence on this conclusion (Low, 1989), this perspective has enriched our understanding of the sociopolitical and power dimensions of the bodily expression of nerves and the medicalization of distress. Many studies also identify strong emotion and gender as a folk explanation of nerves; one example is Dona Davis' (1983) work in outport Newfoundland where nerves is interpreted as an expression of women's worrying and fear about the well-being of their husbands fishing at sea.

The present study addresses both themes in an analysis of culture-specific meanings of *nervios* within an urban Guatemalan setting. This article begins with a review of the study objectives and methodology, presents the setting and findings from the survey of households and case studies based on in-depth interviewing, and concludes with a discussion of the explanations and interpretations of *nervios* within the community and among women sufferers.

THE EL PROGRESO PROJECT

The data for this study were collected in a resettled *colonia* on the edge of Guatemala City organized in 1980 as part of the 1976 post-earthquake reconstruction process (Low, 1988b). The *nervios* interviews were conducted as part of a health study focused on the social and cultural determinants of child growth and development that began in

1981. Francis E. Johnston and Yetilu de Baessa identified El Progreso as a "typical" urban resettlement area with a population large enough to produce an adequate sample of households with young children living in the poorest of socioeconomic conditions. They completed a 1980–1981 census as a baseline for the selection of the 555 participant families and selected the mixed cohort, cross-sectional, and longitudinal samples (Johnston, Low, de Baessa, & MacVean, 1985). The survey material on *nervios* used this sample of families with children in an effort to record illness behavior and health beliefs and practices that could influence family health.

In 1982 I became involved in the El Progreso project as the coordinator of the urban ethnography. At that time I initiated a series of observations on community development, medical services, and family adaptation that indicated that *nervios* was a common health problem. In 1984, we received funds that enabled us to add an intensive family ecology interview of 32 households to the quantitative study of socioeconomic, cognitive, and anthropometric variables. These interviews, many of which are more than 50 transcribed pages, provide detailed information on health beliefs and practices, domestic economy, family activities, and life-style characteristics as well as discussions of *nervios* episodes, attributed causes, and preferred treatments.

Method

Two sets of data on *nervios* were collected over a 4-year period. The first was a *nervios* survey completed as part of the longitudinal study of the growth and cognitive development of children in the *colonia.* The survey questionnaire, administered by a trained interviewer, focused on the family environment, including mother-child interaction, and the measurement of the physical and intellectual characteristics of the child. The *nervios* data were collected during one complete cycle of the interview process and included the entire sample of families measured in 1 year (June 1982 through June 1983). The questions were usually answered by the mother of the child who was being monitored, but in some cases the older sibling or father was the caretaker present during the interview. The survey included the following questions: (a) Have you or any of your family members suffered from nerves? (b) When did you begin to suffer from nerves? (c) What do you think made [makes] you sick? (d) How often do you suffer from nerves? (e) What symptoms have you had [do you have]? (f) How do your nerves affect you (in relation to your daily activities)?

The second set of *nervios* data were collected from 1985 through 1986 by Frances Porras, a psychology and anthropology graduate of the

Universidad del Valle, as part of an in-depth substudy of 32 households. Pairs of children whose nutritional status could not be predicted by the socioeconomic conditions of their homes were matched by socioeconomic variables and included in this substudy. The intensive interview included 215 questions covering health of the child, family composition and living situation, social interaction, domestic economy, dietary habits and food beliefs, and migration and life histories of the parents; it took from 3 to 10 home visits to complete. The health section included 17 questions about *nervios*. The case histories presented in this article are based on these in-depth interviews.

The study also uses data from the initial census and survey of 1980–1981, includes statistical means and community descriptions from the 1981–1986 quantitative study of child growth and development, and draws on the urban ethnography of 1982–1983.

The Setting

El Progreso is a *colonia de reconstrucción* (reconstructed community) situated about 2 km from the main highway of Guatemala City and is in the municipality of the capital. The area totals 16 *manzanas* distributed in seven sectors; each *manzana* has 20 lots, approximately 81 square meters each, except for those at the edge of the ravine. The area has natural limits that separate it from other neighborhoods: an entrance marked by a grove of pines and ravines on all other sides. The community is separated into two parts by a difference in elevation divided by the only vehicular road, and was developed with two distinct housing programs: minimum unit housing in the upper sector and sites and services in the lower sector. Other than the walkways of cement, drainage system, and lights, the area retains aspects of other marginal areas such as few roads, poor services, faulty drainage, trash and litter dumped in the ravines, and stray animals along the roads.

The 1979–1980 census of the neighborhood reported approximately 10,000 inhabitants. A house count in 1985 identified 2,020 houses, about half constructed of wood—frame or *lepa* (rough planks)—and the other half constructed of cement block. Most male residents work in manual labor or in temporary jobs; most females are housewives, although they often supplement the household income through selling in the market or providing domestic services in their homes. The mean number of children is three per household; the father is absent in 16% of all households. Functional literacy and completion of primary education are infrequent; the mean number of years of school is 2.5 for females and 3 years for males.

The mean monthly income of Q160 (U.S. $160 in 1982) supports five or six persons in a household; however, this income is not stable because the wage earner may often be unemployed or marginally employed. The current economic crisis has further devalued household earnings, and the high rate of inflation has increased unemployment in the poorest economic sectors. Economic instability produces a situation in which the purchase of a television that can be sold or returned is seen as a preferable investment than the payment of a mean lot rent of Q25–27 (U.S. $25–27), which has no tangible benefit because of restrictions on house or lot sales. Most residents are behind in their land payments and do not foresee an improvement in their finances in the near future.

There are limited social services in El Progreso; the majority of those that exist were begun by the National Reconstruction Committee and the team of three social workers who organized the residents as part of the self-governance program. There are eight Pentecostal churches, one Catholic church, two public schools, a school for children with learning disabilities, and a private school founded by a religious order and the state. At the public schools there is a lunch program for 300 children. The Sisters of Calcutta run a small childcare center and a home for the elderly. Foster Parent Plan has an aid program that invests money in a cooperative fund for loans that will improve the economic conditions of a family, while a Dutch program emphasizes house-building projects. The facilities are used to a limited extent by members of the neighborhood and are supplemented by services available in the central city. The problems reported by the residents that are not addressed by these services are the lack of adequate employment, the expense of transportation to the city, and the difficulty of keeping children in school when they are needed to care for their younger siblings or to work supplementing the meager family income.

The health services in the *colonia* are minimal. They include a local midwife who assists mothers with home births and provides home remedies, a free clinic open in the morning by the Sisters of Calcutta, and a health post where a 3rd or 4th-year medical student sees local residents for Q2 fee (U.S. $2 in 1982). Most residents complain that the medical services are inadequate and expensive. Although the Sisters of Calcutta clinic is free, residents must buy the medicines prescribed in an expensive pharmacy in the city, and for many families Q2 is more than a day's wage so they hesitate to spend it to see a young student doctor. The alternative is to pay the bus fare into Guatemala City to see a doctor at the public clinic at Roosevelt Hospital where the wait may take the entire day, and the necessary treatment or medicine may still not be provided. Healing services are held in the local evangelical churches and are attended by their members and supplement the use of Western and/or folk medical services. The most common solution is to not seek health care and rely on herbal remedies available in the local market. Medical pluralism, that is, health practices that combine Western medicine and indigenous folk medicine, is characteristic of health care and illness behavior in rural Guatemala (Cosminsky & Scrimshaw, 1980) and continues in an attenuated form in the urban environment.

The political, economic, and cultural context of contemporary Guatemala frames everyday life in El Progreso. Although respondents identify themselves as ladino[1] and use Spanish in all interviews and in public life, there still are traces—in dress, language, decoration of the home, choice of occupation, and dietary and health beliefs and practices—of the indigenous, rural backgrounds from which many of them have come. The majority of the residents have lived in Guatemala City for more than 20 years; however, very few were actually born in the city, and many came after the earthquake in order to qualify for a lot. The importance of the ladino/indigenous contrast discussed by Hawkins (1984) remains a viable metaphor for modernity and class in this new urban community.

The national reality of violence and political oppression also touches daily lives; most residents know someone who has been killed or has been recruited to work in the police or military guard. In the life histories many men agonized over their decision not to work for the police because of the danger, even though the alternative meant remaining jobless, unable to support their families. In the case histories, some women reported the violent death of family members, in some cases from crime in the city, and in other cases at the hands of the police. Violence and fear of violence were common unspoken reasons for changes in activities and a sense of anxiety about the future.

Economic pressures, always present for the poor, have been compounded by the economic crisis of 1982 that left most of Central America with raging inflation, an inability to repay international debts, and failing industrial economies. The crisis is directly observable in the increasing number of unemployed men and youths in the *cantinas* and streets, and in a related increase in crime and vandalism. The impact of the economic and political conditions in which they live, although difficult for respondents to articulate in their interviews, can be indirectly felt and interpreted by what was not said and by the metaphor of illness, particularly *nervios,* expressed in their bodies and the discourse of daily lives.

---

[1]*Ladino* refers to the cultural identification with Spanish/mestizo culture and cultural traits that takes on a special meaning when contrasted the identity of *indigena.* Within the urban context, the ladino identity has higher social status; often social mobility in the Guatemala City is expressed as becoming *ladino.*

Nervios in El Progreso

The *nervios* analysis reported in this article is a reexamination of preliminary data presented in Low and Hammer (1983) and Low (1985a) in light of the in-depth interview material collected in 1985–1986. Trained Guatemalan research assistants interviewed 362 families, of which 322 families were used,[2] representing symptom reports of 308 females and 207 males for a total of 515 individual cases. Of these 515 individuals, 322 or 62.5% reported having *nervios,* with 83% of the *nervios* cases reported by females. Of the 308 females, 269 or 87.3% reported that they suffered from *nervios,* compared with 53 or 25.6% of the 207 males. The mean age for females with *nervios,* based on 263 reports, was 33 years, and for females without *nervios,* based on 33 reports, was 31 years. The mean age for males with *nervios,* based on 49 reports, was 36 years, and without *nervios,* based on 5 reports, was 46 years. Mean age varied little overall between people with *nervios* (33.44 years) and people without *nervios* (33.16 years). The major difference, then, in the distribution was gender, with 3.5 times more females suffering from *nervios* than males.

In Guatemala, sufferers talk about their *nervios* as an illness and discuss the symptoms, cause, and treatment as they would most any other Western medical or folk illness. Sufferers in El Progresso rarely seek medical care for their *nervios*: 44% reported that *nervios* has no effect on their daily activities or work, 24% must rest, and 16% reported that they cannot do anything, are tired or cannot work. Eight percent reported that they have to work and cannot rest even though they would like to, and only 4% seek medical care.

The symptoms associated with the incidence of *nervios* presented in order of highest to lowest frequency include headache, despair or desperation (*desesperación*), face pain (including jaw, mouth, and teeth pain), trembling, anger (*se enoja, cóleras, se altera*), anxiety, twitching or jerking of the body (from the verb *brincar*), stomach pain, high blood pressure, body pain, itching, and insomnia. All symptoms that were reported by more than 1% of the sample are presented by gender in Table 1. Because of the discrepancy in the number of symptoms reported by males and females it is difficult to distinguish a clear pattern of symptom preference that is not confounded by the small number of

---

[2]Of the 362 collected cases, 40 cases were not used; of these 40, 19 were reports on children and 21 were without proper identification numbers and could not be matched to the demographic SAS data files. The decision not to use the children was based on the few number of cases and the focus in this article on gender, rather than age.

Table 1. Symptom Associated with *Nervios* by Gender

Symptom	Number of reports (percent)		
	Male	Female	Total
Head pain (headache)	22 (3.3)	167 (25.5)	189 (28.8)
Despair, desperation	7 (1.1)	72 (11.0)	79 (12.1)
Face pain	7 (1.1)	59 (9.0)	66 (10.1)
Trembling	8 (1.2)	46 (7.0)	54 (8.2)
Anger	10 (1.5)	40 (6.1)	50 (7.6)
Anxiety	2 (0.3)	10 (1.5)	12 (1.8)
Twitching	1 (0.2)	9 (1.4)	10 (1.6)
Stomach pain	2 (0.3)	8 (1.2)	10 (1.6)
High blood pressure	1 (0.2)	9 (1.4)	10 (1.6)
Body pain	2 (0.3)	7 (1.1)	9 (1.4)
Itching	2 (0.3)	6 (0.9)	8 (1.2)
Insomnia	0 (0.0)	8 (1.2)	8 (1.2)
Violence	5 (0.8)	3 (0.4)	8 (1.2)
Upset by noise	0 (0.0)	7 (1.1)	7 (1.1)
Leg and arm pain	3 (0.5)	4 (0.6)	7 (1.1)
Low blood pressure	0 (0.0)	7 (1.1)	7 (1.1)
Difficulty breathing	2 (0.3)	5 (0.8)	7 (1.1)
Nausea	0 (0.0)	7 (1.1)	7 (1.1)
Numbness	1 (0.2)	6 (0.9)	7 (1.1)
Shriveling (*encoger*)	1 (0.2)	6 (0.9)	7 (1.1)
Other	2 (0.3)	5 (0.8)	7 (1.1)

Number of reports includes all symptoms mentioned. List includes symptoms reported by more than 1% of the sample. Total number of symptoms reported was 656, 88 for males, 568 for females.

reported male symptoms (88 male symptoms and 568 female symptoms for the entire sample); however, violence was reported more frequently by males, and stomach pain, body pain, itching, leg and arm pain, and difficulty breathing were reported by more than the 25% of the sample that the males represent. This list of male symptoms, which includes violence and bodily pains and aches, corroborates a commonly cited pattern that men use physical (read "masculine" in Western culture) categories of symptom presentation while women employ both emotional (read "feminine") and physical symptom presentation (Barnett, Bierner, & Baruch, 1987; Verbrugge, 1985).

The attributed causes of *nervios* focus on emotional, reproductive, and family and work related explanations. Presented in order the specific causes were as follows: rage and anger (*cólera, se enoja*), grief and sorrow (*pena*), birth control pills, other illness, birth of a child, worries (*preoccupaciones*), problems, fright (*susto*), pregnancy, caring for children, nightwork, earthquake, and death of a child. Table 2 includes a list of all causes by gender reported by more than 1% of the sample. Thirty-four individuals reported that they didn't know the cause of their *nervios*. Taken together, *cólera* and *pena* account for 25% of the attributed causes; females attributed their *nervios* to emotional causes slightly more often than males—27% for females versus 17% for males. Reproductive and childcare problems (birth, pregnancy, birth control pills, abortion, caring for children, and conflicts with children) are the second most frequent cause of *nervios* (19% overall), but not surprisingly, 22% of females mentioned these causes, compared with only 4% of males. Other causes reported by females include the death of a family member (child, parent, or spouse), fright (*susto*), earthquake, and too much work. Males, on the other hand, more frequently reported work-related problems (nightwork or work), worries, insomnia, and accidents.

Table 2. Causes of *Nervios* by Gender

	Number of reports (percent)		
Cause	**Male**	**Female**	**Total**
Rage and anger	4 (1.3)	42 (13.5)	46 (14.8)
Grief and sorrow	4 (1.3)	29 (9.3)	33 (10.6)
Birth control pill	1 (0.3)	19 (6.1)	20 (6.4)
Other illness	1 (0.3)	16 (5.1)	17 (5.4)
Birth of a child	0 (0.0)	13 (4.2)	13 (4.2)
Worries	5 (1.6)	7 (2.3)	12 (3.9)
Problems	1 (0.3)	10 (3.2)	11 (3.5)
Fright (*susto*)	0 (0.0)	11 (3.5)	11 (3.5)
Pregnancy	0 (0.0)	10 (3.2)	10 (3.2)
Caring for children	1 (0.3)	8 (2.6)	9 (2.9)
Nightwork	5 (1.6)	3 (1.0)	8 (2.6)
Earthquake	0 (0.0)	7 (2.3)	7 (2.3)
Death of child	0 (0.0)	7 (2.3)	7 (2.3)
Accidents	2 (0.6)	4 (1.3)	6 (1.9)
Insomnia	2 (0.6)	3 (1.0)	5 (1.6)
Work	3 (1.0)	2 (0.6)	5 (1.6)
Too much work	0 (0.0)	5 (1.6)	5 (1.6)
Death of parent	0 (0.0)	5 (1.6)	5 (1.6)
Death of spouse	0 (0.0)	4 (1.3)	4 (1.3)
Abortion	0 (0.0)	4 (1.3)	4 (1.3)
Conflicts with children	0 (0.0)	4 (1.3)	4 (1.3)

Number of reports includes all causes mentioned. List includes causes reported by more than 1% of the sample. Total number of reported causes was 311, 47 for males, 264 for females.

Causes, then, also reflect some gender distinctions in that females seem to report more emotional, reproductive, and family-related problems, while males seem more concerned with work and worries.

The Guatemalan interview schedule separated the questions of the initial cause of *nervios* from a question on when it occurs. The responses to this second question, "How often do you suffer from nervios?", were more consistent. Forty percent of the *nervios* sufferers stated that anger triggers their illness; a common response was "I get them [*nervios*] when I am angry." The gender distribution was also fairly equal in that 36% of the males and 40% of the females reported anger as a trigger of *nervios*. Other triggers that were mentioned include time-related occurrences, for example, "I always have *nervios*," "I have them everyday," "I have them once in awhile," and "I have them once a week"; environmental stimuli, such as noise and unusual sounds; problems, fright (*susto*), worries, anxiety, and insomnia; and behavioral statements such as "I have them when I drink." Table 3 presents the frequency of each of these triggers by gender. Of these triggers drinking is clearly gender related in that only males reported this trigger, whereas anxiety and insomnia had an equal number of male and female responses. Worries and problems, on the other hand, were only reported by females. Triggers appear to have a less clearly defined gender logic, at least in terms of the Western conception of the gender being correlated with male/physical and female/emotional expression, whereas the symptom presentation and causation does exhibit this frequently reported pattern. One caution should be offered at this point; since the number of males with *nervios* is so much smaller than the number of females, it is difficult to make statistical comparison or to test for significance. These patterns can be taken only as indications and, in fact, suggest that at least in El Progreso, *nervios* is more often a gender-linked illness.

El Progreso Case Histories

These case histories are drawn from the 32 in-depth interviews collected from 1985 through 1986. Four cases are presented: a case of mild *nervios*, a more serious case of *nervios*, a case in which the mother of the respondent has *nervios* but the respondent does not, and a case in which neither the respondent nor her family members have *nervios*. These cases are presented as illustrations of the kinds of families and processes that may be involved in *nervios*, but are not necessarily representative of the range of families or family life in El Progreso.

Table 3. Triggers of *Nervios* by Gender

Trigger	Number of reports (percent) Male	Female	Total
Anger	20 (5.5)	126 (34.5)	146 (39.9)
Always, everyday	7 (1.9)	53 (14.5)	60 (16.4)
Noise, sounds	3 (0.8)	18 (4.9)	21 (5.7)
Once in a while	6 (1.6)	13 (3.6)	20 (5.2)
Problems	0 (0.0)	14 (3.8)	14 (3.8)
Fright (*susto*)	0 (0.0)	11 (3.0)	11 (3.0)
Worries	0 (0.0)	8 (2.2)	8 (2.2)
Anxiety	4 (1.1)	4 (1.1)	8 (2.2)
Insomnia	3 (0.8)	4 (1.1)	7 (1.9)
Twice a week	0 (0.0)	5 (1.4)	5 (1.4)
Drinking	4 (1.1)	0 (0.0)	4 (1.1)

Number of reports includes all triggers mentioned by *nervios* sufferers. List includes triggers reported by more than 1% of the sample. Total number of triggers reported was 365, 56 for males, 309 for females.

Case 1: Mild Case of Nervios

Ella lives in a small wooden house with two rooms and an extension that is used as a store, with her husband and four children, ages 5 to 12. In addition, her nephew has been living with them for over a year. Her husband has worked in a brewery for the past 7 years. Ella borrowed Q400 (U.S. $400) 2 years ago from Foster Parent Plan to open a store and has been paying it back slowly. She is a home-based person, always has been. She is seen as cool, frugal, and distant. She seems concerned about her own health, even more than with the health of her children; however, she is knowledgeable about medicine and medical care. The steady income from the store makes it possible to use medical services when she wants and to purchase medication.

Ella was born in Quiche and lived there during her childhood. They came to stay in the city with a friend, and eventually rented a room where she lived with her mother and two brothers. She met her husband because both families were renting in the same house, and although they never married they have been living together for 13 years. He is a Catholic and attends church, but she does not accompany him.

Ella has a mild case of *nervios*. She says that *nervios* is something you get as a pain in the face. She feels her *nervios* as a pulling of her cheeks. There are other people who go crazy when they get *nervios,* she says, they throw everything and you have to calm them down. She thinks that both men and women suffer from *nervios* and she has even seen little children tremble with *nervios*. She thinks that people usually start suffering when small and then keep on suffering. Some people get cured, yet others just get worse.

She has been told by people in the neighborhood that she gets her *nervios* because of anger, yet she is able to lead a normal life. Another woman in the neighborhood gets crazy when she has *nervios* and tears her clothes. It is very hard to stop her, and afterward, when she gets over it, she does not remember anything.

She treats her own *nervios* with pills. The vendors leave "nerve pills," *Nervesa,* and she sells them in the store. So she takes them from the store when she needs to. She comments that when a person has *nervios*, "you have to give them a medicine that is effective." Her niece would start crying because of *nervios,* and they would give her a pill to calm her, either *Nervesa* or *Nervotiamina.* The interviewer asked Ella if she would check with a doctor, and she replied that she knows it is always good to consult, but first you have to pay for the appointment, and then you have to buy the medicine. "So it is better to take simple things without consulting. It is cheaper, and you get well." She does not know anyone who has gone to a doctor for this illness. The only way to get well is to take pills: "If you take *Nervesa* today, you awake fine in the morning." When asked what she would do for her *nervios* if she was still living in Quiche, she replied that she would take pills or herbs, like *zacatillo* that are good for getting cured.

Case 2: Severe Case of Nervios

Linda lives in a one-room wooden house with her husband and six children, 11 months to 7 years of age. She was previously married and had three children, but when that marriage broke up the children stayed with their father. She only sees these children from afar, which she feels is the best way. She explains that right now her second husband is not with them. He went to work in the United States, but she received a message from him the other day. He must have gotten caught and is coming back. The live on "whatever they can get." She is sending her children to a day-care center and is making *dobladitas* to sell. Her children also go out to sell or work helping a neighbor. She owes money for *tortillas* and vegetables, and is grateful that people have been willing to wait so long.

Part way through this interview the husband appeared and was also interviewed. The husband was born in Guatemala City and also was married before. Linda was born in Santa Lucia Cotzumalguapa and came to Guatemala to work. She decided to come on her own because her sister was already living here, and she wanted to see what it was like to live in the city. At the same time a women asked her to come to the city to work for her washing and cleaning. That was the first of many jobs that she has had since she has been here. The interviewer comments that Linda is the type of person who knows how to get around in order to give her children an adequate diet. She gets help from several sources and even when she has no money she gets things on credit. Her husband is a good worker, but has a drinking problem, and his salary varies according to demand for work.

Linda gets *nervios* when she has a worry or is suffering. She gets a headache, the roof of her palate gets swollen and her lips tremble. When she was expecting her second child the doctor told her that she had *nervios*. She was spitting foam when she got angry.

Her *nervios* is caused by problems. Her husband drank for some time and gave her a "rough time," screamed at her, and that affected her a great deal. She thinks that *nervios* bothers most women. When her husband has problems he plays the victim; now he is nagging constantly because of how he suffered as a child and how he got caught trying to cross over to the United States. One of her daughters also suffers from *nervios* and also gets headaches and pains in her teeth.

When Linda has *nervios* the pain starts on her forehead, above the nose, and goes around the head and gets worse right above the back of the neck. It generally starts when she worries about what food to give her children. She tries to control herself; she goes to the pharmacy and buys two envelopes of *calmantes*, two for 5 cents (about U.S. $.05). Her husband, on the other hand, does not control himself. She thinks that he also suffers from *nervios* because he drank so much. Now he is not drinking because of the children. He says that he has changed. She believes that if one fights in front of the children "they get a trauma."

She thinks that a doctor knows more about *nervios*. She does not like to go to the doctor though, and prefers to make her own homemade medicine, such as *agua de lechuga* (lettuce water). She cooks the lettuce and then takes the water and it calms her. Or she takes the *calmantes* that she buys. This treatment is enough because her *nervios* is not very developed. Other people who have a very advanced case of *nervios* could not be cured this way. She usually buys her drugs in the city at the Farmacia Municipal because she gets things there at half price. If she could go to the doctor, she would expect him to give her an injection or some other treatment.

She feels that *nervios* is very common. Most people she knows have *nervios*. If she were still living with her mother in Nimaya, Santa Lucia Cotzumalguapa, her mother would make some homemade medicine with herbs from the mountains. Her mother would also get into a *tamascal* (sweat bath) and sweat out the illness.

Case 3: Mother Has Nervios

Alba and her three children, ages 1 to 4, live in a one-room house. Her mother, Juana, lives part of the time in Huehuetenango, but comes every 2 to 3 months to see how they are doing and to bring them food from the countryside. Alba considers her mother and children as her only family. She had a sister who was only 16 when she was killed in the Terminal market.

Alba is a very hard worker whose life is spent earning enough pennies to feed her children that day. She has never been married, but she has lived with three different men. The father of her first child died when the child was 1 year old; then she lived with her second child's father until he left for the United States. She has not heard from him since he left. Then she lived with her third child's father, but he left her when the baby was 9 months old. Her mother helps her with paying the house rent. Each day she cooks food in the morning and heats milk for her children that she leaves for them when she goes out in the afternoon. Each afternoon she collects bottles and newspapers, which she sells at the Terminal market. She then buys her food at the end of the day when the prices are the cheapest. She also has chickens, and her son raised 12 ears of corn. The two boys help doing chores and watching the youngest child.

Alba says *nervios* can come from cavities or if you get angry or if you suffer from an illness called *nervios.* She has seen people with swollen faces, and it has happened to her. They told her at the hospital that this comes from cavities; it affects the nerves (*nervios*) of your face. When her face gets swollen, she gets a headache. You get *nervios* because you do not visit the doctor. If you are in treatment with medicine, you do not get ill. You can fall ill with *nervios* because of happiness, sadness, or a problem. She has heard this, but what she has observed is that when her mother gets angry, one eye starts hopping. And her mother says that "her nerves are altered" and that her face hurts. This happens whenever her mother gets very angry.

Women get *nervios* more often because they get angry at their kids all the time, but both men and women can get it. Even children are affected. She has noticed that when her oldest child is very angry, he throws up and his head starts hurting and it is because of *nervios.*

Her mother's case of *nervios* allows her to do housework, so long as she does not hear noise, fights, or children crying. If there is the least problem, she stops feeling well. There are more cases of *nervios* in the city because there is more noise than in a small town. In a town children are kept busy working in the countryside so there is no opportunity for them to disrupt the order. When her mother has *nervios,* she makes a tea with lettuce water or if she has gone to the doctor she will take the medicine that he has prescribed. Her mother gets better when there is no noise, but when her children do not mind her, then her mother gets *nervios.* When her mother is in Huehuetenango she is better because she is among older people and is more relaxed.

When asked what she would do if she had *nervios,* Alba replied that she would start by asking a neighbor or would take a pill for the *nervios*. But for the moment, she does not consider herself afflicted. She does not get altered by the children. Her mother does because she is older and has no patience. She would also look for help from a doctor. She would explain what she felt and then he would decide whether or not it was *nervios* and act accordingly. But she has worries and does not have *nervios.* If she lived in the countryside, she would probably take "medicine of the mountains"; that is what she has been told the people of the towns do.

Case 4: Does Not Have Nervios

Issa lives with her husband, mother-in-law, and four children ages 3 months to 6 years in a wooden house that was given with the lot. She has problems with her mother-in-law with respect to child rearing. Her mother-in-law does not like her to scold the children, but she has to because she wants them to be educated. Her mother-in-law does not help around the house. She leaves after breakfast and spends the whole day visiting.

Her husband is from Guatemala City. Issa was born in Jutiapa and came to the city as a young woman to work for a lady. She and her husband have been together for 9 years. He is out of work now, but was working as a *cadenero* (similar to a land surveyor). He has also worked at a place where they make prefabricated walls, but he had to pay so much transportation that it was not worth working for so little money. Issa makes *tortillas* to sell every day, and sells enough that the *tortillas* they eat are free.

She says that *nervios* comes because you have a problem and get tense. You get *nervios* and you get a headache. "For instance, one is busy and a child gets hurt. You worry and run to find out what happened. You torment yourself and hit the children. Later you come down with a headache from *nervios* because you got tense." Many times it is because the person is a very angry person.

Both men and women suffer from *nervios.* Some doctors help and others do not. Issa knows a lady who suffers from *nervios*. She trembles all over, and the doctor has not been able to help. He gives her medicine, but her body has already gotten used to the pills and they do not cure her.

She thinks that there are more *nervios* problems in the city. "We are surrounded by cars. Suddenly you are in the street and you hear gun shots; all this makes you nervous. You are in danger and have to be alert. In danger not only from the bullets, but even when you cross the street. Small town life is more tranquil and therefore healthier."

She knows a lady who got angry (*cólera*) with her husband. She wanted to hit him, but could not, so she remained with *cólera* and her mouth twisted up. She explains that when one gets tense, the muscles contract and the liquid moves and starts gathering in one place. "This kind of thing does not happen all the time, but on some days. You wake up and you do not know what is going to happen that day. You may have a scare or a *cólera* and when this happens, *nervios* attacks." If she had *nervios* she would consult first with the people in her house and then with a doctor. She would expect him to talk to her, to ask questions leading up to the problem that caused her *nervios*.

These four case histories illustrate how differently individual sufferers and nonsufferers perceive, experience, explain, and interpret *nervios*. Anger, the most common cause and trigger reported in the survey, does appear as a component in most of these discussions, as does headache, the most common symptom, but when viewed from the point of view of a person the variation seems greater than the commonalities. This discrepancy in survey findings and case histories has been commented on by Cosminsky (1977) in her work on Guatemala when she found that there were more reports of emotion-caused illness in the case histories.

Nonetheless, some themes emerge. The role of anger as related to conflicts with one's spouse or children does appear as a causation factor in most of the cases. The relationship of worrying about the economics and the realities of feeding one's children or maintaining a job seems to be a subtle subtheme in many of the stories. And there are both direct and indirect references to danger and accidents in the discussion of bullets, cars, and noise that appear in some histories. The discussions of noise and city life, however, may be related to the fact that all four of these women were not born in Guatemala City, but moved there to work as young women.

Most women self-prescribe lettuce water or "nerve pills" rather than see a doctor, although they think that you "should" see a doctor in most cases. This finding should be interpreted in the context that the women were being interviewed by a college graduate of higher socioeconomic class, and thus may have been trying to please the interviewer in these statements. The fact that very few women consult a doctor for their *nervios,* except in "severe" cases, speaks more eloquently about what they think a doctor can do and whether they consider *nervios* serious enough to spend the money, time, and energy to seek medical services. The case history discussions of *nervios* are quite sophisticated, in the sense that these women know a lot about *nervios* and have a clinical model that works for them. Their treatments and etiological schemes reflect the medical plurality of their health culture, and the pattern of affliction reproduces the basic gender, economic, and political conflicts of everyday life.

Nervios Explanations and Interpretations

The present data suggest that there are five culture-specific explanations and interpretations of *nervios:* (a) biological—cavities, vitamin and food deficiencies, and a muscular response to tension; (b) psychological/phenomenological—worry and emotion expressed and communicated through the body as an illness metaphor; (c) social—response to abusive and difficult relationships with family and friends; (d) cultural—pattern of folk illness in a ladinoized form; and (e) political and economic—response to political violence and economic hardship and deprivation. Each explanation partially contributes to an understanding of this illness within this socially marginal, urban Guatemalan community. The following discussion explores these diverse explanations and interpretations and their interrelationships, thus illustrating the complexity involved in understanding an illness that may have multiple causes and meanings within a medically pluralistic culture.

Stress, Distress, Susto, and Cavities

In the initial analysis of *nervios* in El Progreso, Karen Hammer and I argued that *nervios* was related to the stress of everyday life and was a *ladino* term for *susto,* an indigenous folk illness common in Latin America (Low & Hammer, 1983; Low, 1985a). To some degree, these explanations still hold true. One of the most salient aspects of the meaning of *nervios* in the Guatemalan context is related to the high reported incidence and the predominance of anger and emotion as its folk etiological explanation. Assuming that *nervios* is a signal of distress (Low, 1985a), and a response to a stressful situation, it is not surprising that *nervios* is occurring with such high frequency. El Progreso is a recently resettled community; most of the residents either lost their homes during the 1976 earthquake or have migrated from the countryside to work in the city.

Further, political unrest in Guatemala and the current economic recession disrupt daily life. Stress-related diseases often appear during migration and periods of social change (Dressler, 1985; Pollock, 1988). The high incidence of *nervios* in this community therefore suggests that it may be an indication of these changes and a metaphor for the impact of sociopolitical and economic conditions (Armstrong, 1983; Scheper-Hughes & Lock, 1986). Further, it seems that *nervios* may be another example of the medicalization of distress (Lock, 1987; Low, 1988c), that is, the transformation of a difficult social reality into an illness expressed through the medium of the body. Thus a medical discourse about cause, prognosis, and treatment of the illness is created, rather than a political or economic discourse focusing on the social situations responsible for the distress.

The Guatemalan interviewees, however, commonly refer to their anger or rage as causing their illness, and if not anger then grief and sorrow. These statements are reminiscent of references to the emotionally based diseases of indigenous Mesoamerican peoples. Brintnall (1979) stated that in traditional Aguacatec religion, illness is caused by angered ancestors, that is, is sent by the ancestors as a punishment for angry relationships among living family members. Cosminsky (1977), working in Chuchexic, commented that greater emphasis was placed on the emotional causes, like anger, of illnesses when using a case study method. Foster (1982), writing about illness in Tzintzuntzan, states, "Strong unpleasant emotional experiences such as anger, fright and grief may lead to that well-known Mexican folk illness, *bilis* . . . The victim causes his own illness by not controlling his emotions" (p. 83). Fabrega and Manning (1979) suggested that in the theory of disease in Chiapas, emotional states occupy the logical analog to germs in biomedicine. Other researchers in Central America, Mexico, and Puerto Rico have reported a similar association of *nervios* with anger and strong emotional states (Finkler, 1985b; Guarnaccia & Farias, 1988; Rothenberg, 1964).

The most common Latin American folk illness, *susto* (fright), is also associated with strong emotions (Watanabe, 1982) and intrasocietal conflict (Logan, 1979), and is signaled in some cases by trembling (Tousignant, 1979). *Colerina,* another folk illness observed in a peasant community in the Peruvian Andes, manifests itself through feelings of restlessness, inability to concentrate, loss of appetite, sleep disturbance, and wild dreams. "The severity of the illness is related to the strength of the *pena* felt by the sufferer, and hence it is related to the depth of his grief reaction, to the strength of his feelings or resentment or frustration, or to the violence of his anger" (Stevenson, 1977, p. 305). *Pena* in the Ecuadorian sierra is caused by suffering and sadness and can also lead to an outburst of violent emotion or *colerin* (Tousignant, 1984).

The emphasis on the emotional causes of *nervios* and the similarity of symptomatology with other emotionally based folk illnesses suggest that *nervios,* in the context of Guatemala, may be a gloss for a set of symptoms previously or alternatively labeled by an indigenous medical term. Since the study was completed in an urban area, it is possible that *susto* would be the more common form of complaint in a rural village and that in the urban setting *susto* takes on a different cultural meaning. *Nervios,* a quasi-medical term, communicates more effectively in the cultural context of the urban environment. The pattern of etiology and expression of illness, however, has not substantially changed. Illness is still attributed to anger and other strong emotions; simply the label has been "ladinoized" (Low & Hammer, 1983; Low, 1985a).

The issue of whether *nervios* is a gloss for *susto,* or a ladino version of *colerina, bilis,* or any other form of folk illness, is confounded by fright (*susto*) appearing as a symptom of *nervios*. Further, at least two researchers (Barnett, 1989; Clement-Brutto, 1988) have provided evidence that *nervios* and *susto* coexist in a variety of Latin American populations. It is probably more accurate to conclude, along with Signorini (1982) and Crandon (1983), that there are many "diseases of adaptation" (Klein, 1978) and that a range of symptoms when labeled *susto* reinforce an indigenous ethnic identity and when labeled *nervios* reaffirm a ladino identity. Crandon (1986) argued that in Bolivia deciding what to call a set of symptoms may be actively manipulated in relation to the social situation and desirability of being identified as either ladino or indigenous. Ethnic identity is also of concern in urban Guatemala, particularly among a group of poor, recent migrants who are trying to establish themselves as part of the socially mobile incipient middle class (Low, 1988b). Rather than a gloss or alternative to *susto*, then, *nervios* is the ladino illness of choice, reaffirming an urban, upwardly mobile ladino identity.

Rubel, O'Neill, & Collado-Ardon (1984) concluded that *susto* also marks a state of physical disease; their work suggests that it is important to consider the physiological as well as the cultural aspects of the problem. Frances Porras, the interviewer for the case histories and a psychologist by training, suggests that the idea that anger can induce *nervios* is a very accepted concept in Guatemala because it is a means of channeling anger in an acceptable way. Open anger is considered culturally inappropriate and people do try to control themselves and have a hard time not saying what they want to. In El Progreso people live very close together and are constantly in situations where one has to either fight or "close one's mouth." "Maybe this is why the respondents' face muscles are tense and what causes their headaches'' (Porras, field notes, 1985).

Another interpretation of the symptomatology of *nervios* comes from the respondents' own explanation that *nervios*-related face pain and headache are caused by the poor dental health of El Progreso residents. Cavities are mentioned in Alba's (Case 3) folk model of *nervios,* and cavities, infections, and tense facial muscles could be part of the pain experienced in some of the cases. However, without other evidence it is difficult to determine whether these problems are prevalent in the *nervios* population.

These explanations—that *nervios* is a response to a stressful sociopolitical situation and a medicalization of distress, that it is a ladino illness expression that in contrast to *susto* reinforces a person's ladino identity, that it is a culturally appropriate way to express anger, and that some *nervios* symptoms may be caused by jaw-clenching tension and bad teeth—address *nervios* as a general syndrome. However, they do not consider the gender-specific nature of *nervios* in the El Progreso population. The following, then, is a discussion of *nervios* as a women's illness and its meaning within the logic of gender relationships.

Gender-Based Nervios in Guatemala

The history of the gender-based concept of *nervios* in Guatemala derives from both Western European and indigenous cultural traditions. Early explanations of nerves are found in the writings of Galen, who identifies nerves as physical entities, related to the brain, but also argues that the ''agents of nervous communication were animal spirit or essences that were produced in the brain and coursed through the nerves'' (Davis & Whitten, 1988, p. 1210). In Galen's theory, humors could interfere with or change these spirits and essences such that nerves could have a mental was well as physical effect (Davis & Whitten, 1988). Further, ''the passions could send the spirits about their task as messengers'' (Davis & Whitten, 1988, p. 1210). Hippocratic–Galenic–Persian medicine became the orthodox medicine of Western Europe in the medieval period and was brought to the New World by the Spanish and Portuguese. According to Foster's extensive historical research, it was taught as part of classical education by the early 16th century (Foster, 1987; Risse, 1987) and continued to be taught in Latin American medical schools until the early 19th century (Foster, 1987). Humoral medical practices were diffused at a popular level through the publication and distribution of ''home care manuals [*recetarios*]'' based on Galenic principles (Foster, 1987, p. 358).

Galenic nerves in Western European and North American medicine became linked to women's physiology, psychology, and susceptibility by the 19th century (Cayleff, 1988; Davis & Whitten, 1988). According to Cayleff, nerves was first equated with women's reproductive organs and later to their psychological nature, that is, their vulnerability and psychological fragility, and these attributed causes corresponded to changing gender power relations (Cayleff, 1988). By the mid-19th century the shift in the organization of work and household economy resulted in gender-appropriate tasks and spheres of influence that were seen as complementary, reflecting perceived differences in women's moral superiority and men's greater rationality. "These social relations were, additionally, a primary way of signifying relationships of power assigned along gender lines" (Cayleff, 1988, p. 1202).

This model of women's vulnerability, both physiologically and psychologically, and the corresponding power inequality also influenced the interpretation of orthodox Galenic medicine in urban Latin America. Luiz Duarte, in an unpublished paper entitled "What It Means to Be Nervous" has argued that the predominant model of the person among the Brazilian urban lower classes derives directly from these 19th century ideas about nerves and nervousness, in contrast to the educated and upper classes' use of a psychological model. He suggests that the adoption of this model of the person draws heavily on the difference between men and women, casting these gender differences in terms of physical, moral, and mental forces. "Woman's moral quality corresponds to her basically *nervous* quality, which accounts for the fact that they are the most common victims of the wide range of disturbances related to nervousness" (Duarte, nd. p. 11).

The second stream of influence on the development of a gender-based concept of *nervios* in Guatemala derives from Mayan preconquest medical beliefs that identify an excess of emotion or an emotional experience as a natural cause of illness (Orellana, 1987). Women, as well as children, are thought to be weaker than men such that strong emotions, such as anger or fear, are debilitating and can cause fright (*susto*) or other emotionally caused illness (Orellana, 1987). These two medical traditions thus tie together gender, emotion, and illness both through the Western medical ideology of nerves/vulnerability/women and through the indigenous emotion/illness/women relationship.

Both of these medical traditions are reinforced by the inequality of contemporary gender relationships based on the *machismo/vergüenza* complex of Mediterranean and Spanish American cultures (Pitt-Rivers, 1966), and the Catholic family model of the man as the respected and obeyed husband and father and the woman as the humble and suffering wife and mother (Brandes, 1988; Browner & Lewin, 1982). Women in Guatemala say that they expect to suffer and serve, that *pena* (grief, sorrow) is their *cargo* (burden) in life. *Nervios,* within the logic of the family relationship, is merely one aspect of this culturally and religiously sanctioned suffering in a medicalized form.

Other researchers in Latin America have reported that *nervios* is a women's illness related to a sense of harassment in rural Mexico (Finkler, 1985b) and is a common disorder among abused and neglected women in an Ecuadorian Indian community (Finerman, 1987). In North America, most of the nerves examples are gender related either through menopause and worry in Newfoundland (Davis, 1983, 1986) or as a somatic complaint of poor, unemployed, and disabled women (Nations, Camino, & Walker, 1988; Van Schaik, 1989); and immigrant women who carry the double burden of work and household chores (Dunk, 1989). Gender-specific patterns of symptoms and folk illnesses have been reported for most parts of the world with explanations that draw on power inequality, inability to express negative emotions, and inability to fulfill social and cultural roles, particularly as related to family responsibility and childbearing (Del-Vecchio Good, 1980; Horton, 1984; Lefley, 1979; Morsy, 1978; Muecke, 1979; Nichter, 1981). All of these interpretations apply to the plight of women who have *nervios* in Guatemala. Both the case histories and the survey materials report physical abuse and neglect of women by their partners, worry about having to care for children and at the same time produce enough income to feed them, concern and conflict related to reproduction and child rearing, and the need to control emotions, particularly anger. In Guatemala, the headaches and face pain of *nervios* are culturally appropriate bodily expressions of these difficult life problems, and even the symptomatology reproduces the cultural ideal of the woman "keeping her head down" in relation to her dominant, and often abusive or absent, partner.

Nerves, Gender, and Emotion

The most difficult part of explaining *nervios* in Guatemala, however, lies in its link to emotion. The arguments that the Mayan theory of disease has always been emotionally based and that the weakness of women was their inability to control their emotions in the Western tradition are historical explanations. Although they are related to emic patterns of expression, they do not explain linkages to contemporary social and political processes. Lutz (1986), in her discussion of emotion as a cultural category, noted that emotion is often thought of as female, unintended, and uncontrollable, and the political implications of this accepted thought are being challenged in recent analyses of women's emotional disorders (Richters, 1988). The literature recently has focused on the hypocognized or hypercognized emotions as a way to discuss why some cultures emphasize some emotions and restrict the expression of others (Knauft, 1985; Levy, 1984; Myers, 1985; Poole, 1985), and in this sense Guatemala, and most of Central America, could be said to hypercognize anger. Yet it is unclear where this explanation or model of emotion leads in terms of emotion and illness.

Within medical anthropology, somatization of emotion has become an important explanatory model for examining how bodily complaints in the absence of psychopathology are an expression and means of communicating social stress (Kleinman, 1982). Kleinman (1986) argues that when we have a sick body, we are a sick body; the lived experience ties together "anger to dizziness" (p. 146) and becomes the symbolic bridge between sickness and emotion. I have used a version of the somatization argument in my discussion of *nervios* as an expression of social stress and personal distress. But in the Latin American context, sufferers do not separate mind and body, and instead experience emotion and bodily sensations as continuous. Thus, the biomedical model that treats soma and psyche as distinct entities, allowing for the somatization of emotion and the psychologizing of physical complaints, is only an alternative rather than an explanatory cultural model for describing sickness. Other researchers have reported folk illnesses that are caused by malignant emotions (Coreil, 1983; Farmer, 1988) and explain the etiology in terms of interpersonal relations and/or emic disease concepts. But in order to fully examine the illness/emotion/gender relationship, a theory of emotion that integrates these different levels of experience with bodily expression needs to be developed.

REFERENCES

Armstrong, D. (1983). *Political anatomy of the body.* Cambridge: Cambridge University Press.

Barnett, E. A. (1989). Notes on *nervios:* A disorder of menopause. *Health Care for Women International, 10*(2-3), 159–169.

Barnett, R. C., Bierner, L., & Baruch, G. K. (1987). *Gender and stress.* New York: Free Press.

Brandes, S. (1988). *Power and persuasion.* Philadelphia: University of Pennsylvania Press.

Brintnall, D. (1979). *Revolt against the dead.* New Yor: Gordon and Beach.

Browner, C., & Lewin, E. (1982). Female altrusim reconsidered: The Virgin Mary as economic women. *American Ethnologist, 9,* 61–75.

Cayleff, S. (1988). "Prisoners of their own feebleness": Women, nerves and Western medicine—a historical overview. *Social Science and Medicine, 26,* 1199–1208.

Clement-Brutto, S. (1988). *Environmental stress and individual survival: Coping with powerlessness in El Salvador and rural Kentucky.* Unpublished manuscript.

Coreil, J. (1983). Parallel structures in professional and folk health care: A model applied to rural Haiti. *Culture, Medicine, and Psychiatry, 7,* 131–152.

Cosminsky, S. (1977). The impact of methods on the analysis of illness concepts in a Guatemalan community. *Social Science and Medicine, 11,* 325–332.

Cosminsky, S., & Scrimshaw, M. (1980). Medical pluralism on a Guatemalan plantation. *Social Science and Medicine, 14,* 267–278.

Crandon, L. (1983). Why susto? *Ethnology, 22,* 153–167.

Crandon, L. (1986). Medical dialogue and the political economy of medical pluralism: A case from rural Bolivia. *American Ethnologist, 13,* 463–476.

Davis, D. (1983). *Blood and nerves: An ethnographic focus on menopause.* St. John's, Newfoundland: St. John's Memorial University Institute of Social and Economic Research.

Davis, D. (1986). The meaning of menopause in a Newfoundland fishing village. *Culture, Medicine, and Psychiatry, 10,* 73–94.

Davis, D. L., & Whitten, R. G. (1988). Medical and popular traditions of nerves. *Social Science and Medicine, 26,* 1209–1221.

Del-Vecchio Good, M. J. (1980). Of blood and babies: The relationship of popular Islamic physiology to fertility. *Social Science and Medicine, 14,* 147–156.

Dressler, W. W. (1985). Psychosomatic symptoms, stress, and modernization. *Culture, Medicine, and Psychiatry, 9,* 257–294.

Duarte, L. F. D. What it means to be nervous: Competing concepts of the person in Brazilian urban culture. Unpublished manuscript, Museu Nacional, Universidade Federal do Rio de Janeiro, Brazil.

Dunk, P. (1989). Greek women and broken nerves in Montreal. *Medical Anthropology 11,* 29–45.

Fabrega, H., & Manning, P. K. (1979). Illness episodes, illness severity and treatment options in a pluralistic setting. *Social Science and Medicine, 13,* 14–52.

Farmer, P. (1988). Bad blood, spoiled milk: Bodily fluids as moral barometers in rural Haiti. *American Ethnologist, 15,* 62–83.

Finerman, R. (1987). Inside out: Women's world view and family health in an Ecuadorian Indian community. *Social Science and Medicine, 25,* 1157–1162.

Finkler, K. (1985a). *Spiritualist healers in Mexico.* South Hadley, MA: Bergen and Garvey.

Finkler, K. (1985b). Symptomatic differences between the sexes in rural Mexico. *Culture, Medicine, and Psychiatry, 9,* 27–58.

Foster, G. M. (1982). Responsibility for illness in Tzintzuntzan: A cognitive–linguistic anomaly. *Medical Anthropology, 6,* 81–90.

Foster, G. M. (1987). On the origin of humoral medicine in Latin America. *Medical Anthropological Quarterly, 1,* 355–393.

Guarnaccia, P. J., & Farias, P. (1988). The social meaning of *nervios:* A case study of a Central American woman. *Social Science and Medicine, 26,* 1223–1231.

Hawkins, J. (1984). *Inverse images: The meaning of culture, ethnicity and family in postcolonial Guatemala.* Albuquerque: University of New Mexico Press.

Horton, C. F. (1984). Women have headaches, men have backaches: Patterns of illness in an Appalachian community. *Social Science and Medicine, 19,* 647–654.

Johnston, F., Low, S., de Baessa, Y., & MacVean, R. (1985). Growth status of disadvantaged urban Guatemalan children of a resettled community. *American Journal of Physical Anthropology, 68,* 215–224.

Klein, J. (1978). Susto: The anthropological study of diseases of adaptation. *Social Science and Medicine, 12,* 23–28.

Kleinman, A. (1982). Neurasthenia and depression: A study of somatization and culture in China. *Culture, Medicine, and Psychiatry, 6,* 117–190.

Kleinman, A. (1986). *Social origins of distress and disease: Depression, neurasthenia and pain in modern China.* New Haven, CT: Yale University Press.

Knauft, B. M. (1985, December). *At peace with violence: Hypocognition in a violent New Guinean society.* Paper presented at the annual meeting of the American Anthropological Association, Washington, DC.

Lefley, H. P. (1979). Female cases of falling-out: A psychological evaluation of a small sample. *Social Science and Medicine, 13,* 115–116.

Levy, R. I. (1984). Emotion, knowing and culture. In R. A. Shweder & R. A. LeVine (Eds.), *Culture theory: Essays on mind, self and emotion* (pp. 214–237). Cambridge, MA: Cambridge University Press.

Lock, M. (1987). Protests of a good wife and wise mother: The medicalization of distress in Japan. In E. Norbeck & M. Lock (Eds.), *Illness and medical care in Japan.* Honolulu: University of Hawaii Press.

Logan, M. H. (1979). Variations regarding *susto* causality among the Cakchiquel of Guatemala. *Culture, Medicine, and Psychiatry, 3,* 153–166.

Low, S. M. (1985a). Culturally interpreted symptoms or culture-bound syndromes: A cross-cultural review of nerves. *Social Science and Medicine, 21,* 187–196.

Low, S. M. (1985b). *Culture, politics and medicine in Costa Rica.* South Salem, NY: Redgrave.

Low, S. M. (1988a). Biomedical practice in response to a folk illness: The treatment of *nervios* in Costa Rica. In M. Lock & D. Gordon (Eds.), *Biomdicine reexamined* (pp. 415–438). Dordrecht: D. Reidel.

Low, S. M. (1988b). Housing, organization and social change: A comparison of programs for urban reconstruction in Guatemala City. *Human Organization, 47,* 15–24.

Low, S. M. (1988c). The medicalization of healing cults in Latin America. *American Ethnologist, 15,* 150–168.

Low, S. M. (1989). Health, culture, and the nature of nerves: A critique. *Medical Anthropology, 11,* 91–95.

Low, S. M., & Hammer, K. (1983, November). *Nerves in Guatemala: An examination of cultural meaning.* Presented at the annual meeting of the American Anthropological Association, Chicago, IL.

Lutz, C. (1986). Emotion, thought and estrangement: Emotion as a cultural category. *Cultural Anthropology, 1,* 287–309.

Morsy, S. (1978). Sex roles, power, and illness in an Egyptian village. *American Ethnologist, 5,* 137–150.

Muecke, M. A. (1979). An explication of "wind illness" in northern Thailand. *Culture, Medicine, and Psychiatry, 3,* 267–300.

Myers, F. (1985, December). *The logic and meaning of anger among Pintupi aborigines.* Presented at the annual meeting of the American Anthropological Association, Washington, DC.

Nash, J. & Safa, H. (1985). *Women and social change in Latin America.* South Hadley: Bergen & Garrey.

Nations, M. K., Camino, L. A., & Walker, F. B. (1988). "Nerves" folk idiom for anxiety and depression. *Social Science and Medicine, 26,* 1245–1259.

Nichter, M. (1981). Idioms of distress. Alternatives in the expression of psychosocial distress: A case from South India. *Culture, Medicine, and Psychiatry, 5,* 379–408.

Orellana, S. L. (1987). *Indian medicine in highland Guatemala.* Albuquerque: University of New Mexico Press.

Pitt-Rivers, J. A. (1966). *The people of the Sierra.* Chicago: University of Chicago Press.

Pollock, K. (1988). On the nature of social stress: Production of a modern mythology. *Social Science and Medicine, 26,* 381–392.

Poole, F. P. (1985, December). *The surfaces and depths of Bimin-Kushusmin experiences of "anger."* Presented at the annual meeting of the American Anthropological Association, Washington, DC.

Richters, A. (1988, July). *Women, emotions and disorders.* Presented at the International Congress of Anthropological and Ethnological Science, Zagreb, Yugoslavia.

Risse, G. B. (1987). Medicine in New Spain. In R. L. Numbers (Ed.), *Medicine in the New World* (pp. 12–41). Knoxville: University of Tennessee Press.

Rothenberg, A. (1964). Puerto Ricans and aggression. *American Journal of Psychiatry, 120,* 962–970.

Rubel, A., O'Neill, C. S., & Collado-Ardon, R. (1984). *Susto, a folk illness,* Berkeley: University of California Press.

Scheper-Hughes, N., & Lock, M. (1986). Speaking the "truth" to illness. *Medical Anthropology Quarterly, 17,* 137–140.

Signorini, I. (1982). Patterns of fright: Multiple concepts of susto in a Nahua–Ladino community of the Sierra de Puebla (Mexico). *Ethnology, 21,* 313–323.

Stevenson, I. N. (1977). Colerina: Reactions to emotional stress in Peruvian Andes. *Social Science and Medicine, 11,* 303–308.

Tousignant, M. (1979). Espanto: A dialogue with the gods. *Culture, Medicine, and Psychiatry, 3,* 347–361.

Tousignant, M. (1984). Pena in the Ecuadorian sierra: A psychoanthropological analysis of sadness. *Culture, Medicine, and Psychiatry, 8,* 381–398.

Van Schaik, E. (1989). Paradigms underlying the study of nerves as a popular illness term in eastern Kentucky. *Medical Anthropology 11,* 15–28.

Verbrugge, L. M. (1985). Triggers of symptoms and health care. *Social Science and Medicine, 20,* 855–875.

Watanabe, J. W. (1982, December). *Realities of the soul: Ethnic identity and cultural convention.* Presented at the annual meeting of the American Anthropological Association, Washington, DC.

THE BURDEN OF RESPONSIBILITY: DUTY, DEPRESSION, AND *NERVIOS* IN ANDEAN ECUADOR

Ruthbeth Finerman, PhD
Department of Anthropology, Memphis State University

Saraguro Indian women possess relatively high status in their community. Nevertheless, they experience high rates of the culturally interpreted illness *nervios*. This syndrome produces symptoms characteristic of stress-induced depression and is identified by Saraguros as the product of suffering and misfortune. Descriptive and quantitative interview data indicate that episodes of *nervios* correlate with experiences of gender role failure, and the condition is identified as a coping mechanism for excessive responsibility and unrealistic social expectation. This syndrome also appears to serve as an effective strategy for enhancing power and social status.

Contemporary literature on gender and health commonly voices the assertion that the socially and politically powerless (usually identified as women) express their frustration over status deprivation through high rates of illness and a range of culture-specific disorders. It is suggested that illness may be exploited as a means of empowerment by commanding the attention and sympathy of socially dominant household and community members (cf. Hamer & Hamer, 1966; Kimball & Craig, 1988; Kleinman & Kleinman, 1985; Lebra, 1972; O'Neill & Selby, 1968; Stewart & Sullivan, 1982).

The use of illness as a coping mechanism has been extensively documented (Foster & Anderson, 1978; Jaco, 1972; Kennedy, 1967; Parsons, 1979; Sigerest, 1977). Nevertheless, the manipulation of health to

Research was supported, in part, by the anthropology departments of the University of California at Los Angeles (UCLA) and Memphis State University. Assistance of the Museo de Antropologia, and the Instituto Nacional de Patrimonio Cultural is gratefully acknowledged. I greatly appreciate the assistance of Douglass Price-Williams and Allen Johnson of UCLA, and Linda Bennett of Memphis State University. Special thanks to my husband, Ross Sackett, for his scholarly insights and his infinite patience. As always, deepest gratitude is owed to the people of Saraguro, whose generous support throughout the years has made research possible and personally fulfilling.

procure care and attention need not be the exclusive prerogative of the socially subjugated members of a population. Individuals facing excessive role responsibility may also be predicted to employ devices providing temporary freedom from personal, household, or community demands and expectations.

A corresponding issue rarely addressed in research on illness as a coping mechanism concerns the problem of efficacy. Is the manipulation of health status a *successful* strategy for securing sympathy and consideration, and how effective is it? Quantitative and qualitative measurements of the social response to illness would verify its power as a means for stress relief. Similarly, few studies have assessed the potential for saturation or overuse of devices for attracting concern and sympathy (Alexander, 1982; Chrisman, 1977). Under what circumstances might health status lose its value as a medium for gaining care and attention?

Descriptive and statistical data collected over a 10-year period in the Andean community of Saraguro indicate that gender role demands and intense pressures to conform with social expectations generate stress, negatively affecting women's health. Saraguro Indian women are perceived to wield control over the domestic sphere, and they are increasingly thought to dominate the local economic sector. Although enjoying relatively high social status (Belote, 1984; Finerman, 1988), Saraguro women nonetheless sustain a high incidence of *nervios* (nerves), a culturally interpreted psychosocial disorder extensively documented throughout Latin America (e.g., Butler, 1982; Garrison, 1977; Guarnaccia, 1985; Harwood, 1981; Low, 1981, 1985; Scheper-Hughes, 1988; Stevenson, 1977; Tousignant, 1984). In Saraguro *nervios* takes the form of a stress-related syndrome exhibiting symptoms characteristic of depression. The disorder is traced in this population to women's efforts to maintain social and economic power, and to the pressures of meeting gender role demands and the unrealistic expectations of family and community. Constituent elements of the syndrome are evaluated along with factors that shape its emergence as a strategy for achieving a temporary "time out," or respite from role responsibilities. The efficacy of *nervios* in stress reduction, and the potential for overreliance on the syndrome to alleviate tension are also considered.

THE CULTURAL SETTING: GENDER ROLES AND POWER

Approximately 17,000 Saraguro Indians populate the southern Andes of Ecuador. At present, more than one-half of this population live on agricultural lands surrounding the county seat of Saraguro, while others have migrated to nearby highland and lowland territories. The town itself supports more than 3,000 artisans and shopkeepers of Spanish and mestizo (mixed) descent, who all bear the local designation of *blancos* or "whites." Saraguros are fully bilingual in Quichua and Spanish, and are easily distinguished from town residents by their maintenance of traditional dress and hair plaiting.

In comparison with many peasant societies, and in marked contrast with *blanco* town residents, Saraguro women command relatively high social status in both domestic and economic spheres, and their status appears to be growing as a result of changes in the production base of the indigenous community.

Saraguro women traditionally supervise virtually all household activities and tend to control most domestic decisions. These women gain additional power within the home by serving as the primary agent in family health care (Finerman, 1985, 1987). Men and women alike inherit land and property such as livestock, and it is not unusual for a Saraguro woman to possess greater wealth than her spouse. The population maintains a moderately flexible sexual division of labor in production, and in recent years women have been forced to assume increased responsibility for most economic tasks (Belote, 1984; Finerman, 1985). Saraguros combine subsistence agropastoralism with a growing dependence on commercial livestock production. Increased investment in pastoralism has encouraged the migration of Saraguro men to the Amazon lowlands, where pasture lands can support larger herds. Consequently, women are more frequently left in charge of homes, families, noncommercial livestock, and cultivation duties. This added responsibility for production has enhanced women's status in the community.[1]

Traditionally extensive gender role responsibilities and increased status accumulated as a result of newly allocated duties have exacted a cost. Saraguro women voice persistent concerns and frustration over the demands of work and family, and participants in research interviews present chronic signs of stress and fatigue. One of the most common expressions of stress appears in the high incidence of *nervios* among adult Saraguro Indian woman.

STRESS, DEPRESSION, AND *NERVIOS*

Qualitative and quantitative data on *nervios* and family health in Saraguro were collected in six field seasons between 1978 and 1988. During

---

[1]Other social, economic, educational, and political changes have also influenced power and stress levels of Saraguro women. For details see Finerman (1988).

the 1980–1981 season a 1-year survey of family illness and therapeutic care was undertaken through monthly interviews with 140 Saraguro Indian mothers (Finerman, 1985). Out of a total of 2,460 illness episodes reported, 154 cases involved *nervios*. The syndrome was identified as the sixth most common health complaint in the overall survey, and the third most common health problem for adult Indian women (the survey informants themselves). Virtually every research subject was found to have suffered at least one episode of the disorder during the year-long study. Furthermore, every Saraguro woman questioned in the last 10 years has reportedly suffered from *nervios* at least once in her life.

The prevalence of *nervios* among adult Saraguro women dictated the need for detailed follow-up studies, which were completed in 1982, 1984, 1986, and 1988. Over this period more than 35 Saraguro women have completed a variety of interviews and open-ended questionnaries on the syndrome. Research volunteers have been asked to describe the causes of *nervios* and symptoms of the disorder, the population at greatest risk, frequency and characteristics of onset, average duration of episodes, and treatment and recovery procedures. *Nervios* case histories have also been collected from most informants.

Etiology

Saraguro descriptions of the causes of *nervios* focus on perceptions about the loss of physical and/or emotional well-being. Informants consistently identify *sufrimiento* (suffering) as the principal cause of the disorder. Informants indicate that circumstances instigating a personal crisis may disturb metabolic function and damage physiological and mental processes. A few individuals suggest that excessive anger, referred to as *iras* or *rabia,* and a magical fright syndrome known as *susto,* can also induce or aggravate the condition. Two informants indicated that while symptoms of the syndrome remain relatively constant, there are actually two separate classes of *nervios*: cases brought on by suffering, and episodes caused by extreme anger.[2] Both women stated that the former version is most common for women, while the latter form is usually specific to adult men. The vast majority of cases, however, are attributed to suffering.

Data were collected tracing specific circumstances that induce suffer-

---

[2]Anger sickness is detailed for the northern Andes of Ecuador by Butler (1982) and Tousignant (1984) where the disorder is also known as *colerin*. Anger sickness remains rare in Saraguro, and Saraguros themselves are unfamiliar with the term *colerin*.

ing and *nervios,* and the frequency with which such conditions are encountered. Subjects reporting *nervios* complaints in the 1980–1981 survey of family illness were asked to identify incidents that had generated the episode, and key informants completing in-depth interviews on the syndrome were asked to detail case histories and precipitating circumstances for each experience with the disorder.

For Saraguros, the most common incident associated with *nervios* was personal and family illness or death, accounting for more than one-half of the episodes recorded in all surveys. Approximately one-quarter of all cases were attributed to domestic discord, including recalcitrance of offspring and *mal comportamiento* (poor comportment) of their spouses (drinking, debauchery, infidelity, and arguing with wives). The remainder of all episodes documented were associated with sporadic cases of shock or sudden fright, and *perjudique,* or abuse generated by malicious gossip, theft, or financial reversals. The select number of cases reported for adult Indian men were attributed to intense anger, and childhood episodes were traced to magical fright or to family discord.

Although *nervios* is clearly rooted in psychosocial conflict, Saraguros identify an equally powerful organic context that shapes its manifestation in the afflicted. Saraguros display a tendency to somatize affective disorders, transforming the experience of powerful emotions into physiological dysfunction (cf. Foster, 1953; Kleinman, 1980, 1986; Kleinman & Kleinman, 1985; Uzzell, 1974). Saraguros identify an organ called *pulsario* as the offending agent in *nervios.* Literally translated as "pulsation," the organ is described as a small sphere positioned at the upper "mouth" of the stomach, and is said to vibrate under conditions of emotional and physical distress. In extreme circumstances *pulsario* breaks free and travels up to the heart, where it causes chest pain and nausea. In rarer instances the sphere reaches the throat and suffocates victims. Saraguros indicate that *nervios* can be fatal, particularly in cases where it accompanies pregnancy. When questioned, several informants provided anecdotal accounts of pregnant women who, unable to resist the illness because of their weakened condition, succumbed to *nervios* and died. A few women also presented vivid details of incidents in which individuals overwhelmed by *nervios* took their own lives.

Symptoms and Characteristics

While data available at present are inadequate for making a reliable diagnosis, *nervios* in Saraguro appears to display symptoms consistent with those for clinical depression. The most common symptoms of *ner-*

vios reported by Saraguro informants include the following (listed in order of frequency): profound sadness; loss of appetite, sleep, and interest in work and family; fatigue; headaches, mental confusion, and poor concentration; trembling, physical agitation, and tension; menstrual irregularity; fits of crying; nightmares; body aches; irritability; and stomachaches. Less common are symptoms such as chest pain, nausea, diarrhea, dizziness, blurred vision, fevers and sweating, and guilt feelings (for additional details see Finerman, 1988, p. 162). One informant described her experience with *nervios* and its symptoms as follows:

> When I have suffering this brings the *nervios* and it is terrible with the *nervios*. Bad headaches and dizziness, stomach aches, nausea. I lose my appetite totally—the belly swells and I can't eat. I cry all the time, worry all the time, and I lose all interest in work, food, sleep. I can't sleep because I think of my troubles, though I have desires to sleep all day. I lose my patience with everyone and can't go outside because I have fears that I will get angry with others.

Such accounts were common in interviews with Saraguro women. Another informant produced a similar account of her symptoms:

> Sometimes, you know really very often, the children get sick. It is my responsibility to keep them healthy, but with children you are always preparing remedies. When they are all sick they cry, they don't want to eat, and this gives me suffering. When it is really bad I can't think and then I start to shake. My hands tremble so much that I can't hold anything; things just fall to the floor. I sit around and cry, I can't remain calm, and I lose patience with my husband and the children. Strong headaches hit me, sweat falls from me, and I can't eat either. Sometimes it keeps up this way, and I can't work or sleep. The only thing that helps is for the children to eat and recover.

Symptoms presented by Saraguro informants resemble criteria for diagnosis of a major depressive episode as outlined in the *Diagnostic and Statistical Manual of Mental Disorders* (Third Edition-Revised) (American Psychiatric Association, 1987), and those specified in depression inventory questionnaries such as the Symptom Check List-90 (Derogatis, 1975) and Zung Self-Rating Depression Scale (Zung, 1965). Moreover, findings suggest that *nervios* in Saraguro conforms with characterizations of the syndrome as a "language of distress" (Davis & Whitten, 1988; Low, 1985; Nichter, 1981), wherein illness acts as a coping mechanism for the articulation and potential resolution of emotional strain and depression (Carr & Vitaliano, 1985; House, Landis, &

Umberson, 1988; Kimball & Craig, 1988; Kleinman, 1986; Ullrich, 1987).

Individuals at Risk for *Nervios*

According to Saraguro informants, anyone experiencing suffering as a result of misfortune or tragedy is at risk for *nervios.* Although no one is excluded by age or gender, women are universally identified by Saraguros as the most common victims of *nervios.* Women are considered more vulnerable because they are thought to exhibit greater sensitivity in response to emotional turmoil and material loss, factors that commonly initiate an episode of *nervios.* As one informant stated,

> The *nervios* affects us all; it catches children, even when they are in the womb—before they are even born. They suffer if their parents treat them badly at home. Then they get fright, they cry and scream. But that is only the children who have bad parents. Men suffer too, but not so much. But women, when they are older and after they marry and have children, they are the ones who have more suffering, more worry. Even those who were calm as children and never knew the sickness before, they also get the *nervios* when they grow older. Some women suffer all the time, others not so much. It all depends on how many burdens we women have, how many troubles find us. Women with many problems, they are the ones affected by the *nervios.*

On initial questioning, most informants suggest that men rarely succumb to *nervios.* Still, Saraguro women do attribute the prevalence of drinking and alcoholism among males to suffering and, by extension, to *nervios,* although causal links may be reversed. Informants variously indicate that men drink to ward off suffering and *nervios,* that they drink because of their troubles, or that men's troubles and *nervios* itself may arise as a consequence of their drinking. Some note that the drunken men's comportment mimicks the symptoms of *nervios.* Still, others point out that men don't necessarily drink because they are unhappy; they frequently drink to excess in celebration, as a friendly challenge, or to seal a business deal.

Onset, Frequency, and Duration of Episodes

The onset and course of *nervios* appear to be highly variable in Saraguro. Approximately two-thirds of all informants interviewed indicate that onset for the syndrome is gradual, remaining dormant for weeks, months and (in rarer cases) even years before the disorder manifests itself, or before it reaches its fullest impact. The remainder, however, maintain that onset can be rapid and require only moments, or a day at most, to instigate an *ataque* (attack) of *nervios*.

Variations in the perception of onset are attributed to the speed with which events precipitating the disorder actually occur. A series of misfortunes that accumulate over a long period of time might eventually take their toll on vulnerable subjects, whereas sudden tragedy would initiate rapid onset. Personal resistance to trauma is also thought to increase the variability of onset. Informants suggest that individuals sustaining greater tolerance of misfortune may forestall an episode of *nervios,* whereas highly sensitive and emotional individuals readily succumb to the disorder.

Inconsistency was also noted with regard to the frequency and duration of *nervios*. Informants stated that frequency varies by luck and personal character; those who encounter recurrent misfortune and those sensitive to adversity are expected to suffer chronic episodes of *nervios*. More than one-half of those questioned indicated that recovery from *nervios* can be painfully slow, requiring months and sometimes years for complete recovery. Several women produced accounts of acquaintances who never recovered, and a few informants recalled victims said to have died from the condition. However, the remainder of those questioned suggested that recovery can be rapid. Variations in duration of *nervios* were related to swiftness with which precipitating events occur and resilience of subjects, the same factors influencing onset and frequency. Saraguros noted that the speedy resolution of problems and the capacity to adjust to unfavorable circumstances can accelerate recovery. Those informants distinguishing between suffering-induced and anger-induced *nervios* also claimed that the latter is more powerful and difficult to cure.

Treatment

Saraguros rely almost exclusively on mothers, or female heads of households, for the treatment of virtually all family health complaints. Indian women supervise a system of home-based therapy combining herbal remedies, pharmaceuticals, bed rest, dietary supplements, and personalized attention to relieve illness (Finerman, 1985). Not surprisingly, then, home-based care was found to be the most common form of therapy for *nervios*. Women treated more than 85% of all reported *nervios* episodes with homemade plant remedies and family support (Finerman, 1988). A few informants also reportedly consulted medical specialists for *nervios*. However, these women all maintained that practitioners had proved ineffective in treating the disorder, and that homebased care was the only successful procedure for relieving the syndrome.

SOCIAL CONSTRUCTION OF *NERVIOS* IN SARAGURO

Research in Saraguro supports the perception of *nervios* as an expression of stress-induced depression. But does this syndrome necessarily denote failure to cope with social and emotional pressures and low social status? Data suggest that for Saraguros, the reverse may be true. Individuals are seen here to use *nervios* as a potential strategy for resolving psychosocial conflict associated with unrealistic gender role expectations. Furthermore, *nervios* is regarded as a possible means to preserve, and even enhance, personal status.

Women are identified as the most frequent victims of *nervios* in Saraguro, and the disorder appears to coincide with inadequate fulfillment of gender roles. Women in this population bear primary responsibility for safeguarding family health and domestic harmony. Those with absent spouses carry the additional burden of maintaining the financial health of the household. Family illness or death, misbehavior of children and spouses, and economic loss generate grief and emotional distress. Such events may also reflect poorly on women themselves, creating fears of recrimination and loss of status and self-esteem. Consequently, *nervios* is identified by informants as a product of misfortune and suffering. Nevertheless, this syndrome may also be viewed as a measure to escape adversity and salvage status.

Informants expressed the opinion that individuals who succumb to *nervios* should not be blamed for their condition or for the events that provoked their illness. The disorder is regarded as proof that the victim was tried beyond endurance by adversity and fell ill from his or her own suffering. Consequently, blame and recrimination would merely exacerbate the disorder. Individuals suffering from *nervios* should also be exempt from responsibility for continued role failure, since one cannot be expected to function effectively while sick. Informants insisted that *nervios* can make it impossible for victims to respond to family or financial crises because they are already debilitated by their condition.

Encounters with *nervios* can also serve to underscore the indispensable quality of the contribution individuals make to their household and community. Informants noted that, since the sick are unable to perform their normal duties, household and community members would be forced to compensate for the lost labor of *nervios* victims. It is assumed that at such times, family and society would come to fully appreciate the adverse consequences of excessive role demands. Consequently, it is expected that the subsequently increased recognition that *nervios* victims earn can help to sustain and even elevate their power and status.

NERVIOS AS A SUCCESSFUL COPING MECHANISM

The question then remains, is *nervios* a successful strategy for managing stress induced by gender role responsibilities? Interview data from Saraguro indicate that for the majority of cases recorded, this syndrome provided opportunities for an effective, sanctioned release from expectations of task fulfillment. More important, these respites were found to benefit long-term adaptation to stress by supplying the time needed to resolve crises and to reconcile role demands.

The efficacy of *nervios* for procuring attention and freedom from duties is readily illustrated by Saraguro women's case histories. Most episodes recorded demonstrate that the condition provided relief from responsibilities and recognition from concerned family members. Examples of responses to *nervios* are presented below (subjects are identified with pseudonyms).

Case 1: Angelina

When I lived in the Oriente [Amazon] with my husband, my father died here in Saraguro. When I received the notice that he had died, it was like a fist hit me in the stomach. I had attacks, like rapid convulsions. My chest became tight, I felt weak and dizzy and lost my senses. I felt sick that I wasn't there to care for him, as my mother was too old to care for him alone. I had other family with me, and they gave me home remedies to cure me. My husband helped me very much. He kept me calm and looked after me, and he and my family did all the work around the house. My husband even cooked for the children! I got better so that I was able to eat and work again, but I suffered spasms with the *nervios* for almost 2 years. I recovered with the help of my family, and when my husband and family are calm. It is hard for them when I can't work and care for them, so they try to help.

Case 2: Balbina

If a woman finds herself married to a man who, by disgrace, is of bad character, bad comportment, she will fall with the *nervios*. This is what happened to me. When I married, my husband moved into my mother's house with me. Our house wasn't ready yet; it had not been built. So we spent our first years of matrimony there. But this resulted badly because my husband grew very lazy. I had plenty of my own money and land, so we had food to eat. Since he did not need to save money he spent it on rum. He drank and was abusive and I suffered. I sat on my bed all day and all night, crying and staring into the fire in the hearth. I had headaches, and when my husband drank I would shake and my heart pounded in my chest like it would break out of my body. My family didn't want to interfere, and my mother told me I must learn not to be afraid of my husband and spend my days just crying. This helped. Then my father bought medicines and gave them to my husband to give to me. My husband saw that his bad comportment had made me suffer the *nervios* and he stopped drinking. He started to work harder to make money, and saved his money so that our house could be completed quickly. I felt much better after this, and with my home remedies, and I recovered. I still suffer with the *nervios,* especially when my husband drinks, but not so much. He knows I suffer when he drinks and mistreats me, and others tell him so too. So he doesn't drink so much anymore.

Case 3: Carmen

With the children I suffer much with the *nervios*. When they are sick they cry and make much molestation, and don't work. They can't help me with the work; I must do everything. I can't send them to buy something in the town or let them go outside because they are too sick, and my husband and my family criticize me for their sickness. I have much work, and suffer from the children and for the many insults of others, and I get the *nervios*. When this happens bad headaches hit me, I get stomach aches and nausea, dizziness and heart palpitations. I can't think about anything, and can't work well. Sometimes, when this happens my sister or my mother or mother-in-law come and help with the work, and give me remedies. My husband also helps with the children and I stop spinning [wool] and sewing, and other work that gives me dizzy spells. I must rest and eat better, and after a few days I recover. But when the children get sick my *nervios* starts again.

These select examples demonstrate that even women possessing considerable social status (in terms of wealth and responsibility for domestic or economic labor) are subject to *nervios*. The disorder appears not because they lack power, but because they are stressed by excessive role responsibility or social expectations (for family health, production, and domestic harmony). Under favorable conditions *nervios* permits release time from duties, which must be absorbed by others in the household. In the cases presented, and in a majority of case histories followed in research, families forced to compensate for the loss of maternal care and labor appeared highly responsive to measures that would restore the status quo of the household. While informants themselves are understandably reluctant to admit that they gained satisfaction from falling ill, it seems clear that these women achieved measurable gratification from the spousal and familial support they received. The disorder successfully attracted the immediate attention and sympathy of family members, and transient episodes produced substantive, long-term gains in power by increasing the informant's control over the comportment of others.

Nervios carries the additional benefit of performing as a nonstigmatizing disorder, particularly for Saraguro women. While Saraguro men are generally expected to demonstrate a moderate level of stoicism in the face of tragedy, susceptibility to the syndrome is not generally regarded as a sign of weakness or personal failure. For women, the syndrome also tends to affirm emotional stability by demonstrating sensitivity to pain and misfortune. Most informants were skeptical about the suggestion that someone could be unfamiliar with *nervios.* They noted that everyone suffers with sickness, malicious gossip, theft, physical abuse, the death of a loved one, or some other misfortune in their life. Therefore, anyone who claimed they had never experienced *nervios* would be regarded as profoundly insensitive or highly suspect.

The high incidence rate for *nervios* also effectively legitimizes the disorder and minimizes likelihood that sufferers will be burdened with the stigma often associated with other illnesses (Parsons, 1979). Although sickness in itself is an abnormal and troublesome condition, the prevalence of *nervios* may place it in the category of "compulsory diseases" (Foster & Anderson, 1978, pp. 40–41). It is expected that virtually all women, and many men and children, will experience at least one episode of *nervios* at some point in their lives. Consequently, the condition is often described as serious yet commonplace. As one informant stated, "Life is filled with suffering, so everyone has the *nervios*."

FAILURE OF *NERVIOS* IN STRESS REDUCTION

Under some circumstances *nervios* might prove ineffective as a coping mechanism for stress and gender role demands. A number of factors shape family and community responses to the disorder. For example, individuals unable to effectively articulate their distress limit their ability to secure sympathy and assistance. Other individuals, lacking an audience sympathetic to their condition, may fail to attract support in relieving strain. One such case was presented by an elderly informant:

> It has been 11 years now since my husband died. He had a hemorrhage and they took him to the hospital in Cuenca but they couldn't save him. When this happened it was like a knife cut into me. My heart beat, I shook like this—like an earthquake. I cried for months. I just couldn't stop. Even at celebrations I felt bad and I couldn't talk; it was like my voice had gone away. Everyone said I would recover but this wasn't the case. It has been 11 years now and I still suffer. I still cry. What do you think causes this? I can't sleep at night. I lie down in my bed waiting to sleep, but I think of all my pain and troubles and sleep leaves me. I eat nothing, my appetite left me. I have no children now to take care of me. They are all married and live [far away] in the Oriente. Two of my children died; a son and a daughter. I have no one to talk to; family, friends, no one. So I sit alone in the house and cry and stare at the wall.

A further problem associated with reliance on *nervios* as a coping mechanism concerns the potential for overuse of this strategy for stress relief, resulting in what may be termed "the patient who cried wolf." In these cases, individuals who succumb too readily or too frequently to *nervios* may extinguish the response level of family, friends, and even therapists, by taxing their capacity to react enthusiastically to persistent health complaints. Alexander (1982) noted that chronically ill patients might not be freed from role responsibilities or from blame for their condition. An example of this phenomenon is revealed in an unresolved case of *nervios* from Saraguro. This informant discussed her bitterness at failing to attract sympathy for her disorder:

> When I married, at first my husband treated me well. He worked with the animals and then came home and helped me. But he began to drink and this made me suffer. He would spend money on rum and drink and mistreat me. Sometimes he would go to drink with those disgracefuls his friends, and end up asleep in the street. Then he left his work. The children had to stop helping me with my work and take care of the animals. He would also mistreat the children, and they would get very quiet and cry. They didn't have enough to eat because he didn't work and they were sick all the time from the bad comportment of their father. My mother said I had married badly, and was not taking proper care of my children. All this made me suffer and the *nervios* caught me. I cried all the time and couldn't eat, and I couldn't work. The children had to do my work and that of their father. At first he saw how it was, that he was making the children and me sick with pain, and he left off drinking. But after a while he returned to the drink and came home intoxicated, and the

> *nervios* started again. My mother and the older ones said that all this is my own fault; that my suffering is ridiculous and I should stop crying and go back to my children and my work. After this no one cared that I suffered. It meant nothing; my husband drank anyway. That is how it is. He drinks and I suffer. I cry but nothing comes of it; it doesn't help me at all. This life is suffering when you have a husband who doesn't mind you, who drinks and doesn't care.

In this instance, the informant achieved initial success in securing sympathy and control over the behavior of family members. However, as her *nervios* episodes grew increasingly frequent and persistent, accrued benefits gradually gave way to ridicule and neglect from the household and community.

DISCUSSION

Stress has been shown to bear close causal links to illness (Blumhagen, 1982; Brenner, 1981; Janes, 1986; Restak, 1988), and sickness is commonly observed to provide an escape from tension and responsibility. Might stress-induced illness therefore denote failure to cope? The appearance of psychosocial stress in Saraguro suggests that culturally interpreted syndromes such as *nervios* actually represent coping skills for adapting to distress. Although such disorders do permit short-term evasion of duties, they also ensure long-term compliance with social role demands. Sick leave provides sufficient time to adjust to expectations, and social support and emotional reinforcement necessary to encourage role resumption.

Research in Saraguro further demonstrates that stress is not a health concern limited to the socially disenfranchized. Those burdened by overwhelming gender role responsibilities are similarly inclined to suffer from emotional strain induced by efforts to maintain or increase personal status. It is therefore suggested that *nervios* does not merely signify a plea from the powerless. In some instances it also expresses demands for status recognition, cooperation, and control by individuals occupying positions of relative influence.

Case histories from Saraguro reveal that in a majority of instances, *nervios* continues to function as a highly effective coping skill, and failure to attract support remains comparatively rare. Still, continued success hinges on the ability to employ such strategies on a short-term, selective basis. Chronic or persistent incapacitation diminishes the desired effect of the sick role on family and community members, producing the stigmatized status of *nervios* sufferers as "career patients" (Foster & Anderson, 1978, p. 160). It seems clear, nevertheless, that such mechanisms present an adaptive response to conditions of stress and lend meaning to the fulfillment of gender roles.

REFERENCES

Alexander, L. (1982). Illness maintenance and the new American sick role. In N. Chrisman & T. Maretzki (Eds.), *Clinically applied anthropology* (pp. 351–367). Boston: D. Reidel.

American Psychiatric Association. (1987). *Diagnostic and statistical manual of mental disorders (Third edition–revised).* Washington, DC: Author.

Belote, J. (1984). *Changing adaptive strategies among the Saraguros of southern Ecuador.* Unpublished doctoral dissertation, University of Illinois, Urbana-Champagne.

Blumhagen, D. (1982). The meaning of hypertension. In N. Chrisman & T. Maretzki (Eds.), *Clinically applied anthropology* (pp. 297–323). Boston: D. Reidel.

Brenner, M. (1981). The importance of the economy to the nation's health. In L. Eisenberg & A. Kleinman (Eds.), *The relevance of social science for medicine* (pp. 371–395). Boston: D. Reidel.

Butler, B. (1982). Anger sickness: social stress and native diagnosis among Ecuadorian Indians. In M. Aguwa (Ed.), *Women, health, and development* (pp. 121–132). Ann Arbor, MI: Office of Women in International Development, Michigan State University.

Carr, J., & Vitaliano, P. (1985). The theoretical implications of converging research on depression and the culture-bound syndrome. In A. Kleinman & B. Good (Eds.), *Culture and depression: Studies in the anthropology and cross-cultural psychiatry of affect and disorder* (pp. 244–266). Berkeley: University of California Press.

Chrisman, N. (1977). The health seeking process. *Culture, Medicine, and Psychiatry, 1,* 351–377.

Davis, D., & Whitten, R. (1988). Medical and popular traditions of nerves. *Social Science and Medicine, 26,* 1209–1221.

Derogatis, L. (1975). *The SCL-90-R.* Baltimore: Clinical Psychometric Research.

Finerman, R. (1985). *Health care decisions in an Andean Indian community: Getting the best of both worlds.* Unpublished doctoral dissertation, University of California, Los Angeles.

Finerman, R. (1987). Inside out: Women's world view and family health in an Ecuadorian Indian community. *Social Science and Medicine, 25,* 1157–1162.

Finerman, R. (1988). The price of power: Gender roles and stress-induced depression in Andean Ecuador. In P. Whelehan (Ed.), *Women and health: Cross-cultural perspectives* (pp. 153–169). Granby, MA: Bergin & Garvey.

Foster, G. (1953). Relationships between Spanish and Spanish-American folk medicine. *Journal of American Folklore, 66,* 201–217.

Foster, G., & Anderson, B. (1978). *Medical anthropology.* New York: Wiley.

Garrison, V. (1977). The "Puerto Rican Syndrome" in psychiatry and espiritismo. In V. Crapanzano & V. Garrison (Eds.), *Case studies in spirit possession* (pp. 383–448). New York: Wiley.

Guarnaccia, P. (1985). *Ataques de nervios: An idiom of distress in the Latino community.* Paper presented at the meeting of the American Anthropological Association, Washington, DC.

Hamer, J., & Hamer, I. (1966). Spirit possession and its socio-psychological implications among the Sidamo of southwest Ethiopia. *Ethnology, 5,* 392–408.

Harwood, A. (1981). *Ethnicity and medical care.* Cambridge, MA: Harvard University Press.

House, J., Landis, K., & Umberson, D. (1988). Social relationships and health. *Science, 241,* 540–545.

Jaco, E. (1972). *Patients, physicians, and illness.* New York: Free Press.

Janes, C. (1986). Migration and hypertension: An ethnography of disease risk in an urban Samoan community. In C. Janes, R. Stall, & S. Gifford (Eds.), *Anthropology and epidemiology* (pp. 175–211). Boston: D. Reidel.

Kennedy, J. (1967). Nubian Zar ceremonies as psychotherapy. *Human Organization, 4,* 185–194.

Kimball, L., & Craig, S. (1988). Women and stress in Brunei. In P. Whelehan (Ed.), *Women and health: cross-cultural perspectives* (pp. 170–182). Granby, MA: Bergin & Garvey.

Kleinman, A. (1980). *Patients and healers in the context of culture.* Berkeley: University of California Press.

Kleinman, A. (1986). *Social origins of distress and disease: Depression, neurasthenia, and pain in modern China.* New Haven, CT: Yale University Press.

Kleinman, A., & Kleinman, J. (1985). Somatization: The interconnections in Chinese society among culture, depressive experiences, and the meanings of pain. In A. Kleinman & B. Good (Eds.), *Culture and depression* (pp. 429–490). Englewood Cliffs, NJ: Prentice-Hall.

Lebra, T. (1972). Religious conversion and elimination of the sick role: A Japanese sect in Hawaii. In T. Lebra (Ed.), *Transcultural research in mental health* (Vol. 2., pp. 282–292). Honolulu: University of Hawaii Press.

Low, S. (1981). Meaning of nervios: A sociocultural analysis of symptom presentation in San Jose, Costa Rica. *Culture, Medicine, and Psychiatry, 5,* 350–357.

Low, S. (1985). Culturally interpreted symptoms or culture-bound syndromes: A cross-cultural review of nerves. *Social Science and Medicine, 21,* 187–196.

Nichter, M. (1981). Idioms of distress. Alternatives in the expression of psychosocial distress: A case study from South India. *Culture, Medicine, and Psychiatry, 5,* 379–408.

O'Neill, C., & Selby, H. (1968). Sex differences in the incidence of susto in two Zapotec pueblos: An analysis of the relationship between sex role expectations and a folk illness. *Ethnology, 7,* 95–105.

Parsons, T. (1979). Definitions of health and illness in the light of American values and social structure. In E. Jaco (Ed.), *Patients, physicians, and illness* (pp. 120–144). New York: Free Press.

Restak, R. (1988). *The mind.* New York: Bantam.

Scheper-Hughes, N. (1988). *The madness of hunger: Sickness, delirium, and human needs.* Paper presented at the 12th International Congress of Anthropological and Ethnological Sciences, Zagreb, Yugoslavia.

Sigerest, H. (1977). The special position of the sick. Reprinted in abridged form in D. Landy (Ed.), *Culture, disease, and healing* (pp. 388–394). New York: Macmillan. (Original work published 1929).

Stevenson, I. (1977). Cholerina: Reactions to emotional stress in the Peruvian Andes. *Social Science and Medicine, 11,* 303–307.

Stewart, D., & Sullivan, T. (1982). Illness behavior and the sick role in chronic disease. *Science and Medicine, 16,* 1397–1404.

Tousignant, M. (1984). Pena in the Ecuadorian sierra: A psychoanthropological analysis of sadness. *Culture, Medicine, and Psychiatry, 8,* 381–398.

Ullrich, H. (1987). A study of change and depression among Havik brahmin women in a south Indian village. *Culture, Medicine, and Psychiatry, 11,* 261–287.

Uzzell, D. (1974). Susto revisited: Illness as a strategic role. *American Ethnologist, 1,* 369-378.

Zung, W. (1965). A self-rating depression scale. *Archives of General Psychiatry, 12,* 63–70.

NOTES ON *NERVIOS*: A DISORDER OF MENOPAUSE

Elyse Ann Barnett, PhD
Department of Anthropology, Foothill College

The condition of nerves among women in the small Peruvian town of Puente Piedre is described. Both *nervios* (a symptom) and *Nervios* (a disorder) describe a woman's difficulty with nerves. In Puente Piedre, the identification of an anxiety condition among women depends only on the women's age. Younger women with anxiety symptoms are diagnosed as *nervios,* a temporary condition ascribed to a single episode of high blood pressure. Menopausal women with similar symptoms, on the other hand, are thought to have a specific disorder, *Nervios.* In Puente Piedre, *Nervios* clearly is a folk illness limited to women of menopausal age.

In the Peruvian town of Puente Piedre, a young woman walks into a pharmacy, saying that she feels *nervios.* The pharmacist may ask a few questions regarding symptoms such as headaches or dizziness, but basically both the pharmacist and the woman know that a medication to lower blood pressure is needed. The woman is given a single tablet of an antihypertensive medication selected by the pharmacist and is not expected to suffer further sequelae. A middle-aged woman, however, walks into the pharmacy and says that she has *Nervios.* She will receive a tranquilizer from the pharmacist, with instructions either to take a long walk or go to the movies within the week. Thus, *nervios* refers to a symptom of hypertension in the young, and *Nervios* refers to an unrelated emotional disorder among menopausal women.

In Puente Piedre, *nerves* is unique in many ways from similar entities reported elsewhere because it is both a symptom and a disorder. Although the complaints reported by women appear similar, age alone determines interpretation and treatment. Furthermore, men are never affected by either the symptom or the disorder. Men do suffer from hypertension (*presion alta*), but they do not complain of *nervios* even in the presence of high blood pressure. On the basis of ethnographic material collected in Puente Piedre, I suggest that in some cultures, nerves may indeed be interpreted as a female disorder. In Puente Piedre, *Nervios* is a culture-bound disorder of menopausal women.

THE SETTING

Data were collected during a 15-month study of menopause and women's health in Puente Piedre. This *pueblo joven* (shanty town) is located 30 km northeast of Lima, Peru. Beginning as one of the first *pueblos jovenes* outside of Lima, Puente Piedre was the first such settlement to grow into a full-fledged town. The town had grown from a mere 30 families in 1900 to 571 families in 1940. More than 900 families resided in Puente Piedre in 1980. Ninety-six percent of women residents over the age of 40 years had immigrated to Puente Piedre. Seventeen percent of the residents had relocated from the inner city slums of Lima; the majority had immigrated from small traditional mestizo communities in the hinterlands.

Puente Piedre offered relatively improved living conditions for families emigrating from both locations, but the women lived in a culture of "transition" as described by Datan (1971). According to Datan, women in the middle of the continuum from traditional to modern life are likely to have difficulties during their menopause. Datan's assumption is that such women have few effective means of dealing with stress, because they have rejected old coping skills before accepting new ones. For example, a menopausal woman might refuse to see *la brujéria* (the witch doctor) believing that native healers are not acceptable, but she might also refuse to see a Western practitioner because she is not familiar with modern medicine. Indeed, we would expect women of all ages to be more susceptible to stress in the absence of effective coping mechanisms.

Living in a culture of transition appears to have influenced the incidence and treatment of nerves among the women of Puente Piedre. For younger women, single episodes of *nervios* apparently constitute a disorder that has been recently recognized. Although the condition of *Nervios* is recognized among older women throughout Peru, women in the *pueblos jovenes* appear to use drug treatment more frequently than do those in other communities throughout Peru.

DATA COLLECTION

The Maoz-Datan (Datan, 1971) interview, open-ended questions, and the Menopause Index (Kupperman, Blatt, Wiebader, & Filler, 1953) were used to gather information. The Maoz-Datan interview contains multiple-choice questions on adolescence, marriage, childbearing, motherhood, grandparent role, self-esteem, menstruation, menopause, aging, and coping styles. I always encouraged the women to elaborate on their answers. To avoid leading questions about symptoms, an open-ended interview format was used before scoring the Menopause Index. (Symptoms included in the Index consist of vasomotor instability, paresthesias, insomnia, nervousness, melancholia, vertigo, fatigue, arthralgia, headaches, palpitation, and formication—a form of dysesthesia.) During these interviews 85% of the women reported suffering from nerves.

On the basis of preliminary data, I modified the interview to collect data particular to the health and well-being of the women of Puente Piedre. For example, I specifically asked women if they were married, divorced, separated, or living in an "appearances" marriage—one in which both spouses lived under the same roof, but did not speak to one another (Barnett, 1986). I asked women specifically if they had ever suffered from *nervios* whenever they volunteered that they had difficulties with nerves and anxiety. A woman could complete the interview in less than 1 hr, but because most women preferred to elaborate, the interviews often lasted 2 to 3 hr.

Final data were collected from more than 400 women. Although the focus of my original research concerned menopausal women, proper protocol required that I interview all older women initially. Thus, I saw 23 older women first, then I interviewed 97 menopausal women for my own study. Finally, my research assistants and I interviewed an additional 300 women of all ages.

Information was also collected while observing in the local clinic, in the pharmacies, and in daily living situations. I lived with families in the community, and they frequently discussed health and illness. During my observations, I gradually became aware that another condition of nerves affected younger women in the village. Thus, two separate disorders emerged: As described, younger women complained of a symptom, *nervios,* whereas menopausal women reported in illness, *Nervios.*

FOLK MEDICAL BELIEF SYSTEM IN PUENTE PIEDRE

Discussion about health and illness generally focused on traditional folk medical beliefs of *hot* and *cold;* knowledge of these traditional folk concepts is essential to the understanding of young women who complain of nerves and of menopausal women who complain of *Nervios.* The nosology of nerves in women is based on current reproductive history, which is in turn explained by concepts of *hot-cold* medicine.

In many indigenous and mestizo cultures throughout Latin America, hot and cold humors in human physiology are recognized. A balance of these two entities is necessary for good health (Currier, 1966; Simmons, 1955). Traditionally, hot–cold medicine defines foods, beverages, herbs, and medications as being either *hot* or *cold.* Rather than describing any inherent physical characteristics such as temperature, color, or texture, *hot* and *cold* refer to presumed operative effects on human physiology (Currier, 1966).

When anyone in Puente Piedre reports a fever, the local physician asks whether the fever can be measured with a thermometer. The patient can readily state that the fever is measurable or is "inside." Physicians recognize and distinguish the two forms. Women who are *hot* inside are expected to obey certain taboos, avoiding certain foods and not bathing. Lemons, *aji,* and most food spices—normally consumed daily—are not permitted. Most women bathe only weekly, so the taboo on bathing is not as difficult for older women to observe. The interactions of affected women with other people do not change.

A cold imbalance, on the other hand, does modify a woman's interactions with other people. Afflicted women report being *frio* toward family and friends. For example, these women might raise their voices to family members for behaviors that they would tolerate at other times. The women's behaviors at these times are manifestations of an internal state of being cold, rather than expressions of their psyche.

In Latin American cultures, the various stages of women's reproductive physiology also are often defined as intrinsically hot or cold. Menstruation and pregnancy make a woman hot. For example, 40% of the women interviewed in Puente Piedre specifically noted a fever "inside" at the time of their first menstruation. A common scenario in which a woman discovered her first menstruation was described as follows: "I felt hot, very hot. I was burning with fever. So, I went down to the stream and I began to bathe myself. Then I saw blood."

Menopause was defined as cold, and women after menopause were subject to periods of *frio.* Women did not seek medical attention for the condition of *frio,* although some women reported that eating citrus fruits suppressed their irritability.

During *la edad critica,* the transition to menopause, women suffered from extremes of *hot* and *cold.* Furthermore, they frequently did not initally recognize transitions from one condition to the other. Women reported that these years were confusing and unpleasant because they no longer had regular monthly cycles: "Horrible, horrible, horrible. First I had a flow, then I didn't. I didn't know what was happening."

These women seemed distressed not so much by the lack of monthly cycles as by their inability to tell, in the absence of menstrual regularity, whether they were hot or cold. Women repeatedly emphasized to me that if a woman took a bath, only to discover that she was menstruating, that "the blood will go to your head and cause serious headaches during menopause."

Only women who abruptly ceased to menstruate were perceived as experiencing a healthy transition to their nonreproductive years. None of the women accepted irregularity of their cycles before cessation of menses as normal, even though such irregularity is the most common pattern in all menopausal women. Women regarded *la edad critica* as being fraught with risks of ill health. They attributed the high incidence of illness to the frequent imbalance of hot and cold within the woman's body.

Next to headaches, *Nervios* was the most common disorder attributed to hot and cold imbalance among menopausal women. It is unclear whether the women believed that hot and cold imbalance actually caused *Nervios* or that the continual stress of attempting to maintain a hot–cold balance within the body resulted in *Nervios.* Hot and cold imbalance was never mentioned in connection with *nervios* among young women.

Hemorrhage and hypertension, thought to be more prevalent in middle-aged women than in younger women, were interpreted as placing women at particular risk from *Nervios.* Hemorrhage, inferred by local obstetricians from a high rate of spontaneous abortions in middle-aged women, was commonly interpreted by women as extreme hot and cold imbalance. The uncomfortable symptoms of hypertension (such as frequent headaches, fatigue, or visual disturbances) weaken older women's resistance to *Nervios,* according to local folk medical beliefs. In the absence of sphygmomanometers, these symptoms were also interpreted by local physicians as evidence of hypertension.

Women believed that menstrual irregularity, which often occurred at the onset of menopause, posed an even greater risk factor than hemorrhage or hypertension. Women would attempt to force an abrupt transition to menopause in order to prevent *Nervios.* Women felt that it was possible to trigger an abrupt transition to menopause by having a "menopause baby" or by a variety of medical treatments.

NERVES, *SUSTO,* AND *LOCURA* IN PUENTE PIEDRE

The complaint of nerves frequently has been associated with women, rather than with men, in the anthropology literature. Some anthropologists have questioned whether nerves might be present among equal numbers of men (but not reported because of cultural pressures) or whether the same symptoms might be labeled differently for men in some cultures. For example, Low (1981) suggested that men with nerves might label their symptoms as *susto* (fright illness) in some Latin American societies. The study of nerves among persons of Puente Piedre is particularly important because only women are affected, and the disorder is considered separate and distinct from *susto.*

There was never any confusion between conditions of nerves, *susto,* or *locura* among women. A fright, as in *susto,* was thought to pose the danger of losing one's soul. A person who loses his or her soul suffers the classic symptoms of depression in Western medicine: loss of appetite, disinterest in the world, insomnia, and a multitude of somatic complaints. Men, women, and children could suffer from *susto.*

Young women might also be *loca,* crazy. Either the women were born *loca* or they became *loca* after suffering from *susto.* Young women never develop *loca* as a sequela of *nervios.* On the other hand, menopausal women with *Nervios* might well progress to *locura,* a state of permanent craziness.

The great danger posed by *susto* at menopause was the tendency to become *loca* permanently. *Susto,* therefore, presented a greater risk to middle-aged women than to men or younger women in the society. However, if a younger woman's *susto* resulted in premature menopause, the woman was likely to become *loca.* The danger of turning *loca* was frequently reinforced by the well-known case of a woman who had suffered from *susto,* was frightened into menopause, and became *loca.* This woman was alive and roamed the community speaking unintelligible words during the time I lived in Puente Piedre.

PRESENTATION AND TREATMENT OF NERVES

The distinction between *nervios* (the symptom) and *Nervios* (the disease) can be understood by an analogy. In Western society, a psychiatrist differentiates a patient's subjective reports of sadness from the diagnostic entity termed "depression." The person who is "feeling depressed" is expected to remain functional in society and to recover on his or her own, whereas the individual with the condition "depression" may have decreased social capabilities and may be observed for suicidal ideation. By contrast, however, differentiating the two kinds of *nerves* in Puente Piedre never requires a skilled diagnostician: A woman's age defines the disorder from which she suffers. The younger woman is expected to continue with her usual duties and obligations. The older woman, however, must be watched carefully, lest she "go crazy." Indeed, many of the taboos associated with menopause are directed toward reducing the recurrence of *Nervios.* Unlike in the United States and Canada, where emotional disorders are viewed as separate and distinct from physical disorders, in Peru all illness is thought to be organic.

In young women, the symptom *nervios* is often reported as pressure in the head or as a pounding heart beat. The Peruvian's presumptive diagnosis of an isolated hypertensive episode causing *nervios* is different, however, from the diagnosis of hypertension referred to in Western medicine. Although both forms of hypertension are referred to as *presion alta* (high pressure), *nervios* is acute and self-limiting, whereas "simple" *presion alta* is chronic.

It is interesting to note that with only one exception, neither any woman I interviewed nor any of her family members who were present actually had high blood pressure (diastolic pressure above 90 mm Hg). Although even physicians in the town rarely had equipment to take blood pressure measurement and frequently relied on the patient's complaints to prescribe antihypertensive drugs, I did possess such equipment and offered free blood pressure readings to all interviewees and to members of their families.

Generally, men and women with continuous headaches and visual disturbances sought professional medical advice. In contrast, women who suspected that they suffered from *nervios* frequently sent a child to the pharmacy for medication. The same medication, methyldopa, was prescribed both for acute "hypertension," or *nervios,* and for chronic hypertension. The physicians and pharmacists both believed that it was difficult to lower blood pressure excessively with this particular antihypertensive medication; a single dose of methyldopa even given to persons with normal blood pressure is unlikely to cause untoward side effects. Hence, the drug in the dose given for *nervios* never produced any pronounced negative side effects that might have led women to question methyldopa as the optimal treatment for *nervios.*

Nervios was reported by 80% of all menopausal women interviewed. Women identified relapsing episodes of *Nervios* throughout their menopause years, tending to emphasize their experiences with *Nervios* more than any other disorder of menopause. Specifically, when women were asked to discuss their last paroxysm of *Nervios,* they frequently referred to actions that they had taken to prevent "what would have been a terrible case." For example, a woman might report that she suddenly had to go for a long walk to prevent another episode of *Nervios.*

A women who suffered from *Nervios* did not "act like herself." She often felt *abruido* (boredom), a foreboding symptom of *Nervios* that could lead to *locura* if not treated. In addition, menopausal women suffering from *Nervios* reported a variety of manifestations often using idiomatic expressions: *muy mal de humor* (very bad humor), *grita a los hijos* (yelling), *pega otras* (hitting others), *fastidia* (finding fault with everything), and *colera* (anger). In each situation, the woman said that she was "out of control" and later experienced remorse. Women's behaviors in each case resulted from their state of hot–cold imbalance.

When women took estrogens at menopause, they did so primarily to prevent irregular periods, and only rarely to ameliorate any other menopausal symptoms. Women could request hormone prescriptions from their physicians or obtain over-the-counter estrogens. From time to time, women would stop taking estrogens to see whether the danger of irregularity had passed. Thus, women often forced an abrupt transition to menopause pharmacologically.

Unlike women in Newfoundland (Davis, 1983), Peruvian women never referred to estrogen tablets as "nerve pills." Women commonly stopped taking estrogen when they were certain that they would no longer have menstrual cycles. Only tranquilizers were considered to be "nerve pills." Given the confusing data on the efficacy of estrogen replacement therapy in reducing anxiety among menopausal women (Davey, 1981), it is not surprising that women from Newfoundland use estrogen, whereas those from Peru use tranquilizers. Either medication may be effective in dealing with the increased anxiety that can accompany menopause.

Peruvian women also sought a variety of alternative treatments for *Nervios* when possible. All women believed in folk medical practices for *Nervios*. Only traditional mothers, however, generally had the opportunity to pursue such time-consuming options. Thus, traditional mothers followed folk medical treatments and then turned to Western medical practices in cases of incomplete cure. Laborers with less free time often went to physicians and pharmacists first, turning to folk medical practices as a second option.

Women who suffered from *Nervios* reported that they felt overwhelming impulses take walks, go to the movies with friends, or drink cups of special tea. These same actions were even prescribed by physicians as treatment. Doing something to distract oneself from the symptoms of *Nervios* was a common home remedy and was frequently recommended by folk healers and physicians alike. Laborers, however, were likely to seek the advice of a pharmacist and therefore were most often treated with tranquilizers.

The belief in the dangers of *locura* provided many secondary gains for menopausal women with *Nervios*. The predisposition to *Nervios* was treated with special teas and foods, principally vegetables. Obtaining the right tea always involved leaving home and going either to market or to a friend's house. Procuring vegetables meant either a trip to market or tending a garden. Although menopausal women were permitted to consume large quantities of vegetables, such a diet was unusual in Puente Piedre, because people believed that eating vegetables in excess would lead to parasites. Whether treating their *Nervios* with teas or vegetables, women seemed to benefit from both the social experience and the special diet.

The usefulness of entertainment as a therapeutic tool for combating *nervios* was also well recognized. As a result, women with the disorder frequently went to the movies. It was important for women to go either alone or with a friend, although an understanding spouse might offer to escort his wife to the theater door. Older sons had the responsibility of providing the money necessary for their mothers' cinematic excursions.

NERVIOS, GENDER ROLES, AND SOCIAL ORGANIZATION

A transfer of control from the husband to the wife was undoubtedly the most important social function served by *Nervios.* A husband was extremely solicitous of his wife when she suffered from *Nervios,* especially if he desired to maintain a close relationship with his spouse after her menopausal years. Certainly, women who had close relationships with their husbands stressed to me the special support given to them during menopause when they suffered from *Nervios.*

The folk illness of *Nervios* may have helped couples to make the transition from the father supporting the family to the sons providing the primary income. In the absence of a welfare system, older sons assumed financial responsibility for their aging parents. Customarily, sons would give their paycheck to their mother. Thus, women assumed a new position of power by controlling the financial resources of the family. Without acknowledging that women had more independence with their newfound financial security, men could allow women with *Nervios* more freedom.

To prevent women from developing *locura* as a result of *abruido*—a warning sign of intractable *Nervios*—men allowed women the freedom to come and go from their homes as they pleased. Women with *Nervios* were allowed to be alone; at all other times, a solitary woman was perceived as both lonely and at risk of impropriety. Although wanting to be solitary was never considered in a favorable light if expressed by other individuals in society, a wish for privacy was a classic symptom of *Nervios.* Indeed, the desire was much more than a wish—it was a "need" beyond the woman's control.

Although I do not have data to calculate rates of recovery from *Nervios,* I suspect that women who wished to distance themselves from their husbands did so by maintaining the role of the woman affected by *Nervios.* Many of these women maintained a relationship with their spouses "for the sake of their children," and the incidence of *Nervios* legitimated solo activities. Divorce or separation was never socially accepted in Puente Piedre; in cases of extreme marital discord, spouses frequently lived under one roof, never speaking to each other. "Appearance marriages," in which husband and wife lived separate lives in the same household, were often the subject of disapproving gossip in the community. Women who achieved independence from their spouses as a result of *Nervios,* however, did not encounter such stigma.

Children were typically well behaved when their mothers were suffering from *Nervios.* Women reported that their children would avoid squabbles, speak in quieter tones of voice, and be very accommodating. One common manifestation of *Nervios* was *irritabilidad* (being short tempered with others). Children were particularly careful to avoid actions that would provoke *irritabilidad* in their mothers.

In Puente Piedre, the relationship between *Nervios* and *locura* behavior was imprecise. If a women with *Nervios* returned to more "normal" behaviors after menopause, she frequently referred to her *Nervios* as a temporary period of *locura.* Only the woman herself could choose to describe her previous behaviors as being transiently crazy. Other people in society could not make this judgment, although again there was no stigma attached to the condition. When menopausal women spoke of their temporary condition of *locura,* their voices always showed great amusement at their earlier behaviors. Women appeared to use the term *loca* to stress the severity of their case of *Nervios.*

Nervios among women in Puente Piedre, as elsewhere in Latin America (Barlett & Low, 1980; Low, 1981), provided social sanction for otherwise unacceptable behavior. Men did not lose the respect of the community when they allowed their wives with *Nervios* extensive freedoms. The potential for family harmony was preserved by explaining the disruption of more traditional patterns of male dominance by the diagnosis of *Nervios* in the wife. *Nervios* thus functioned to preserve the family, as valued by society, and provided an acceptable alternative to divorce.

DISCUSSION

My study of women in Puente Piedre demonstrates that *Nervios* can be defined as a pandemic disorder of menopause described in terms of folk medical beliefs regarding women's physiology. *Nervios* and *nervios* are both disorders that affect solely women in Puente Piedre. In Puente Piedre *Nervios* entails a precise relationship between menopause and a condition reported to affect one's nerves.

As in earlier case reports (Davis, 1981), the predominance of nerves among Peruvian women appears to reflect folk interpretation of the disorder, rather than the possibility of reporting biases, as suggested by Low (1981). By defining such a causal relationship between menopause and *Nervios,* it becomes clear that in some cultures, it is possible that men do not report cases because, by definition, they cannot be at risk. Men and women may, however, suffer equally from symptoms of anxiety; the symptoms are labeled and treated differently in these cultures.

Low (1985), in her study of modern urban Guatemalans, suggested that *nervios* might have replaced *susto* in the evolution of the society from rural to urban. She postulates that *susto* might be the more common form of nerves in rural villages. At least in Puente Piedre, however, *nervios* did not replace *susto.* Both disorders were recognized, although they were very different in etiology, presentation, treatment, and prognosis. It is possible, however, that *susto* might represent the condition of nerves among men of Puente Piedre, as is the case elsewhere (Low, 1981).

It appears that in some cultures, the specific complaint of nerves may be defined as a female condition, whereas *susto* is prevalent among both sexes. Men might be taught alternative manifestations for anxiety by these cultures or be given only one diagnosis for what, in women, is recognized as three separate disorders. In Puente Piedre, women are diagnosed as having *susto, Nervios,* or *nervios* on the basis of their age and whether or not they can identify a precipitating event, rather than on the basis of any particular symptom complex.

REFERENCES

Barnett, E. (1986). *Perceptions of menopause: The importance of role satisfaction in a Peruvian town.* Unpublished doctoral dissertation, Department of Anthropology, Stanford University, Stanford, CA.

Barlett, P., & Low, S. (1980). *Nervios* in rural Costa Rica. *Medical Anthropology, 4,* 523–559.

Currier, R. (1966). The hot–cold syndrome and symbolic balance in Mexican and Spanish folk medicine. *Ethnology, 5,* 251–263.

Datan, N. (1971). *Women's attitudes toward the climacteric in five Israeli subcultures.* Unpublished doctoral dissertation, Department of Anthropology, University of Chicago, Chicago, IL.

Davis, D. L. (1983). *Blood and nerves: An ethnographic focus on menopause.* St. John's, Newfoundland: St. John's Memorial University of Newfoundland, Institute of Social and Economic Research.

Davey, D. A. (1981). The menopause and climacteric. In Field, W. C. I. (Ed.). *Integrated obstetrics and gynecology for postgraduates* (pp. 646–679). Boston: Blackwell Scientific Publishers.

Kupperman, H. S., Blatt, M., Wiebader, H., & Filler, W. (1953). Comparative clinical evaluation of estrogenic preparations by the menopausal and amenorrheal indices. *New England Journal of Medicine, 15, 688–703.*

Low, S. M. (1981). Meaning of *nervios:* A sociocultural analysis of symptoms presentation in San Jose, Costa Rica. *Culture, Medicine, and Psychiatry, 5,* 350–357.

Low, S. M. (1985). Culturally interpreted symptoms or culture-bound syndromes: A cross-cultural review of nerves. *Social Science and Medicine, 21,* 187–195.

Simmons, O. G. (1955). Popular and modern medicine in Mestizo communities of coastal Peru and Chile. *Journal of American Folklore, 68,* 57–71.

THE UNIVERSALITY OF NERVES

Kaja Finkler, PhD
University of North Carolina at Chapel Hill

The focus on nerves addresses the *universalist–particularist* debate and illuminates the differential experience of nerves between men and women. Using illustrative materials from Mexico and the United States, the hypothesis is advanced that the experience of nerves is not a culture-bound syndrome but is embodied distress, universally experienced by all human beings. Its diffuse symptomatology signals the embodiment of generalized adversity and recreates in the internal world of the body the perceived disorder of the external world. The important task for medical anthropology is to identify the processes by which embodied distress becomes transformed differentially into specific symptomatologies along gender lines. Cross-cultural data are needed to test the proposition.

The aim of this brief article is to present a hypothesis that addresses the universalist–particularist debate. To place under scrutiny a particular syndrome such as nerves is to focus on what is commonly identified as a culture-bound syndrome, meaning a set of symptoms encountered in a culturally discrete context (Simons, 1985), as, for example, nerves in Latin America. We are led to ask: "Is a condition such as nerves indeed culture bound, or is it universally experienced by all humans?" This question bears on the cultural relativity versus the universality of a set of symptoms and on the ways in which the individual's experience of the syndrome relates to the sociocultural conditions of his or her existence. Here we attend to the body as a physiological entity and as it is embedded in society and culture.

I shall explore these matters by examining the meaning of the nerves syndrome as experienced by individuals in their day-to-day existence. I advance the proposition that what has been commonly identified as

Data collection in Mexico was supported by National Science Foundation Grants BNS77/13980 and BNS86/07543 and National Institute of Mental Health Grant 1-RO1-MH42309-01; data collection in a U.S. southern town was supported by a grant from the Research Council at the University of North Carolina at Chapel Hill.

nerves in Latin America and elsewhere is a universal human phenomenon that may differentially affect men and women. To test this hypothesis will require bringing to bear cross-cultural empirical data, which is outside the task of this endeavor. The case materials drawn from my research in rural and urban Mexico and the United States are presented primarily to illustrate the hypothesis.

The nerve syndrome has been variously identified by several investigators who have worked in Latin America (Boyle, 1985; Finkler, 1985a; Low, 1981, 1985), but it is apparent that people refer to a nerve condition in a wide variety of sociocultural settings. In fact, the syndrome has been reported not only for people of Latin American descent (Jenkins, 1986; Low, 1981, 1985; Finkler, 1985a; Garrison, 1977; Guarnaccia, de la Cancela, & Carrillo, in press) but also for Appalachians (Van Schaik, 1985), Newfoundlanders (Davis, 1983), and Greek migrants in Montreal (Dunk, 1985).

Nerves has been interpreted as a distress response that transforms adverse biological and emotional signs into a meaningful illness experience (Low, 1985), as a metaphor for distress (Dunk, 1985), and as an idiom of distress that communicates powerlessness (Guarnaccia et al., in press). Jenkins (1986) suggested that nerves is used by Mexican Americans to label schizophrenia in order to mask a stigmatized condition with a culturally acceptable label and thereby also minimize the differences between the sick person and other family members.

Importantly, all reports on nerves indicate the syndrome entails multiple symptoms, and etiologically it is associated with a miscellany of physiological, emotional, and social conditions (Davis, 1983; Low, 1981). Van Schaik (1985) noted that to complain of nerves is to speak of a large array of social and familial distress.

In my study of patients presenting complaints to Spiritualist healers in rural Mexico (Finkler, 1985a), I found that when people spoke of nerves they were referring to an illness state that they associated with a wide variety of emotional problems, physical symptomatology, and existential conditions experienced in the entire body. Potentially, however, nerves could become manifest in specific afflictions and the illness state could become reinterpreted to explain the onset of a variety of specific impairments (Finkler, 1985a). As an illness state, the nerves condition refers to an agitated state, a state of worry and anxiety, when the entire body trembles and aches and one has the sense that nothing seems to go right. In the popular view the syndrome may be associated with *susto* (sudden fright), sometimes with anger, poor diet, and high blood pressure. Nerves can produce headaches, pain in the *cerebro* (around the medulla area) and other physiologic states (Finkler, 1985a).

During my apprenticeship in a Mexican Spiritualist temple (Finkler,

1985a), I observed healers diagnose nerves for diverse symptoms, including sleeplessness, loneliness, feelings of emptiness in one's stomach, headaches, excessive crying, chest pain, heart palpitations, and pain in the feet, as well as an inexplicable case of amenorrhea. A man who had difficulties with his employer because he hadn't been paid for overtime work was assessed as experiencing nerves, as was his wife because of her husband's distress. Other examples of healers' diagnoses of nerves include when a person lamented his hard life and claimed he was feeling weak, when a woman was mortified because her ward had left her, and when one was not at peace with oneself. In one instance when a medical doctor failed to alleviate stomach problems, headaches, and nausea, the healer assessed the condition as nerves.

According to traditional Mexican belief, illness is intertwined with existential conditions and day-to-day experience (Finkler, 1985a). Patients seeking treatment at the temple claim that nerves cannot be treated by physicians, who, according to the patients, usually dismiss them with "Oh, it's just nerves." Observation of physicians in a hospital in Mexico City revealed that physicians there similarly dismiss nerves with "It's nothing, just nerves," or treat it as a neurological problem, a problem of the nervous system particularly on the synapse level.[1] Generally Spiritualist healers recognize nerves as an illness state that requires treatment. Not surprisingly, whereas only 1 out of 183 cases interviewed in a physician's office located in a rural town (Finkler, 1985a) complained of nerves, about 2% of the patients seeking Spiritualist healing identified their conditions as nerves (Finkler, 1985b).

Importantly, although nerves is initially experienced in the entire body and the whole body trembles, it becomes transformed into an etiological explanation for specific problems. Patients seeking treatment in a major hospital in Mexico City reported experiencing nerves associated with every conceivable symptom, including feelings of desperation, self-diagnosed low blood pressure, high blood pressure, tumor in the neck, feeling of numbness and tiredness, pain in the neck or in the chest, physical exhaustion, irritated colon, sweating, menopause, tonsillitis, headaches, rheumatism, and chest pain,

Patients, like Spiritualist healers, but unlike physicians, diagnose their condition as nerves when they have been subject to an assault by adverse existential conditions and sickness itself. For instance, a woman in Mexico City whose 12-year-old son was murdered by a neighborhood

---

[1]**On the basis of my current (1986–1988) research in a Mexico City government hospital, Mexican physicians tend to view nerves as synonymous with the now commonly accepted concept of stress, or as a neurologic condition.**

gang experienced a case of nerves when she was overcome by a state of anxiety, worry, and shudders to such a degree that she could not recognize her surroundings. In addition, some patients attributed their nerves state to the sickness they were experiencing, as was the case of a woman who experienced nerves as a result of suffering pain in her body. It is important to emphasize that, although a wide range of symptoms are associated with nerves, nerves may be experienced as an outcome as well as a cause of sickness.

Nerves, then, is a generalized condition with a diffuse symptomatology. It encompasses many existential, physical, and emotional disorders. Significantly, the syndrome reflects a congruence between diffuse bodily symptoms and diffuse experiences including sickness itself. Informed by Merleau-Ponty (1963), who proposed that the body communicates to the world and the world becomes expressed by the body, Kleinman (1986) observed, "The body feels and expresses social problems" (p. 194). "The body mediates structure and cultural meaning making them part of our physiology" (p. 195). In keeping with a phenomenological framework, I propose that nerves is the embodiment of adverse existential conditions. If we accept the Merleau-Pontian premise, as I believe we ought, nerves is the embodiment of existential conditions and the experience of suffering in the same way as, for example, a cold is the embodiment of a pathogen.

It is my contention that nerves is not simply an idiom of distress, a metaphor for distress, or a coping strategy informed by rational choice, as has been suggested by the scholars cited earlier. Rather, it is the body acting out the conditions of its existence. Nerves signifies the *embodiment* of generalized adversity and recreates in the internal world of the body the perceived contradictions and disorder of the external world, "when nothing seems to go right," as Mexicans say. When individuals state they are experiencing nerves they are telling the world that they have embodied perceived misfortune and despair. Day-to-day perceived misery is experienced as worry and anxiety, and is labeled as nerves. It is not simply a response to stress, a secondary gain maneuver, or a way of coping. It is embodied distress, an incorporation of the world as perceived by the individual. It is an empirical question whether we will encounter in all cultures a diagnostic category termed nerves; however, I hypothesize that, universally, human beings must confront adversity and contradictions that become incorporated into the body and expressed in states of worry, anxiety, and trembling. Unlike the heart, the seat of emotions in some cultures (Good, 1977) that serves as a dominant symbol for a specific set of problems and contradictions, nerves communicates a person's biography and overall state of perceived inimical existence.

Experiencing nerves does not imply that the individual is alienated from self and society (Low, 1981). On the contrary, it suggests that the individual is experiencing a heightened awareness of adversity in day-to-day life that is incorporated into and expressed by the entire body (Karp, 1985) and socially communicated by the label *nerves*. Or, as Leder (1985) observed, the body articulates a preconceptual grasp of the world. The fact that many people speak of having experienced nerves implies that their own experience of the world becomes validated by the label they give it (Jenkins, 1986; Leder, 1985).

When the world is conceived as having lost its sense of coherence (Antonovsky, 1979), it becomes articulated bodily and identified as nerves. According to Antonovsky (1979), "A sense of coherence does not suggest that life is free of complexities and stresses: it does suggest that one has a sense of confidence or faith, that, by and large, things will work out well" (p. 127). A sense of coherence "does not at all imply that one is in control. It does involve one as a participant in the process of shaping one's destiny, as well as, one's daily experience" (p. 128) that also accommodates to incongruities of daily life. I postulate that when individuals, or lay healers of the Spiritualist kind, diagnose themselves or others as experiencing nerves, be it in Mexico, Appalachia, Newfoundland, or elsewhere, they are experiencing a heightened perception of loss of coherence, and of the contradictions embedded in their lives when "things don't seem to go right."

It is perhaps stating the obvious that all human beings may lose their sense of coherence sometime or other in their lives, when we experience injustice, personal tragedy, and affliction. In contemporary times these universal experiences become multiplied by difficult economic circumstances and asymmetrical power relations both in the public and private spheres that further aggravate personal tragedies, interpersonal conflicts, and loss. Take, for example, the case of May (pseudonym), a poor 44-year-old Black woman in the American South who gave birth to five children and lost one, whose husband left her, who is now mothering two grandchildren and who self-diagnosed her sickness as nerves. She defined her condition of nerves as "bad news":

> I just worries sometimes about things I don't have no control over. I got a bill and I can't pay that bill. My father is sick and he never been down sick, cause of my baby born dead. And you know sometimes I have bad headaches and stuff. I have to take medicine for my nerves. I get, you know, just the least little thing just tear me to pieces and I just get so nervous cause I just cries and you know and the least little thing just worry me, just worry me. I just get so worried. I just cries. Can't sleep at night, walk, walk, walk.

When asked "Are there times when you don't feel nerves?" May responded, "No, it's all the time." She continued, "It just got so I just couldn't go no longer, so they put me down there, stayed down there for two weeks [referring to a mental institution]."[2]

When it gets "just so" nerves may remove one from daily functioning, or when existence is embodied to a degree of being "just too much," nerves may become experienced in more specific symptoms that may lead to a nervous breakdown or to what Latins often identify as *ataque de nervios*. Or it may produce a variety of symptoms, including headaches, chest pain, heart palpitations, back pain, sleeplessness, or other symptoms noted earlier. Our task, however, is to identify the processes by which generalized embodied distress becomes transformed to specific symptomatologies, how patients come to associate their general condition of anxiety, worry, and tremble—nerves—with a particular set of symptoms such as chest pain, heart palpitations, back pain, high or low blood pressure, and headaches, and how the embodiment of distress becomes reinterpreted as etiology or outcome.

Biomedicine in America has medicalized nerves by prescribing pills upon which patients become dependent, as in the instance of the southern Black woman, as well as all her sisters and her mother. Analogously, nerves has also become medicalized by Spiritualist healers who usually prescribe baths, massages, teas, and patent medicine (e.g., paciflorine) to alleviate the nerves condition.

However, although one may recover from the breakdown or other impairments, as in the case of May, by using medicines, the overall experience of nerves can be an ongoing embodiment. When May was asked whether she expected to recover from her nerves condition, she responded, "I am just like they say, 'You got bad nerves, you don't get well from that'." The doctor prescribed for her "nerve medicine" (Tofronil) but she said, "When I get off the medicine, I get real sick because I tried several times to get off, and he says [the doctor] you know no way that I can get off it now."

To be human is to perceive tragedy and experience vicissitudes, distress, injustice, and anxiety (Geertz, 1966). Or, as Berger (1969) informed us, the worlds that humans construct are forever threatened by the forces of chaos, with which religion attempts to deal. Perhaps when religiosity or its secular equivalents fail, adversity and perceived chaos become embodied, and palliation is sought, either with "nerve medi-

---

[2]These data come from a pilot study entitled *Patient's Perceptions of Biomedical Treatment in a Southern Town*.

cine" or baths, massages, teas, or rituals.[3] Spiritualist healers clearly recognize the importance of ritual when they encourage their patients to participate in them to alleviate all impairments. When May was asked whether there was anything else besides the medicine that made her feel better, she responded, "When I go to church, it makes me feel better, after you know I go to church and stuff, hear a preacher, the preaching and stuff, the praying, stuff like that."

Although we may all be threatened by chaos, be confronted by disorder, and embody general untoward episodes that may result in experiencing nerves at some point in our existence, not all human beings obviously experience nerves continuously, or even for lengthy periods of time. We must thus seek to isolate the circumstances that mitigate the embodiment of adversity in the same way we investigate why some and not others succumb to ever-present pathogens in the environment. We must search for the mitigating conditions that cushion the embodiment of nerves across cultures and within a given culture. By so doing, we may begin to understand why in any society some people experience nerves less often than others.

This leads to an important point. Elsewhere (Finkler, 1985b), I have addressed the question of why more women than men report illness, including nerves. I have suggested that women's unequal position in the social structure, which also results in their relative powerlessness cross-culturally (Sanday, 1981) and assaults their self-esteem, renders them more vulnerable than men to sickness in general. Clearly not all women get sick, given their differential positions in all societies; however, a personal experience of perceived adversity becomes heightened, making them more vulnerable to the embodiment of pathogens or distress. Women whose lives possess a sense of coherence, when their life is "as it ought to be," tend not to experience illness, including nerves (Finkler, 1985b). But women whose lives are constantly under duress, because of a chaotic interpersonal relationship with a spouse, adverse social and economic circumstances, or personal tragedies of loss of a child or parent, are more susceptible than men to pathogens and other types of impairments.

Further studies are necessary to analyze the intertwining social, cultural, and psychologic parameters that save some and not others from embodying nerves. I propose that there is a gradual process at work when the individual's perceived world loses its sense of coherence. The first step of embodiment is a generalized anxiety and worry that be-

---

[3]As I discuss elsewhere, ritual may relieve anxiety (Wallace, 1966) but it may also heighten it (Finkler, 1985b).

comes articulated as nerves. I anticipate that if loss of the sense of coherence relentlessly continues to persist, then nerves may become transformed from a generalized to a more specific affliction, with specific symptoms being attributed to a state of nerves.

As noted earlier, it is essential to identify specific distresses in a given society that lead to the embodiment of adversity, and the experiencing of nerves. It is also necessary to charter the processes by which and the conditions under which the generalized state of nerves becomes differentially expressed and manifested in specific symptomatologies in men and women within a given society. It is possible, however, that under some circumstances or in some cultural settings nerves is incorporated as part of the day-to-day routine and is regarded as a natural condition of being human.[4] In the instance when people accept the state of nerves as natural they may fail to develop specific sets of symptoms or translate nerves into etiological explanations to help them make sense of their symptoms (Davis, 1983).

To summarize, in this discussion I have suggested that the condition referred to as nerves is an all-pervasive bodily experience characterized by generalized worry, anxiety, and trembling that is experienced in the entire body because it embodies generalized untoward events. As such, it is a universal human condition that will be found in all cultures and which may be labeled *nerves* or an analogous term. When the nerves condition becomes exacerbated, it may become expressed in a variety of afflictions. I have also suggested that women may experience nerves more frequently than men as they do other types of afflictions. Women are more vulnerable to embodying adversity given their unequal status in society and relative powerlessness vis à vis men. By attending to nerves, we are focusing on the universality of the embodiment of day-to-day life. Future empirical studies of symptoms that characterize the nerves condition will further illuminate this proposition.

REFERENCES

Antonovsky, A. (1979). *Health, stress and coping.* San Francisco: Jossey-Bass.

Berger, P. L. (1969). *The sacred canopy.* New York: Anchor Books.

Davis, D. L. (1983). *Blood and nerves: An ethnographic focus on menopause.* St. Johns, Newfoundland: St. John's Memorial University of Newfoundland, Institute of Social and Economic Research.

---

[4]An analogy could be made to a situation of parasites being endemic in a society, as is the case in Mexico, where people tend to accept parasitosis as a natural condition of the human body.

Dunk, P. (1985, December). *Greek women and nerves in Montreal.* Paper presented at the meeting of the American Anthropological Association, Washington, DC.

Finkler, K. (1985a). *Spiritualist healers in Mexico: Successes and failures of alternative therapeutics.* South Hadley, MA: Praeger/Bergin & Garvey.

Finkler, K. (1985b). Symptomatic differences between the sexes in rural Mexico. *Culture, Medicine, and Psychiatry, 9,* 27–57.

Garrison, V. (1977). The Puerto Rican syndrome in psychiatry and espiritsmo. In V. Crapazano & V. Garrison (Eds.), (pp. 383–449). New York: Wiley.

Geertz, C. (1966). Religion as a cultural system. In M. Banton (Ed.), *Anthropological approaches to the study of religions* (pp. 1–46). London: Tavistock Publications.

Good, B. L. (1977). The heart of what's the matter: The semantics of illness in Iran. *Culture, Medicine, and Psychiatry, 1,* 25–58.

Guarnaccia, P. L., de la Cancela, V., & E. Carrillo, in press. *Ataques de nervios:* An idiom of distress in the Latino community. *Culture, Medicine, and Psychiatry.*

Jenkins, J. H. (1986). *Ethnopsychiatric interpretations of schizophrenic illness: The problem of nervios among Mexican-American families.* Unpublished manuscript.

Karp, I. (1985). Deconstructing culture-bound syndromes. *Social Science and Medicine, 21,* 221–228.

Kleinman, A. (1986). *Social origins of distress and disease: Depression, neurasthenia and pain in modern China.* New York: Yale University Press.

Leder, D. (1985). Medicine and paradigms of embodiment. *Journal of Medicine and Philosophy, 9,* 29–43.

Low, S. (1981). The meaning of *nervios:* A sociocultural analysis of symptom presentation in San Jose, Costa Rica. *Culture, Medicine, and Psychiatry, 5,* 25–47.

Low, S. (1985). Culturally interpreted symptoms or culture bound syndromes: A cross-cultural review of nerves. *Social Science and Medicine, 21,* 187–196.

Merleau-Ponty, M. (1963). *The structure of behavior.* Boston: Beacon Press.

Sanday, P. R. (1981). *Female power and male dominance.* New York: Cambridge University Press.

Simons, R. (1985). Sorting the culture-bound syndromes. In R. C. Simons & C. C. Hughes (Eds.), *The culture-bound syndromes.* Dordrecht: D. Reidel.

Van Schaik, E. (1985, December). *Women, health and culture: The case of nerves.* Paper presented at the meeting of the American Anthropological Association Meetings. Washington, DC.

Wallace, A. F. C. (1966). *Religion: An anthropological view.* New York: Random House.

Section II

MEDITERRANEAN AND NORTHERN EUROPE

NERVES AND PSYCHOSOMATIC ILLNESS: THE CASE OF UM RAMADAN

Laurie Krieger, PhD
PATH (Program for Appropriate Technology in Health),
Washington, D.C.

Belief in the unity of mind and body among poor working class women in metropolitan Cairo is exemplified by the "state of being upset." The Egyptian women of this study use physical symptoms that they believe derive from emotional causes to negotiate and give meaning to relationships with neighbors, friends, and relatives; to jockey for power; to fill emotional needs; to manage presentation of self; and to weave the political fabric of interpersonal life. A detailed case study of Um Ramadan, a woman whose misuse by her husband made her *nerfiza,* illustrates the relationship between emotional upset and physical illness and the use of psychosomatic illness to gain sympathy and exact revenge. The expression of Um Ramadan's symptoms is further analyzed in terms of the underlying cultural constraints placed on Muslim women and the tensions inherent in local gender role relations.

From 1978 to 1980 I conducted participant observation research with women and their families in a poor working-class area of metropolitan Cairo, Egypt. I went to Egypt to study family planning, sexuality, gender roles, and concepts of health and illness for my doctoral dissertation in anthropology. In 1988, I had the opportunity to return to the area several times, enabling me to rekindle old, dear friendships, note changes, and interview many of the same people I had talked with and observed 8 to 10 years earlier.

Although changes in peoples' lives and in the culture abounded, such as the proliferation of "fundamentalist" Islam, many facets of life endured. Among these were beliefs about the relationships among mind, body, and emotion. Even some illiterate women had become, by 1988, astonishingly sophisticated about explaining behavior in clinical psychology terms. Yet their perception that mind, body, and emotion are inseparable was due to the perseverance of traditional belief, rather than to any Western newly rediscovered notion of the holistic nature of mind and body.

Belief in the unity of mind and body is exemplified by the state of being upset, which is often expressed in physical symptoms. The state of being upset may be attributed by people in this area of metropolitan Cairo to many causes (some of which have changed as the culture has changed), and several different forms of being upset exist. Yet all causes may be seen as produced by constraints and demands made on people by the culture or stressful life events universal to all human groups, or by some form of psychological trauma. In 1988, women continued to use certain physical symptoms, which they believed derived from emotional causes beyond their control, for social gains, just as they had 10 years earlier.

Women publicize their emotionally caused illnesses in order to put social pressure on the individual causing their upset and physical illness or to gain emotional support if they have undergone a difficult life experience. The social use of emotional upset and the physical symptoms it causes is but one tool with which women manipulate the social realm.

Both men and women are adept at interpersonal politics, although only women use physical and emotional symptoms extensively. This difference in behavior rests partly on the culture's characterization of women as less in control of their emotions than men, so that women are expected to be more susceptible to such emotional/physical symptoms. Women are also more in need of a wider array of interpersonal political skills because they are more often in a position where their culture does not accord them authority. Furthermore, women in this district seldom work outside the home and gain much of their rewards, punishment, status, and emotional fulfillment through relationships with others.

This article presents the nature of "upsetness" in this Egyptian working-class urban area, explores women's social use of upsetness, briefly describes the study area, presents a case study of Um Ramadan [mother of Ramadan—her oldest son] whose behavior illustrates the points made here, and discusses Um Ramadan's behavior in relation to her culture's beliefs about and uses of being upset.

NATURE OF "UPSETNESS"

Many varieties of being upset exist in this community. For example, there is *z^c laana,* a sad kind of upset.[1] *Nerfiza* is an irritable, nervous kind of upset. In *bititxala'*, a woman becomes upset in a hysterical, nervous way. *Maxduuda* is the type of upset (which in some cases may produce disease analogous to the Latin American *susto*) where the person is frightened by a sudden surprise—different from just being frightened of something. All of these types of "upsetness" have different causes and different manifestations, but all may be expressed both emotionally and somatically. The person "feels upset" not only with the mind, but with the body as well. Expression of emotion by physical symptoms is considered perfectly normal in this district and is based on the underlying conceptualization of the human being as a whole composed of emotions, mind, and body.

The circumstances that cause a woman to be upset are thought to be beyond her control. For example, the death of a close relative will cause a women to be *z^c laana,* or mothering many young, noisy children will make a woman feel *nerfiza.* The sudden death of a girl's young fiancé was believed to have caused her to become *maxduuda,* and consequently physically ill. A violent, authoritarian husband might make the woman either *bititxala'* or *nerfiza.* The lack of personal responsibility for the circumstances causing a woman to become upset was even more obvious in the past,[2] when more women and men than today might attribute "upsetness" in any of its forms not to life circumstances, but to possession by malevolent *ginn* (genies).

A woman is not expected to be able to control the expression of her "upsetness" in physical symptoms. The woman can, however, control how she uses the emotional and physical manifestations of being upset to get what she desires in the social sphere. She may, for example, advertise her physical or emotional upset to get needed emotional support, to win a more powerful position within her marriage, or to elicit the support of her relatives and friends against an authoritarian husband who is obviously upsetting her and making her physically ill. The social use of illness stemming from being upset occurs frequently, but is only one of many interpersonal political skills.

---

[1]In this article, the Arabic letter "Qaf," pronounced as a glottal stop in Egyptian colloquial dialect, is transliterated by an apostrophe. The Arabic letter "ayin," which has no equivalent in English, is transliterated by superscript lower case c. Long vowels in Arabic are transliterated here by the equivalent English vowel, doubled.

[2]"The past" may be as recent as 1980, when I concluded my first research project.

SOCIAL USE OF "UPSETNESS"

The social use of emotional and physical symptoms of "upsetness" rests on two aspects of the culture: (a) Personal and familial reputation are extremely important, resulting in the necessity for careful presentation management, and (b) people negotiate and manipulate the meaning and emotional content of relationships with skill and sophistication (for examples of this see Krieger, 1984; Nelson, 1974; Wikan, 1980). Much of social life, therefore, revolves around the control of information transmitted to others, because, as in any political situation, any information presented to others may be used against one or for one's own aims.

Women's revelation and even advertisement of their "upsetness" takes on special meaning in a culture where information control assumes such importance. In this area of metropolitan Cairo, and in the Middle East, circum-Mediterranean, and elsewhere as well, reputation is extremely important. Reputation is the concept of an individual held by people who know or have heard of her or him. The group judges the individual's behavior, attributes traits to her or him (e.g., good or sexually promiscuous), and consigns him or her to the appropriate social category (e.g., good person or bad person).

Females are especially vulnerable to attacks on their reputation because much or most of their worth depends on their reputation for celibacy before marriage and chastity after marriage. An unmarried girl whose reputation for sexual purity becomes besmirched through gossip (even if untrue) will find it difficult to marry well, or possibly at all.

Reputations are formed and augmented during gossip-laden conversations in which the subject of the gossip is not present. Reputations, however, are also "managed" by women and men during interactions with neighbors, friends, and relatives. Women consciously and carefully craft their social presentations of self. They may even enlist the aid of close relatives to rehearse with them the story that the family will convey to the "public," that is, neighbors, friends, and more distant kin, or even to other close kin whose interests diverge from the woman's. Women in this section of greater Cairo are involved in gossip networks because they seldom work outside the home and because, as women, they are rooted in relationships with family and neighboring women. People of both genders, however, are quite careful about what they disclose to others about themselves, their families, and even their friends.

Two examples clarify this. One woman discussed the arguments she was having with her neighbor, the former mother-in-law of the woman's divorced daughter, about her daughter's reputation, only with her near kin and her closest friend outside her kin group. With others outside her family she behaved as if she and her neighbor were on fine terms so that her feud and its subject would not be discussed. In a second example, a brother in his early 20s was furious with his 13-year-old sister and beat her severely for "dating" a boy, a practice in which girls in this neighborhood in 1980 (and in 1988 as well) were not allowed to indulge. He discussed with his parents and siblings his sister's unacceptable behavior, but never mentioned it to anyone outside of his immediate family. He maintained silence in this matter out of regard for his family's reputation, which would have suffered were it known that a female member had engaged in what is considered to be prohibited sexual behavior. Had the sister's behavior become known to people who did not have a stake in the reputation of the family, and consequently in the girl's reputation, gossip—resulting in a vast amount of speculation about the girl's peccadillo—would have proliferated.

In addition to the social manipulation involved in reputation management, both women and men engage in sophisticated manipulation of the emotional content and meaning of relationships in many different situations that do not involve sexuality or the use of emotional upset or physical illness. For example, a husband who competed with his wife for their children's affection gave the small children tiny sums of money and bought them sweets, then asked them whom they preferred, their mother or father? The preschool children, already adept at information control and manipulation of relationships, took the money and sweets and obediently responded that they loved their father best. They then went to their mother and whispered in her ear that they really preferred her, but wanted money and sweets. (For other examples of manipulation, see Krieger, 1984; Wikan, 1980.) Through behavior that these people themselves would often categorize as "manipulations," people negotiate relationships, jockey for power, attempt to fulfill their emotional needs, and weave the political fabric of interpersonal life. Use of emotional upset and its often accompanying physical symptoms represents but one armament in the arsenal of interpersonal political skills.

Although women tend to be at least the match of men in interpersonal political negotiations, women often have more need to exercise tight information control and presentation management because overall they have less authority over their own lives than men do. Unless a woman has no male relatives, she is always under the protection and jurisdiction of some man. Before marriage it is her father or brothers who bear the responsibility for her and her behavior. After marriage the male authority figure is her husband.

Beliefs about male and female natures also illuminate the relationship of emotion to gender. Although people in this district consider mind, emotion, and body a united whole in everyone, traditionally men are viewed as more centered on the mind, while Egyptians of all social classes consider women to be more emotional. Women are also believed to be less in control of their physical appetites as well. Such a typology of male and female natures prevails in much of the Middle East (e.g., Beck & Keddie, 1978) and allows women both to experience emotional upset more visibly and to use the experience for social and psychological gain.

In this social environment, the publication of illness due to a circumstance that has made a woman *z^c^laana* (upset with sad affect) will usually elicit sympathetic reactions and support from the woman's social network. Illnesses caused by more angry types of upset may be due to mistreatment by a relative. Judicious advertisement of the illness and its cause may serve to manipulate public opinion against the wrongdoer and, through gossip, ultimately pressure him or her into more acceptable behavior.

The case history of Um Ramadan, an exceptionally bright woman who excels at social negotiation illustrates these points.

FIELD SITE

In 1978 Um Ramadan lived, as she does today, in the urban portion of a district that is largely rural. The urban portion is part of the Cairo metropolitan area, and its residents consider themselves Cairenes. Almost all the men in this area commute by ferry, city bus, minibus, automobile, or foot to jobs in the city of Cairo.

In 1976, 57.8% of the women of the urban part of the district were illiterate (as is Um Ramadan). Only 26.6% of the men of this portion of the district were illiterate, however (GMPS 1982, as quoted in van Roemburg, 1987). This meant that virtually all women in my sample were married to men who could and did read the newspaper.

The district (by which I mean only the urban portion) has no sewerage, with the result that its dirt and few broken macadam streets are often flooded with sewage, water, and undistinguishable foul-smelling liquids. Almost all residences are low apartment buildings crammed next to each other, each housing from two to five families. Most houses face each other across narrow dirt alleyways, but some buildings are located on the few paved streets. The government built or caused to have built several large housing projects. Even in these complexes, however, buildings do not reach more than four or five storeys.

All apartments have at least one balcony equipped with a clothes line. Women stand on their balconies to hang out clothes to dry, catch a breath of relatively cool air during the hot spring and summer, and talk and gossip with neighbors. Although the commodiousness of the apartments depends not only on their size, but on the number of people living in them, in general apartments are extremely small and cramped by North American standards. In this setting, familial privacy is difficult to attain and one's neighbor's business becomes one's own.

Almost no married women in my sample worked outside the home, although many brought in income by working as independent seamstresses, an income-generating labor that they could do without leaving home. Women also devised other ingenious income-generating strategies, such as serving as informal rental agents for apartments in their neighborhood.

Husbands were employed as unskilled or semiskilled workers, with the exception of two husbands who, in 1978–1980, were fulfilling their compulsory 2-year military duty. Husbands were gone for most of the day at work, so that the neighborhoods in the district belonged to women and children much of the time.

UM RAMADAN: A CASE STUDY OF NERVES AND PSYCHOSOMATIC ILLNESS

An anthropologist entering a new culture often finds that the first people who will talk with her or him, and often who throughout the anthropologist's stay will spend the most time with her or him, are people who are marginal to their own cultures. These informants have an emotional need for companionship that they are incapable of filling within the confines of their culture. Anthropologists have often wondered whether reliance on such people who do not really "fit in" with their own cultures may not provide a rather skewed picture of the culture under study. It was my good fortune to be introduced, during my first field trip in 1978 to the poor metropolitan Cairo area that was to be my field site, to an extraordinary woman, Um Ramadan.[3] Far from marginal to her culture, Um Ramadan was at the center of many social relationships. At that time a grandmother in her late 30s, she was widely respected by neighbors and relatives for her experience, as well as for her intelligence. During my stay (1978–1980) Um Ramadan demonstrated admirable skill in fulfilling all aspects of her social role: house-

---

[3]Um Ramadan is a pseudonym.

wife, mother, grandmother, neighbor, friend, sister, daughter, cousin. She was also chronically ill with largely psychosomatical ailments, as she still was during my visits to her in 1988.

The story of Um Ramadan, collected over 2 years of participant observation, life history, and other types of interviews, illustrates the role of *baladi* women's psychosomatic illness brought about through "nerves."[4] The problems that caused Um Ramadan to become upset and that precipitated the somatization of her psychological discomfort were largely problems causes by conflicts inherent in her culture. It was perhaps precisely because Um Ramadan was so adept in her cultural milieu that she suffered most from its contradictions. Although Um Ramadan cannot control the somatization of her psychic pain and genuinely suffered and suffers from her physical complaints, she is skilled at manipulating the illness and its underlying psychological cause to her best social advantage. Um Ramadan is not alone in the use of psychosomatic illness and its underlying cause of psychic upset to gain desired social ends. Most of the approximately 50 women in my study sample displayed at least one instance of this technique during my nearly 2 years with them.

Both Um Ramadan's mother and father had been married previous to their marriage to each other. Um Ramadan had several half-siblings from her parents' earlier marriages. While Um Ramadan was still a girl, her father married a second woman, which greatly vexed Um Ramadan and her mother. Both wives lived in the same house in the district—although in separate rooms—along with their husband. Um Ramadan's mother had conceived only Um Ramadan with Um Ramadan's father. Um Ramadan believes that the absence of male progeny caused her father to marry a second wife. After a period of intense sadness and hostility toward the new wife and Um Ramadan's father, Um Ramadan and her mother adapted to the situation. The second wife gave birth to two sons and two daughters.

Before her 18th birthday, Um Ramadan was married to a literate man more than 15 years her senior who worked as a guard for a private company (in Egypt the government rather than the private sector is the largest employer). Her father arranged her marriage to this man against her wishes, for she confessed to the shameful (in her culture) love for one her father's brother's sons, who ordinarily in the Middle East is a preferred marriage partner. Despite the cultural norm, her father ob-

---

[4] ***Baladi*** **is an urban social class whose members are more traditional than "moderna" Western-looking urbanites. *Baladi* people are usually, but not necessarily, poor.**

jected. It is very likely that the marriage that was forced on her was punishment for breaking the prohibition against falling in love before marriage.

Um Ramadan's marriage was unhappy almost from the beginning. Her husband was not nearly as intelligent as his unwilling wife. He began early in their marriage to respond to his wife's adroit negotiations and manipulations of their relationship with authoritarianism that often included physical violence to his wife and children, because he apparently felt that he was no match for his wife in social skills and, it seemed to me in 1978–1980, he keenly felt the disparity in intelligence. Um Ramadan, on the other hand, in 1978–1980, made no attempt to make allowances for her husband's limitations; rather, she exploited them. This infuriated her spouse even more and he responded by yelling insults and occasionally beating her.

Um Ramadan's first pregnancy, within the 1st year of her marriage, resulted in a miscarriage in the second or third trimester. She was very *zᶜlaana* for a period of time after this, but she conceived again soon after her miscarriage and successfully gave birth to her oldest child, a daughter, followed the next year by her eldest son, Ramadan. Um Ramadan had nine living children in 1978.

Um Ramadan values motherhood more than any of her other roles. She expressed this repeatedly during our acquaintance. For example, when explaining her thwarted love for her cousin to me, she shrugged her shoulders about her marriage, in which we both knew she was miserable. She then said, "You don't think of the past. My children are my whole world—can a mother not love her child?"

Although he went to work about 80% of the time, Um Ramadan's husband, Abu Ramadan [father of Ramadan], was ill for the entire 2 years I lived in Egypt. His diagnoses included heart disease, high blood pressure, and pneumonia. He spent several months in the hospital for the last illness. Abu Ramadan occasionally expressed his dissatisfaction with the marriage when he was particularly angry with his wife. He would say that he hoped he would die from his illnesses and then his wife would see if she could do without him. Abu Ramadan died in 1982. Um Ramadan has not remarried.

During the 2 years I lived in Egypt, I visited Um Ramadan and her family virtually every day. During this time Um Ramadan had many illness episodes. I recorded all of Um Ramadan's illness episodes during my stay in her district. During the first year I spent with her, all of her illnesses occurred either during a time of crisis in her marriage or when she was upset by the behavior of one of her children, or during a time of psychological stress (such as the wedding day of her eldest daughter—a marriage she and her husband had forced on this daughter to protect the daughter's reputation).

One of the illness episodes from the 1978–1980 period and one from 1988 will illustrate Um Ramadan's pattern of upset–physical illnesses, the uses to which she put them, and the underlying cultural stresses her symptoms expressed.

During the first year of my field work Um Ramadan and her husband went through a particularly stormy period in their marriage. Abu Ramadan complained constantly about his wife's spending, which he considered extravagant. Um Ramadan insisted that she bought only necessities and that her husband was out of touch with current food and basic commodities prices, and that her increased spending was due to Egypt's inflation. Um and Abu Ramadan daily had noisy arguments during which Abu Ramadan often insulted his wife, calling her by some nasty, if colorful, epithets (in which colloquial Arabic abounds). Finally, her husband shouted that he would do the daily marketing (a responsibility of the wife in this district). Um Ramadan perceived this as a grave insult to her status as wife and housekeeper, particularly because the neighbors were privy to information conveyed during the loud conjugal arguments.

Um Ramadan became ill. She said that her husband *biyz*^{c}*aalni* ("makes me *z*^{c}*laana*") and made her *nerfiza* so that she became ill. She complained to her children and to me that her knees were hot and swollen, her stomach hurt, her chest was weak, and she had a headache and was dizzy. She wanted to go to a doctor new to the district, but with a good reputation. His office was about a 2-mile walk away, and it was evening.

I volunteered to accompany Um Ramadan. The doctor examined her and, writing the diagnosis in English, declared that the patient had rheumatoid arthritis and psychosomatic symptoms. He told Um Ramadan that she had arthritis in her knees and was apparently upset about something, because nothing else was wrong with her. Contrary to my expectations, Um Ramadan was overjoyed at the diagnosis.

When we returned to her home, and for weeks afterwards, Um Ramadan would tell her neighbors and friends, "The doctor told me that I am sick because of *z*^{c}*aal*. He said that if Abu Ramadan doesn't stop making me *z*^{c}*laana*, I will get very sick and I could die!" Abu Ramadan was very angry at this presentation of his behavior. He countered not that the illness was organic, but that his wife was crazy because she had a psychosomatic illness. In the neighbor women's homes, however, both with and without the presence of Um Ramadan, Abu Ramadan was characterized and discussed as a bad husband who upset his wife and made her sick. Within a few weeks of this pressure, Abu Ramadan had ceased to nag about money and his wife did the daily shopping once more.

The second example is more recent. During the four visits I made to Um Ramadan during 1988, she complained constantly of a severe headache, which she said was due to grief at the sudden and unexplained death of her 21-year-old son less than 1 year earlier (he, to all appearances in good health, had simply not woken up one morning). Um Ramadan appeared, indeed, very sad. She wore and continues to wear a cloth around her head because of the headache. The cloth's presence is intended to help the headache (which apparently it does not), but it also advertises Um Ramadan's lamentable condition to anyone with whom she comes into contact. Relatives visit Um Ramadan, ask about her headache, and condole her on the loss of her son.

DISCUSSION AND CONCLUSION

In the first instance, Um Ramadan became upset because of severe strain in her marital relationship. During this period, she actually appeared quite distraught. Her illness was, both to her and to a physician, a natural outcome or accompaniment of her upsetness. She used the symptoms, however, to cure what she believed to be the cause of her illness: her husband's angry behavior. The advertisement of her symptoms was crucial to this. She could not have applied social pressure had she remained silent about her illness and its cause. She also derived emotional support and a bit of revenge through sharing her "misuse" by her husband with others.

In the second instance, Um Ramadan was very *z*ᶜ*laana* about her son's death and needed emotional support. She sees her physical symptom as an uncontrollable outcome of her grief. She told me that "nothing helps" her headache. Yet she continues to wear the cloth, which to all in her district identifies a headache sufferer. Even strangers could be expected to inquire about her headache. This would provide Um Ramadan with an opportunity to tell the person about her son and derive some sympathy. The headache cloth is a constant reminder to friends and relatives that they are in the presence of a truly grieving mother. Um Ramadan thus derives the emotional support she wishes by advertising her physical complaint originating from her emotional state.

The examples from Um Ramadan's life illustrate the tensions in gender roles. Um Ramadan had, of course, been married to her husband against her will. It is not surprising that she experienced illness on her daughter's wedding day when this time it was she who forced an unwilling bride to marry. The issues were also very similar, that is, marriage to protect the bride's reputation. Had Um Ramadan's love for her cousin reached malicious nonfamily members, her chances of any marriage might have been severely damaged. The marriage probably served the additional purpose of punishing a girl with wayward "shameful" feelings. Um Ramadan's daughter, as mentioned earlier, also had her own problems with reputation that the daughter's former mother-in-law exploited. Thus marrying off such a daughter served both as punishment and insurance of reputation. The strain on Um Ramadan was great, however. Um Ramadan's physical symptoms effectively prevented her unhappy newly married daughter from complaining because it is wrong to bother your mother when she is obviously ill.

Gender issues are key to the struggle between Um Ramadan and her husband. Um Ramadan felt that she could not directly challenge her husband's authority in their marriage, because her culture accorded him the authority to control the spending of his income. Husbands, however, are not supposed to make their wives sick; rather, their responsibility for their wives' behavior includes responsibility for the wives' welfare. In the absence of the right to command as much of her husband's income as she desired, and with Abu Ramadan using the authoritarian right to control his wife's behavior, Um Ramadan used shame to illustrate his failure to fulfill his obligation to preserve her welfare.

The example of Um Ramadan's headache casts light on culture change and upsetness. Traditionally, women who have become ill from being upset and require emotional support have recourse to a *zar*, a women's ceremony for placating the *ginn* who are able to prolong or exacerbate a woman's upsetness–illness. When I asked Um Ramadan why she did not go to a *zar* to see if that would help her sadness and headache, she informed me in classical Arabic, which neither she nor I understand, that *zars* were but an *idée fixe.* People believe a *zar* will help their symptoms, so it does. Um Ramadan had previously visited many *zars,* so I asked her to explain the change in her opinion. Um Ramadan cited the transmission of Islamic beliefs (Islamic fundamentalist teaching) to people through television and by word of mouth, so that now she knew "the truth": *zars* do not really help people and are not part of Islam.

With the new religious climate depriving women of a traditional outlet for receiving emotional support for upsetness–illness, and current Islamic movements' reinforcement of traditional gender roles, it is possible that the mechanism of using upsetness–illness for social and emotional gains may assume even greater importance in women's interpersonal politics. As more women cease to rely on *zars* for emotional support and social recognition of their illnesses, their reliance on their social networks to provide this support may increase.

REFERENCES

Beck, L., & Keddie, N. (1978). *Women in the Muslim world.* Cambridge, MA: Harvard University Press.

Krieger, L. (1984). *Body notions, gender roles, and fertility regulating method use in Imbaba, Cairo.* Unpublished doctoral dissertation, Anthropology Department, University of North Carolina at Chapel Hill.

Nelson, C. (1974). Public and private politics: Women in the Middle Eastern world. *American Ethnologist, 1,* 551–563.

van Roemburg, R. (1987). *The reproductive behavior of rural–urban migrants in a popular district in Cairo.* Unpublished master's thesis, Human Geography of Developing Countries Program, Catholic University of Nijmegen, Netherlands.

Wikan, U. (1980). *Life among the poor in Cairo.* (A. Henning, Trans.). London: Tavistock Publications. (Original work published 1976).

NEVRA IN A GREEK VILLAGE: IDIOM, METAPHOR, SYMPTOM, OR DISORDER?

Mari H. Clark, MA, MEd, PhD
Department of Anthropology, University of North Carolina at Chapel Hill

The folk model for *nevra* (nerves) in Methana, Greece, is discussed in terms of the contradiction between the ideal of solidarity, central to the local family ideology, and the reality of interpersonal conflict in daily life. Contradictions in values resulting from rapid socioeconomic change are also considered. *Nevra,* a broad, ambiguous, negotiated concept, expresses a wide range of symptoms and serves as a culturally condoned medium for expression of otherwise unacceptable emotions. The notion of *nevra* provides a metaphor for social disorder such as interpersonal conflict between close kinfolk and value conflicts between generations. Case studies of social interaction demonstrate the relationship of *nevra* to various kinds of social disorder as well as to what Western psychiatry labels emotional disorders. *Nevra* is also related to other idioms of distress: the evil eye, possession by the devil, excessive drinking, and pilgrimages to religious shrines.

Nerves, Gender, and Aging

Nevra (nerves) is an idiom of distress, a metaphor for social disorder within the family, and a symbol for value contradictions resulting from rapid socioeconomic change for the villagers of Methana in the Greek Peloponnese. The results of my study of *nevra* in Methana are largely consistent with earlier cross-cultural research on nerves, discussed by Davis and Low in the introduction to this issue. What was unexpected was the insistence, by most Methanites, that women were no more likely than men to suffer from *nevra.* This was surprising because a number of studies have shown nerves to be more frequently a medium of expression of distress for women than for men because of women's limited options for self-expression resulting from cultural definitions of their roles (see Danforth, 1979; Dunk, 1987; Low, 1985; Nichter, 1981).

Discussions of gender roles in Greece also suggest that women are expected to worry about the household, the children, and daily affairs. Men can go to the coffeehouse to drink and talk with their buddies and forget their problems (see Dubisch, 1986; du Boulay, 1986; Hirschon, 1978; Sutton, 1985). The ideal role of a Greek woman is that of the suffering mother, modeled after *Panagia* (the mother of Christ) (Caraveli, 1980; Dubisch, 1988b). The extreme expression of this role is the death of a woman from worry about her child (Dubisch, 1988b).

However, what Methanites view as more significant than gender, in determining who has *nevra,* are aging, stressful life experiences, and heredity interacting with individual character. Those who have been marginalized in this setting are the older men and women who lost their power and status as a result of rapid socioeconomic changes. There have been broad societal changes in values and life expectations from a focus on relations with people to relations with things and "keeping up with the Joneses." Methanites, young and old, perceive these changing expectations as a "new" type of stress that causes nerves.

Approach and Methodology

I approached the study of *nevra* on Methana with a focus on Methanites' understanding of nerves as *lived* events and experiences (Scheper-Hughes & Lock, 1986). I examined both the folk model of *nevra* and its negotiation in social interaction (Quinn & Holland, 1987). My study was based on focused interview and participant observation data gathered in the broader context of household research conducted in a village of 40 households from 1972 through 1974 and from 1985 through 1987 (Clark, 1988). I did focused interviews with 24 individuals who differed in age, gender, and education. They included people who had experienced *nevra* and others who had not. Participant observation data included all 40 households as well as many in other villages and in Athens over the years that I spent in the field. The three cases I discuss below are herein from focal households where I spent a great deal of time and was able to observe ongoing conflict and *nevra* episodes.

Nevra in Greece

The literature on *nevra* in Greece is very limited (Dunk, 1987). Similarly, interpersonal conflict within families, that has been strongly associated with *nevra* in other settings, has received little attention from scholars of Greek society with the exception of the honor killings of unchaste sisters or daughters and adulterous wives (e.g., Campbell, 1983; Loizos, 1978; and Safilios-Rothschild, 1972; but also see Bialor, 1963; Herzfeld, 1980).

There are some data on Greek *nevra* scattered amidst literature focused on other themes. Accounts of folk beliefs about health and healing in rural Greece indicate that often emotions are believed to cause illness. Worry is said to cause heart pain, high blood pressure, stomachache, dizziness, and headaches (Blum & Blum, 1965). The *Anastenaria,* a possession ritual performed in Northern Greece, serves, in part, as therapy for *nevrika*—a nervous disorder caused by anxiety, grief, and despair (Danforth, 1979).

An American psychiatrist described "culturally institutionalized modes of dealing with distress" in Northern Greece that would have been diagnosed as paranoia and projection in the United States. He noted "a constant externalization of all that is felt to be painful and a continual assignment of responsibility to forces or individuals outside the limits of oneself" (Skinner, 1965, p. 480; also see Blum & Blum, 1965; Lee, 1953; and Safilios-Rothschild, 1972, 1973, for similar observations). Skinner observed that compared with Americans, Greeks generally found more people with whom to discuss their distress and were more likely to enter psychoanalysis starting with somatic complaints presented to a general practitioner (Skinner, 1965). The social stigma of mental illness in Greece has often led to its denial and explanation in terms of more acceptable physical complaints (Blum & Blum, 1965; Safilios-Rothschild, 1968). Gender stereotypes held by practitioners may have limited the access of males to psychoanalysis and counseling in Greece as well (Safilios-Rothschild, 1969).

Studies of the evil eye in Greece describe symptoms similar to those for *nevra* (Blum & Blum, 1965). The evil eye is the power of an individual to cause harm to other people, creatures, and things through his or her gaze. A person cannot control this power and unintentionally causes harm by envious glances (Blum & Blum, 1965, 1970; Dionisopoulos-Mass, 1976; Herzfeld, 1981). Evil eye accusations provide a means of expressing dislike of a kin who one is morally obligated to support (Herzfeld, 1981). The ritual cure for the evil eye can restore order to the body and to the social situation (Herzfeld, 1986).

THE SETTING

Changing Local and Political Economy

Methana is a mountainous, volcanic peninsula in the easternmost part of the Greek Peloponnese. It is a 2-hr journey, by boat, from the international port of Pireas that serves Athens—the nexus of the social, political, and economic life of the country. Because of the steep, broken terrain and the small size of the terraced fields, even in 1987, local farmers tilled the soil with scratch plows pulled by mules and harvested their grain with sickles. Many farmers from the 10 villages on Methana also earn cash through summer businesses and wage labor in the port town where therapeutic mineral springs attract Greek summer visitors with a variety of health complaints. Others work year round in small manufacturing and food processing plants on the nearby plain of Trizina or in various construction trades.

As is the case in the rest of Greece and elsewhere in the Mediterranean, the mountainous rural villages of Methana have steadily declined in population since World War II with the migration of many villagers to Athens and to foreign countries (Sutton, 1983). At the same time, the port town of Methana has expanded and, for all practical purposes, has become a suburb of Athens.

The standard and style of living in Methana's villages have changed significantly since World War II. As a result of limited mechanization of activities in the fields and the house as well as greater opportunities to earn cash through nonfarming activities, Methanites, like many other rural Greeks, have more leisure time and more cash for consumer goods and services.

While in the past houses were "shelters" and units of production, more recently houses have become "villas" and units of consumption reflecting social status (see Clark, in press-b). In the prewar days, most people had simple one- or two-room houses with little furniture and few household goods. By the mid-1970s, many households had refrigerators, televisions, more furniture, household goods, and clothing. By the late 1980s, nearly all households had these goods and telephones. Many villagers had expanded their houses with the addition of separate kitchens, bedrooms, and bathrooms. Many people owned trucks and motorcycles. These changes were part of a widespread shift in spending patterns in rural Greece, from the spartan frugality of the prewar past to postwar consumerism that began in the 1960s (Karapostolis, 1983).

There also have been major administrative changes in Greece from dictatorship to socialist rule. From 1967 through 1974, a military dictatorship fiercely enforced strict laws and censored mail, films, printed matter, and all of the broadcast media. In the mid-1980s, the socialist government had reduced many of the earlier limits on individual freedom, eliminated media censorship, and established equal legal rights for women.

Older Methanites viewed all these changes as mixed blessings. On the one hand they often said, "Now we live like people; in the past we lived like animals." On the other hand, many insisted that people had become selfish, greedy, and cunning. Many felt that the new government had given individuals more freedom than they could manage and the result was a lazy younger generation that expected a pension for doing no work and pursued a decadent life-style. Others reluctantly admitted that they themselves had spoiled their children in their attempt to give them an easier life than their own.

These broad, rapid societal changes affected who suffered from *nevra* as well as the conditions under which they expressed *nevra.* The changes themselves were causally linked with distress and nerves in Methanites' folk model of *nevra.*

Family Ideology

Along with the many rapid changes in the lives of Methanites there were also some very important continuities, such as the family ideology. Underlying Methanites' family ideals was the belief that a person has to fulfill familial responsibilities in order to be a good Greek Orthodox Christian. Descriptions of "a person from a good family" and "a good Christian" were nearly identical. The Greek Orthodox Church places a strong emphasis on marriage and family. Marriage is one of the most important sacraments (Constantelos, 1982).

Methanities' ideals regarding the family emphasize the responsibilities of family members. Most important are carrying on the family line through progeny, providing for family members' spiritual and material well-being, maintaining and increasing the prosperity of the family for the children's dowry and inheritance, arranging good marriages for children, caring for parents in their old age, and performing the essential rituals upon their death.

First and foremost a family is supposed to have "a good order," that is, its members should be loving to one another, hard working, and regular in their work and all their affairs so they can fulfill their familial responsibilities. A "good" family displays the qualities of respect for each other, understanding, agreement, good behavior, hospitality, tranquility, and generosity.

By providing an estate and making certain that children marry a person from a good family, parents help their offspring to take a proper place in the social order. Increasingly education has become another essential part of a child's future "estate." These ideals, with their emphasis on reciprocal responsibilities of parents and children, placed greater emphasis on the parent–child relationship than on that of the husband and wife.

Villagers said that in a "bad" family there is continual arguing, bad feelings, no offer of hospitality, berating and making accusations about others, holding grudges, telling lies, swearing, dirtiness, and disorder. Such a family is not united. Each person goes where he or she wishes. Family members do not work together. They are quick to take people to court. In the past, if they heard about a marriage arrangement before it had been settled, they tried to break it up out of jealousy. These descriptions of "good" and "bad" families reflect ideals for interpersonal relations based on working hard, cooperating within the family, maintaining good relations with other families, and not interfering in other families' business. However, ideals and practice often differed.

Family and Household Organization

Most people had close kin ties with every house in the village through descent, marriage, or spiritual kinship. The economic, social, and ideologic importance of the family has been repeatedly stressed in ethnographic studies in Greece (Campbell, 1964; du Boulay, 1974; Friedl, 1962; Hirschon, 1983). Methana is no exception. The family household[1] was the major point of articulation between the individual and society. On Methana, the stem household form has maintained a strong presence. A stem household consists of two, co-resident, lineally related, married couples and their unmarried children. Most commonly the youngest son brought his wife to live in his parents' household.

Household organization also responded to the aforementioned changes and continuities. In the past, the stem household operated in terms of patriarchal ideal in which authority was based on age as well as gender.[2] The elder couple in the stem household managed the allocation of labor and the distribution of resources. Couples generally had five or more children, whom they expected to contribute to farming activities and to obey their parents or expect a beating.

By the 1970s most younger couples were taking over the management of stem households or forming their own nuclear households. The patriarchal ideal was slowly giving way to one based on equality that offered the younger generation a greater voice in household affairs. The elder generation could no longer dominate household production and distribution because most of the resources (mountain farmland, crop trees, vineyards) that they controlled were no longer valued by the young. The younger couple had opportunities to earn wages and manage independently. By the

---

[1]By using the terms "family" and "household" interchangeably, Western scholars have confused family structure with household composition. assuming that the residential unit, the kinship unit, and the domestic functions are one and the same (Bender, 1967; Wilk & Netting, 1984; Yanagisako, 1979). For this reason, I distinguish "family," a kinship grouping that is not necessarily localized, from "household," a co-residential activity group (Wilk & Netting, 1984).

[2]I refer here to the standard definition of "patriarchy," as a social system based on the absolute authority of the father or elderly male over the family group. See Clark (1988, Chapter 3) for further discussion.

1970s, most couples had only one or two children whom they expected to attend school and have time to play. Most parents were very indulgent with their children, giving them almost everything they demanded.

Conflict Within and Between Households

The topic of conflict within the household was one that Methana villagers were not eager to discuss unless it was about someone else's domestic strife. It is evident from the descriptions of "good" and "bad" families that good relations within and between families were central to their family ideology. Conversely, conflict had a very negative meaning. Yet, in actual practice, conflict, in the form of quarreling, grumbling, or dispute, was a part of everyday life. The structure of the stem household and disagreements over inheritance as well as the rapid changes in the standard of living and expectations created conditions for interpersonal conflict, particularly between the generations.

Interpersonal conflict on Methana was not necessarily obvious from looking at behavior alone. The style of discussion and decision making within many households was often more confrontational, less polite, and just plain louder than that of the Midwestern American household settings that I have known, as was interaction between households. Serious conflict in the village was most often punctuated by silences—people passing and not speaking and, at the same time, using gossip as a weapon against each other. On occasion it exploded into arguments, fistfights, property damage, and even murder.

The stem household residence pattern also generated conflict. The son resented the prolonged authority of his father. His wife often felt that she was treated like a servant by her in-laws. In old age the older couple reluctantly gave up their control of the household and complained about the way in which the younger generation treated them. The older and younger couples had different ideas about how various tasks should be done and how they should spend their time. Rarely did the relations in stem households approach the ideal of the cooperative loving family discussed earlier.

In stem households, there was frequently tension if not quarreling between the mother-in-law and the daughter-in-law. They continually struggled over the affection, attention, and support of the male who was the older woman's son and the younger woman's husband. This placed him in a no-win situation. If he sided with his mother, his wife was upset. If he sided with his wife, his mother was upset and gave his wife a hard time.

Looking at the model of behavior provided by the family ideology and the presence of interpersonal conflict in actual social relations, the contradictions are obvious. A "good" person was not supposed to engage in interpersonal conflict and yet conflict was a part of everyday life. One means of dealing with this contradiction was through the notion of *nevra.* "Bad" people engaged in conflict willfully. Those afflicted with *nevra* could not help themselves. Claims of possession by the devil, affliction by the evil eye, and excessive drinking were alternative idioms of distress and metaphors for social disorder.

THE FOLK MODEL OF *NEVRA*

The Notion of *Nevra*

The term *nevra* is used on Methana to refer both to the nerves in the body and to various states of emotional agitation vaguely associated with the nerves. *Nevra* as an emotional state represents a departure from the desired state of calm and tranquility. The word "tranquility" is the response most frequently given when one asks "How are things going?" or "What has happened since I last saw you?" It indicates that "All is well; everything is in order."

Villagers said that there are no distinct types of *nevra.* A person simply has more or less *nevra.* They insisted that everyone has a little bit of nerves and some people have a lot of nerves. They explained that some people were more easily irritated than others but everyone occasionally got irritated and lost his or her temper. One woman gave the example of getting angry when she saw that someone's goats had eaten part of her vegetable garden. She got very upset as she looked at the damage. Her anger went away when she returned to her house and stopped thinking about her lost tomatoes and beans. A person who is *nevrikos* is easily irritated or distressed but is not necessarily suffering from *nevra* (in the sense of "lots of nerves").[3]

Generally when someone spoke of a person as "having *nevra*," it was understood that this referred to "having lots of nerves." They described a person with *nevra* as "not normal." Such people are easily agitated and must take care to avoid such irritation because they will get more and more *nevra* and eventually go crazy or become psychopathic. As an illustration, one villager brought out a newspaper article about a man in Athens who, after medical treatment for psychological problems, went home and murdered his wife. Having lots of nerves can also harm vari-

---

[3]There was some difference of opinion about the relationship between having *nevra* (nerves) and being *nevrikos* (easily irritated) depending on whether the person viewed the term *nevra* in the broad sense of general propensity to become irritated or distressed or in the narrower sense of extreme irritability (lots of nerves).

ous parts of the body and even kill a person by causing high blood pressure, low blood pressure, heart attacks, strokes, and ulcers.

Villagers spoke of (lots of) *nevra* as a physical debility—"weak nerves" in the physical sense of the term. They suggested that one could strengthen the nerves through hard work. They considered *nevra* as an illness only when one had lots of nerves. Some commented that *nevra* was the most serious illness because there was no real cure.

Just as a fever or blood pressure rises and falls so does the emotional state of *nevra.* A person in an agitated state, "at the top of the nerves," is not aware of or responsible for his or her behavior. The villagers contrasted this behavior with that of a "bad" person who berates or beats someone intentionally. As a person with *nevra* calms down and is no longer agitated, "the nerves fall."

Nevra Symptoms

Despina,[4] who suffered from *nevra,* described some of the feelings experienced during an episode:

> At the time that the nerves break one gets sick, one suffers something like a fever, like a swelling, without realizing it. Their ears roar, their head, they feel like they have something wrong in their mind. Slowly, slowly, they suffer a melancholy. They do not want company. They want to die. They feel as if they are lost from the world. Their life is nothing and it seems to them, personally, that they have nothing, that there is not anything for them. They want to be alone. The person is lost. She [or he] doesn't know where she [or he] is going.

Despina's mother-in-law, Calliopi, who also suffered from *nevra,* said that often she could not sleep at night because of her *nevra*: "It is like having ants biting at your head."

The kinds of overt behavior said to identify a person with *nevra* included getting angry, yelling, acting stubborn or spiteful, speaking rudely or abruptly, being hot-headed, and being troubled. Also associated were insomnia, headache, neck pain, restlessness, lack of appetite, melancholy, talking to oneself while walking down the road, and wandering aimlessly. Villagers emphasized that people react in different ways during *nevra* episodes, depending on their individual character. Some cry, some yell, some break plates, some beat up other people, and a few try to commit suicide or murder.

---

[4]This and other names used in the text are pseudonyms.

The individuals most likely to have lots of nerves are those with a character that is hard, arrogant, stubborn, or very sensitive. People likely to have few nerves are those who have a great deal of patience and who are calm. Most villagers insisted that one could not say that either women or men suffered more from *nevra*. A few suggested that *nevra* was more of a problem for women who were housewives and stayed in the house all day because they had lots of time to worry about their problems. Most people felt that older people had more *nevra* because a person who has lived a long time has experienced more of the distress that causes *nevra*.

Causes of *Nevra*

Reference to the *nevra* "breaking" was the most common description of the onset and the state of agitation during a *nevra* episode. This phrase and a few others allude to the stresses that irritate the nerves and prevent a person from maintaining the desired state of calm. Villagers also said that nerves "struck" a person and the nerves could be "ruined." They occasionally referred to a person's nerves being "crushed." All the verbs suggest that some external forces are doing violence to the person through the medium of the nerves. Thus the person with *nevra* is a victim of these forces and not responsible for her or his own agonistic actions.

Villagers said that a major cause of *nevra* was *stenokhoria* (worry, distress) about responsibilities to one's family and various problems such as difficulty in relations with one's spouse, a lost love, a broken engagement, a divorce, a stillborn baby, the death of a spouse, one's children getting in trouble or doing poorly in school, lack of money, failure of a business, or failing to achieve some other highly desired goal. For example, in 1972 I visited the house of an old woman who rarely recognized her own relatives, talked about events of the past as if they were the present, and had to be constantly watched by her daughter-in-law so that she did not wander off or hurt herself. Villagers explained her condition as caused by the *stenokhoria* that she suffered when her daughter was jilted by a fickle fiancé.

Some of the people with lots of nerves were said to have inherited this condition from their parents or grandparents—it ran in the blood. An elderly man suggested that there are two types of blood—hard and soft. Those who inherit hard blood have lots of *nevra*. A woman explained that her husband's brother had inherited *nevra*. Sometimes he was fine, other times he was violent. Once he even threw rocks at her and threatened to kill her for no apparent reason.

The social environment in which a child was raised was considered to be an important influence on *nevra*. As one woman phrased it: "When the child grows up with anxiety, with quarreling, with distress, inside the house, his nerves suffer."

Another source of distress leading to *nevra* within the household was chronic poor relations with another household member—one's spouse, one's child, or one's mother-in-law. As one woman described it, "To have a person annoy you every day, contrary, talking as if you were not all right—it breaks your nerves."

Others insisted that it was important to say what one felt, not to hold it in because at some point it would make one sick. However, people should not do so when they are agitated by *nevra* but when their mind was clear to discuss the situation. For example, when a young woman had an argument with her brother, with whom she shared an apartment in Athens, she waited until they both calmed down to try to resolve their differences.

Fatigue was another factor said to contribute to *nevra.* A tired person gets irritated more easily and is less willing to avoid disturbing others. A woman who ran a souvlaki stand with her husband in the summer said that she and her husband argued much more during the summer when they were both exhausted from serving customers.

A more recent type of stress said to cause *nevra* is from frustrated aspirations for the "good life"—material goods, entertainment, and higher status. Informants said that contemporary life was filled with anxiety about having as much as the next person does; it was like jealousy. Everyone insisted that fewer people had problems with nerves in the past when life was simple. People had few possessions, were not aware of other options, and were content with what they had. Young people looked forward to saint's day celebrations and weddings for entertainment and were satisfied with that. Older villagers suggested that today's children expected to have money to go to the *kafeteria*[5] and the disco as well as to buy stylish clothes and cigarettes. They were distressed if their parents did not give them these things. Even tiny children demanded candy and toys. And even with all of these things, they were never satisfied.

Some suggested that *nevra* in children and youth was the result of their being spoiled, given everything they want and not being expected to do any work. It was also explained by the influence of peers who had been spoiled. Other children had *nevra* because of their worry about

---

[5]The first *kafeteria* in the port town of Methana opened in the early 1980s; it was similar to those that had popped up all over Athens and its suburbs as youth gained more freedom and buying power. In contrast to the traditional *kafenion* (coffeehouse) where men drank, gambled, and debated, the *kafeteria* was a place where the younger generation went in groups for entertainment.

school. Villagers suggested that anyone who does not realize that a person can never get everything he wants in life, and gets distressed when he or she fails to attain a goal will suffer from *nevra.*

Some women were said to suffer from *nevra* before and just after their menstrual period. Men suffered from *nevra* when they were sexually frustrated. Some, but not all, women had *nevra* with menopause, particularly those who had an early onset. As noted earlier, people in general were expected to have more *nevra* as they grew older and had more distressing life experiences. Discussing aging and nerves, one woman observed that "life has more distress than good things in it."

Some people insisted that aspects of the physical environment contributed to problems with nerves, particularly the chemicals added to the foods they ate. Many felt that air pollution, noise, traffic, crowds, and having to deal with more people causes greater anxiety and more problems with nerves in the city than in the village. A woman who had migrated to Athens and ran a business there with her sister said that she came to the village to become calm when she suffered from *nevra.*

One woman suggested that some people feign *nevra* when they do not actually suffer from it, as a means to get their own way and to receive more careful treatment from others. It became a way of life for them. Eventually people realized that it was not really *nevra* but a type of exploitation of others.

Treatment for *Nevra*

Everyone indicated that tranquility is essential to eliminate the symptoms of *nevra.* Many recommended that the person suffering from *nevra* go to a quiet place, away from people and whatever bothers the person. They also said the person should not talk during a *nevra* episode. Likewise, one should not try to talk to a person in that state because the person could not reason properly while irritated and would be upset by whatever was said to him or her. Some suggested that the person needs to occupy him- or herself and not sit around worrying about problems. Work and visiting were two options. Friends could help the person forget his or her troubles by talking about other things.

They said that there was no traditional folk medicine for *nevra.* The only medication that they knew of was tranquilizers. If a person has a lot of nerves and is unable to calm them in any other way, he or she has no choice but to go to a doctor (a general practitioner) to get tranquilizers. Most people agreed that it is bad for a person to take tranquilizers all of the time and it is only a momentary solution to the actual problem.

One woman described taking tranquilizers for stomach nerves that had resulted from long-term poor relations with her co-resident in-laws.

Others in the village had also taken tranquilizers for various symptoms associated with *nevra*—insomnia, fits of screaming, or melancholy.

Some people took their relatives with *nevra,* as well as other ailments and disabilities, on pilgrimages to monasteries and shrines of various saints and the Virgin Mary, known for their miraculous cures (see Dubisch, 1988a). A villager described a pilgrimage where he saw a woman with *nevra* cured. As a result of *stenokhoria* she had not spoken in months. The saint came to her in a dream and told her that she would begin talking, and that she must make another pilgrimage to the shrine.

Some villagers concluded that certain cases of *nevra* were due to possession by the devil and they sought the assistance of an exorcist and/or a priest. When there was a chronic case of *nevra,* family members often pursued several lines of explanation and treatment including the exorcist, the priest, and when all else failed, the psychiatrist.

NEVRA IN SOCIAL INTERACTION

Case 1: Mother-in-Law Versus Daughter-in-Law

Despina Vanioti came from a poor family in another village and lived in her husband's parents' home. She had been unruly as a child and in her youth had dreamed of marrying a handsome, wealthy man who lived in Athens. She turned down various marriage offers including one from a wealthy farming family near Athens. Even though her father yelled and beat her, she refused to go there. Time passed. She grew older and it was more difficult to find a spouse for her. When she was 30, she was pressured to marry her present spouse, Kiriakis, a poor farmer with little ambition.

From the start there was conflict between Despina and her mother-in-law, Calliopi. Calliopi was known to be *nevriki,* as was her grandmother before her. The two women continually argued. Despina suffered from *nevra*—severe headaches and the feelings described earlier. She went to a doctor and was given tranquilizers for her problem. She continually complained about her mother-in-law when she grazed her sheep in the company of other village women. They always consoled her.

Despina's husband, Kiriakis, was a quiet man who said very little. He was content to have his father manage the household. He escaped the bickering in his house by sitting in the village store and drinking with the other men. He regularly became drunk. Eventually he became an alcoholic and failed to do his work on the farm. It was at this point that Despina suffered the most from *nevra.*

She was also distressed about her only son, fearing he might associate with bad companions. She worried that he would get hurt during his 2 years of military duty, was extremely upset when he failed the university entrance exams, and agonized when he had a motorcycle accident. The boy was also *nevrikos.* He lost his temper easily and yelled at his mother and grandmother. Despina and her son also argued frequently. After her son married a quiet young Athenian woman with a dowry apartment, Despina suffered less from *nevra.*

When Kiriakis's father died, power relations shifted in the household. Despina managed to persuade Kiriakis to go to a clinic for treatment for his alcoholism. Calliopi had less control over household affairs and began suffering more from *nevra.* The doctor had been prescribing tranquilizers for her for many years. She decided that she was also suffering from the evil eye. Calliopi said that she was afflicted by it so frequently that it had become like an illness. The woman who frequently performed the ritual to remove the evil eye told me that Calliopi was only suffering from her *nevra.* But, to calm the old woman, she pretended that it was the evil eye and performed the ritual.

Whenever there were visitors in the house, the mother-in-law and daughter-in-law competed for their attention and continually interrupted each other. Calliopi complained that Despina never spoke to her and never did anything for her. Her daughter had to come up from the port town to do her laundry. Despina even kept the old woman's cup, bowl, and spoon separate from the rest of the dishes. Calliopi lay in bed complaining, refusing to go out, and praying that she would die so she could join her husband. She wished Despina a long life so that she too might suffer in her old age. Many nights when Calliopi had episodes of *nevra,* she moaned and yelled all night long so her son and daughter-in-law could not sleep.

Despina, Calliopi, and Kiriakis all used physical complaints as an expression of and response to distress about the struggle for power within the household between mother-in-law and daughter-in-law. Both women were strong minded, and the clash inherent in the structural relations in a stem household was intensified. Although Calliopi recognized that she suffered from *nevra* and took medication, she often used the alternative idiom of the evil eye to explain her behavior and feelings and to blame it more directly on her daughter-in-law, who she believed had given her the evil eye. As predicted by the folk model, the son became *nevrikos* growing up in this setting of continual quarreling.

It was not always the case that the stem household form led to such conflict among its members. In many households the daughter-in-law quietly accepted her mother-in-law's instructions. Not all mothers-in-law were as cantankerous as Calliopi. It also might appear, from this case, that *nevra* was an idiom of distress and a metaphor for social disorder only for women and that men used other means such as excessive drinking. However, as the next case illustrates, the interactional expression of symptoms was not so neatly divided along gender lines.

Case 2: The Worried Mother and Her Melancholy Son

Penelope Ghizelis was in her mid-60s. She had married when she was 25 to a fairly poor man with several siblings whose father was a widower. Penelope was a shy, sensitive woman who was very uncomfortable when visitors came to the house. Other than working in the fields at her husband's side, she stayed in her neighborhood in the company of her close kin.

Penelope had great hopes for her older son's future and that of her daughter who had married a fruit merchant in Pireas. Despite her great hopes, however, she found herself rejected by her daughter's sisters-in-law and by her own beloved elder son as a backward village woman. One day her elder son, Paraskevas, even broke Penelope's distaff and threatened to do the same with her loom, saying that it was backward to spin and weave even though she took great pride in her skill as a weaver.

Paraskevas was known as a *nevrikos* fellow who got upset if things were not done his way. Some people said that he took after his grandfather on his father's side who was also extremely *nevrikos.* His aunt said it was because his mother had spoiled him, her favorite, as a child.

Paraskevas fell in love with a girl from an Aegean island when he was 26 and wanted to marry her. His father went to the island to negotiate the dowry and found that she did not have one. Penelope refused to allow her son to marry a girl with no dowry. Paraskevas did not care if she had a dowry or not since he made good money as an electrical engineer in the merchant marine. He obeyed his parents and did not marry the girl. But he became very depressed about his lost love. He refused to eat and became very thin. He would not go anywhere or do anything. He said his life was not worth anything and he wanted to die. His mother, who was already distressed about his behavior, became worried about his health.

When he had a motorcycle accident and was taken to Athens to get a cast, Penelope was convinced that he had died and they were not telling her. She would not eat, refused to talk to people and became very weak. Her neighbor told her that she was a fool; she was killing herself.

Penelope went to stay with her daughter in Athens who already had the burden of in-laws, Paraskevas with his *nevra* and broken leg, and her own two small children as well as a husband who demanded that his meals be ready as soon as he returned from work. She soon sent Penelope to a private hospital for mental patients. Penelope had always been a healthy woman and had never gone to a doctor in her life. She died in the hospital from the drugs she was given to sedate her. No one said, "Ah how noble that she died worrying about her son; what a model mother!" Instead they sadly noted how pointless her death had been; what a waste of a young, strong woman's life.

Paraskevas began to suffer even more from *nevra* because of his distress over his mother's death. However, he did not admit this. Instead, he insisted that his nerves had broken long ago when the vessel on which he was working nearly sank with him trapped in the engine room. Paraskevas stopped working. He wandered aimlessly, sought out churches, made pilgrimages to shrines, and became convinced that he had been possessed by the devil. For a time he stayed with his sister and her husband then he moved in with his father in the village where he spent a large part of his time drinking his father's wine. To help him forget his worries, friends in the village invited him to meals with them and engaged him in house construction work. At times he was better. At other times he suffered from *nevra.* At the baptism feast for his younger brother's child, he got drunk, broke beer bottles where people were dancing, said he wanted to break everything in the house, and called his sister a whore, thus breaking up the celebration.

In this case there was conflict over contradictions in changing values symbolized by the broken distaff, the broken engagement, the broken-up celebration, and the broken nerves of mother and son. Both the mother and her son expressed their frustrated aspirations through *nevra* which took the form of withdrawal and depression. Although Penelope's *nevra* was the result of her distress about the mental and physical health and behavior of her favorite son, it was also a form of protest about his behavior. Paraskevas's initial *nevra* was due to his distress about a goal frustrated by his mother—marriage to the woman of his choice. It was as if both mother and child waged a hunger strike to force the other to feel guilty and to force that person to act differently.

In breaking up the celebration for his brother's child's baptism, Parakevas overtly expressed jealousy of both his married siblings and frustration with his own single status that resulted from his parents' interference. He finally explained, and thus denied responsibility for, his behavior, through the alternative idiom of possession by the devil. As in the case of Calliopi, other villagers assumed that his chronic *nevra* was inherited.

Case 3: Tammy and the Exorcist

Tammy, who was 19, had lived in New York until she was 11. Her father decided that America was not a safe place for his children because of the growing drug problems there. His wife and children all wanted to stay in America because they had friends there and did not want to give up the life-style that they had enjoyed. Tammy had a twin brother who was the favorite of both parents. She had two other brothers as well.

Tammy started having emotional problems while she was still in New York. Eventually her doctor referred her to a psychiatrist. He diagnosed her as schizophrenic and said that she would have to take medication for the rest of her life. Her parents gave her medication for several years. Later Tammy saw the film "The Exorcist" and decided that she had been possessed by the devil. She began to "see" the devil in various dreams and visions. She refused to take medication and would not return to the psychiatrist. Instead she read books about the martyrdom of the saints.

After they returned to Greece, her parents did not send Tammy to secondary school, giving the excuse that she refused to wear glasses and would ruin her eyes. Even after she had lived in Greece several years, she refused to be called by her Greek name of Toula. She insisted on retaining her American name—Tammy. She dreamed of returning to America. She also talked about wanting to marry and feared no one would marry her because she was fat and ugly. She was actually a slim, attractive girl. Thus she ignored her emotional problems and behavior as a reason for frightening away prospective boyfriends and replaced them with imaginary physical problems.

While they were building a house in the port town, Tammy, her parents, and her brothers stayed with her grandparents in the village. They hoped that the tranquility of the village would be better for her. In the port town and the village they were reluctant to allow her to go out by herself because she spread false tales about her parents and their treatment of her. Her brothers refused to take her with them when they went out for a stroll in the port town because she made strange sexual comments and innuendos that embarrassed their friends and made fools of them.

When Tammy was particularly distressed, her eyes looked very wild and often rolled back in her head so that only the whites could be seen. Sometimes she expressed a physical attraction to her father and other times she told him to go away or she would kill him. She insulted her grandfather's neighbor, saying she was fat and ugly and had huge breasts. Later she returned to apologize, saying that the devil had made her do it. She said that she often saw the devil and he told her to do bad things. Once he even made her urinate in the church and spill some of the Eucharist wine which she took from the area near the altar where women are not supposed to set foot. Occasionally she disappeared, wandering off to other villages or up on the mountainside, forcing her mother, grandfather, and other relatives to search for her. When they found her, she expressed fear that her father would beat her for running away.

Tammy's mother was an insecure woman who had great difficulty making a decision about anything. She complained a great deal about what a burden her daughter was, often in Tammy's presence. Sometimes, in her own frustration with the burden that she felt, she criticized Tammy in ways that inevitably irritated her and sometimes threw her into a rage.

Tammy's parents found an exorcist in the port town who said he had "a gift" and could help Tammy get rid of the devil. He frequently visited the house and read cards. Sometimes he gave her a knife to wave above the cupboards to chase out the devil. He always locked all the doors and closed all the windows of the house during these sessions.

Many other villagers were very skeptical about the exorcist and viewed him as a charlatan taking advantage of people with problems in order to make money. Many people urged Tammy's parents to take her to a psychiatrist for proper care, saying, "She is sick, she needs help." Not everyone was sure that her condition was caused by *nevra,* but most said, "What else would it be?" Everyone agreed that it was an illness.

Among other things, Tammy said she had been told by the devil that her twin brother would die and she would take over his spirit. One day, shortly after he returned from military service, he was killed in a motorcycle accident. His parents were grief stricken. They wailed that their best child had been killed. The father threatened to commit suicide and the mother wept continually in the months that followed. The other children did their best to soothe their parents, as did their relatives.

Some people suggested that their son had been killed because they brought the exorcist into their home—a person associated with the devil who was bound to cause discord. Tammy's uncle persuaded his brother to go to a nearby monastery to see what they should do about the situation and to seek help for Tammy. In the meantime the exorcist had been driven out of the port town by the police on the grounds that he did not have a permit for his "business." Tammy's parents gave her medication to sedate her while they were dealing with the agony of their son's tragic death. Her mother also took her on pilgrimages to religious shrines, hoping that one of the saints would perform a miracle and cure her.

In this case, Tammy appeared to be expressing distress about relationships within her family and jealousy of her twin, the favorite son. Clearly the mother and daughter agitated one another. As did Paraskevas, Tammy and her parents used the alternative idiom of possession by the devil to explain what to them was aberrant behavior. They were unwilling to accept the pscychiatrist's diagnosis of schizophrenia.

This was no doubt influenced by the stigma attached to mental illness in Greece.

In dealing with her behavior, Tammy and her family pursued several explanations and treatments which were at the same time idioms of distress about the situation. Possession by the devil was most appealing because it removed blame from them and offered a cure through the exorcist. The pilgrimages to the religious shrines and Tammy's continual reading about the saints offered the hope of intervention and miraculous cure by the saints. Tammy's mother had also considered the possibility that other women had been envious of her four beautiful children and the affliction was the result of the evil eye. The psychiatrist offered no cure and identified Tammy as deviant.

The villagers viewed Tammy's case as the most serious of the three and some believed that it was incurable. A few suggested that she was mentally retarded. Most felt that she needed professional care. Although there may have originally been *nevra* as an idiom of distress about the disruption of leaving America, her conflict with her parents, and her jealousy of her twin brother, her behavior appeared to symbolize deeper troubles that were irritated by but not caused by her social relationships. Her behavior challenged existing categories and caused people to continually reinterpret her condition.

CONCLUSION: NERVES RE-EXAMINED

It is clear that *nevra* has meaning for Methanites in several senses. *Nevra* is a label identifying describable felt physical/emotional states. *Nevra* is also an idiom of distress through which individuals can react to and express their distress about interpersonal conflict and other conditions that are otherwise unacceptable to discuss or complain about. As such it may be a means to gain sympathy and support and possibly even change the distressful circumstances. However, repeated expressions of distress may make the situation worse, individually and interactionally, as in Case 1.

At another level, *nevra* is a metaphor for the agonistic behavior that is not supposed to occur between family members and other close kin, according to the family ideology. There is a recognition of conflict but it is recontextualized and the responsibility for otherwise inappropriate behavior is projected elsewhere, as is also the case with the alternative metaphors of the evil eye and possession by the devil. Blaming the *nevra* rather than the person also appears to reduce the intensity of interpersonal conflict.

It is important to emphasize that the concept of *nevra* does not entirely absolve an individual for chronic agonistic behavior. A person with lots of *nevra* is seen as one with a flawed character—a poor prospective marriage partner and parent, a difficult neighbor and coworker, and a person who has lost control as a result of heredity, life stresses, or failure to control anger. This applies to men and women.

Even more abstractly, *nevra,* the evil eye, and possession by the devil symbolize the contradictions inherent in the social order—the disorder, the lack of "proper" order. Some or all of these levels of meaning may operate at the same time, as the case histories illustrate.

The Methanites' model of the nature of *nevra* does not separate mind and body or culture and nature, just as Greek Orthodoxy has no spirit–flesh dualism. The bodily senses are spiritualized, not dematerialized, through the spiritual energy communicated through the sacraments (Campbell & Sherrard, 1968; Scheper-Hughes & Lock, 1987). Villagers' emphasis on the importance of individual character in determining whether and how persons are affected by *nevra,* combined with inheritance of character and problems of *nevra,* suggests that they are identifying what Western psychiatry would divide into biological, psychological, and social factors causing *nevra.*

Not everyone who was subject to similar interpersonal conflict, frustrated life goals, and other problems exhibited lots of *nevra.* Thus it appears that factors in addition to social interactional ones led some people to *nevra* that was recognized as an illness.

The ambiguity and negotiability of *nevra* are evident in the view that everyone has a little *nevra* and a few people have a lot of *nevra.* Like most aspects of social relations, it is a matter of degree and depends on the circumstances. Those who feign *nevra* carry the negotiability of *nevra* to its limits.

The three *nevra* cases histories varied in severity, age, and circumstances. They included both men and women. In Cases One and Two, more than one individual responded to family conflict through the idiom of *nevra* as well as other idioms—possession by the devil, the evil eye, excessive drinking, and religious pilgrimages. In the third case, biological as well as social interactional factors appear to have been at work, generating unexplainable behavior labeled as *nevra.*

In all three cases, interpersonal conflict played a significant role in generating *nevra.* All the individuals had both physical complaints and emotional upset though they expressed them in different ways. Their *nevra* was both a psychophysiological reaction to various types of interpersonal conflict within their families and an idiom of expression of distress about their situation. In general, physical symptoms provided a means of expressing distress and projecting responsibility for one's misbehavior and misfortune to other individuals and forces, consistent with the Greek sense of self described by Lambiri-Dimaki (1983), Lee (1953), Safilios-Rothschild (1972), and Skinner (1965). Thus the label of *nevra* enabled easily irritated individuals and others in the community to explain and excuse behavior antithetical to the family ideology, within limits.

Why does *nevra* on Methana appear to differ from that of other areas where nerves has been more closely associated with women as an idiom of distress? In this particular village, women had more avenues for expressing themselves than the Greek Canadian housewives studied by Dunk (1987) or the Athenian housewives described by Sutton (1985). Many had been born in the village and were surrounded by close kin. Every day women screamed and cursed at their goats, their children, and sometimes their husbands. They found sympathy from other women when they grazed their goats together. They visited each other's houses and talked about their problems. Women played an active role in the economy, owned productive resources through the dowry system, and had a voice in decision making.

Along with other Greeks, Methanites experienced sharp, rapid socioeconomic changes, especially after World War II. Thus it was the aging villagers, male and female, who became increasingly marginalized from the way of life pursued by their children, many of whom resided in Athens. Where, in the past, old people were shown respect for their knowledge from experience, the young increasingly regarded them as ignorant and backward because they were uneducated farmers. The elders' power base was undermined by the greater market participation, increasing opportunities, and changing values of the younger generation. Thus it is not surprising that they associated *nevra* with aging.

Related to this, the folk model of *nevra* and the cases showed the Methanites' conscious association of *nevra* with these rapid socioeconomic changes. They viewed *nevra* among children and increased *nevra* among adults as the outcome—a sort of modernization anxiety.

This analysis of *nevra* on Methana demonstrates the importance of examining both the folk model of nerves and its social interactional use in order to describe and explain nerves cross-culturally as idiom, metaphor, symptom, and, in a few cases, disorder. It indicates that future research should also look more closely at male *nevra* and idioms of distress and examine aging as a factor, particularly in countries experiencing rapid socioeconomic change. Finally, it suggests that we must be careful to avoid overlooking the biological aspects of nerves, as symptoms and emotional disorders, in our concern to address the social and emotional aspects of nerves, as metaphors and idioms, that have been ignored in biomedical models of illness.

REFERENCES

Bender, D. (1967). A refinement of the concept of household: Family, coresidence, and domestic functions. *American Anthropologist, 69,* 493.

Bialor, P. (1963). Tensions leading to conflict and the resolution and avoidance of conflict in a Greek farming community. In J. Peristiany (Ed.), *Contributions to Mediterranean sociology* (pp. 107–126). The Hague, Netherlands: Mouton.

Blum R., & Blum, E. (1965). *Health and healing in rural Greece.* Stanford, CA: Stanford University Press.

Blum R., & Blum, E. (1970). *The dangerous hour: The lore of crisis and mystery in rural Greece.* New York: Charles Scribners' Son.

Campbell, J. (1964). *Honor, family and patronage: A study of the institutions and moral values of a Greek mountain community.* Oxford, England: Clarendon Press.

Campbell, J. (1983). Traditional values and continuities in Greek society. In R. Clogg (Ed.), *Greece in the 1980s* (pp. 184–297). London: Macmillan.

Campbell, J., & Sherrard, P. (1968). *Modern Greece.* New York: Praeger.

Clark, M. H. (1988). *The transformation of households in Methana Greece, 1931–1987.* Unpublished doctoral dissertation, University of North Carolina at Chapel Hill.

Clark, M. H. (in press-a). From shelters to villas: Changing household and settlement form in Methana, Greece. In S. B. Sutton (Ed.), *Farmers, shepherds and sailors: Regional development in the southern Argolid of Greece.* Stanford, CA: Stanford University Press.

Clark, M. H. (in press-b). The transformation of households on Methana. In A. Papataxiarchis (Ed.), *Selected papers from the Symposium on Horizons of Anthropological Research in Greece.* Mytilene: University of the Aegean.

Caraveli, A. (1980). Bridge between two worlds: The women's ritual lament as communicative event. *Journal of American Folklore, 93,* 129–154.

Constantelos, D. (1982). *Understanding the Greek Orthodox Church.* New York: Seaberry Press.

Danforth, L. (1979). The role of dance in ritual therapy of the Anastenaria. *Byzantine and Modern Greek Studies, 5,* 141–163.

Dionisopoulos-Mass, R. (1976). The evil eye and bewitchment in a peasant village. In C. Mahoney (Ed.), *The evil eye* (pp. 42–62). New York: Columbia University Press.

Dubisch, J. (1986). Introduction. In J. Dubisch (Ed.), *Gender and power in rural Greece* (pp. 3–41). Princeton, NJ: Princeton University Press.

Dubisch, J. (1988a). Golden oranges and silver ships: An interpretive approach to a Greek holy shrine. *Journal of Modern Greek Studies, 6*(1), 117–134.

Dubisch, J. (1988b). *What mother is crying now? Prolegomena to a poetics of womanhood in Greece.* Manuscript.

du Boulay, J. (1974). *Portrait of a Greek mountain village.* Oxford, England: Clarendon Press.

du Boulay, J. (1986). Women—images of their nature and destiny in rural Greece. In J. Dubisch (Ed.), *Gender and power in rural Greece* (pp. 139–168). Princeton, NJ: Princeton University Press.

Dunk, P. (1987). *Greek women and broken nerves in Montreal.* Manuscript submitted for publication.

Friedl, E. (1962). *Vasilika: A village in modern Greece*. New York: Holt, Rinehart, and Winston.
Herzfeld, M. (1980). Social tension and inheritance by lot in three Greek villages. *Anthropological Quarterly, 55*(2), 91–100.
Herzfeld, M. (1981). Meaning and morality: A semiotic approach to evil eye accusations in a Greek village. *American Ethnologist, 8,* 560–574.
Herzfeld, M. (1986). Closure as cure: Tropes in the exploration of bodily and social disorder. *Current Anthropology, 27*(2), 107–120.
Hirschon, R. (1978). Open body/closed space: The transformation of female sexuality. In S. Ardener (Ed.), *Defining women* (pp. 68–88). London: Croom Helm.
Hirschon, R. (1983). Under one roof: Marriage, dowry and family relations in Piraeus. In M. Kenny & D. Kertzer (Eds.), *Urban life in Mediterranean Europe* (pp. 299–323). Urbana: University of Illinois Press.
Karapostolis, V. (1983). Consumption patterns in rural Greek communities: A sociological approach. *Ekistics, 50,* 442–448.
Lambiri-Dimaki, J. (1983). Greece in the 1980s: Changing evaluations of the roles of men and women. In J. Lambiri-Dimaki (Ed.), *Social stratification in Greece* (pp. 182–206). Athens: A. Sakkoulas.
Lee, D. (1953). Greece. In M. Mead (Ed.), *Cultural patterns and technical change* (pp. 77–113). Deventer, Holland: UNESCO.
Loizos, P. (1978). Violence and the family: Some Mediterranean examples. In J. P. Martin (Ed.), *Violence and the family* (pp. 183–196). London: Wiley.
Low, S. M. (1985). Culturally interpreted symptoms or culture-bound syndromes: A cross-structural review of nerves. *Social Science and Medicine, 21*(2), 187–196.
Nichter, M. (1981). Idioms of distress. Alternatives in the expression of psychosocial distress: A case from south India. *Culture, Medicine, and Psychiatry, 5,* 379–408.
Quinn, N., & Holland, D. (1987). Culture and cognition. In D. Holland & N. Quinn (Eds.), *Cultural models in language and thought.* New York: Cambridge University Press.
Safilios-Rothschild, C. (1968). Deviance and mental illness in the Greek family. *Family Process, 7*(1), 100–117.
Safilios-Rothschild, C. (1969). Psychotherapy and patients' characteristics: A cross-cultural examination. *International Journal of Social Psychology, 15*(2), 120–128.
Safilios-Rothschild, C. (1972). Honor crimes in modern Greece. In C. Safilios-Rothschild (Ed.), *Toward a sociology of women.* Lexington, MA: Xerox College Publishing.
Scheper-Hughes, N., & Lock, M. (1986). Speaking truth to illness: Metaphors, reification, and pedagogy for patients. *Medical Anthropology Quarterly, 17*(5), 137–140.
Scheper-Hughes, N., & Lock, M. (1987). The mindful body: A prolegomenon to future work in medical anthropology. *Medical Anthropology Quarterly, 18,* 6–41.
Skinner, J. C. (1965). Symptom and defense in contemporary Greece: A cross-cultural inquiry. *Journal of Nervous and Mental Disease, 4,* 478–489.
Sutton, S. (1983). Rural–urban migration in Greece. In M. Kenny & D. Kertzer (Eds.), *Urban life in Mediterranean Europe* (pp. 225–249). Urbana: University of Illinois Press.

Sutton, S. B. (1985). Family and work: New patterns for village women in Athens. *Journal of Greek Studies, 4*(1), 33–47.

Wilk, R., & Netting, R. N. (1984). Household—changing form and function. In R. N. Netting, R. Wilk, & E. Arnould (Eds.), *Households: Comparative and historical studies of the domestic group* (pp. 1–28). Berkeley: University of California Press.

Yanagisako, S. J. (1979). Family and household: The analysis of domestic groups. *Annual Review of Anthropology, 8,* 161–205.

LIVING ON THEIR NERVES: NERVOUS DEBILITY IN NORTHERN IRELAND

Jeffrey A. Sluka, PhD
Department of Social Anthropology, Massey University
Palmerston North, New Zealand

Divis Flats was a high-rise public housing project on the Falls Road in Belfast, Northern Ireland. It was frequently described as the worst ghetto in Western Europe, and was widely reputed to be a political hotbed, an Irish Republican Army stronghold, and one of the most violent housing estates in the United Kingdom. The complex exhibited some of the worst manifestations of Northern Ireland's considerable political, economic, social, health, and housing problems, and had been the scene of some of the worst violence that had occurred since the outbreak of the political "troubles" (as the war in Northern Ireland is euphemistically called) in 1969. Generalized ghetto conditions in combination with political violence created a powerful environment for the development of nervous complaints, and many people in Divis Flats, but particularly women, suffered from "nervous debility" or "bad nerves." Although this problem derived from multiple causes—political, economic, and social—*terror* stands out as the single most important causal factor. This article describes and analyzes the causes and experience of "nerves" and explores the relationship between gender and nerves in a Northern Irish ghetto.

There is a growing literature on the etiology and experience of "nerves," and physicians and social scientists alike are increasingly recognizing that this is a widespread complaint that occurs in many different cultures with diverse cultural interpretations (Low, 1985). In recent years, scholars have emphasized the importance of cultural variation and social structural factors in the etiology and experience of nerves (e.g., Davis & Guarnaccia, 1987; Low, 1985). Davis and Guarnaccia (1987, p. 2) have noted that nerves is "an emically derived, popular, variable, multipurpose complaint which transcends mind, body, and culture," and argue that the phenomenon "is best understood through anthropological investigation and analysis."

My purpose in writing this article is to explore, describe, and analyze both the causes and experience of nerves in Divis Flats—a Catholic-Nationalist ghetto on the Falls Road in Belfast, Northern Ireland, where I conducted research over an 11-month period in 1981–1982. The research was based on participant observation and interviews with 76 households in the community, and the monograph emerging from this was an anthropological study of the social dynamics of popular support for the Irish Republican Army (IRA) and Irish National Liberation Army (INLA) (Sluka, 1989). Although the research focused on political culture, the schedule used in the household interviews included a section on health conditions, which brought to my attention the fact that many people in Divis, particularly women, suffered from "bad nerves."[1]

Although the research on which this article is based was not directly on the experience of nerves, it appears that most anthropologists who have written about this subject have approached it indirectly. Their interest in nerves has usually been stimulated by their experiences in the field when informants identified this as an important phenomenon (Davis & Guarnaccia, 1987). My experience was similar. Because most of the households interviewed spoke of depression and bad nerves, it was clear that these were important subjective experiences and serious health problems in the community and deserved to be studied.

SETTING

Divis Flats was a high-rise public housing project built between 1966 and 1972 as part of slum clearance and urban redevelopment of the inner-city areas of Belfast. It was an inner-city ghetto community located only a few hundred yards west of Belfast City Hall, at the bottom of the Falls Road—the largest Catholic enclave in Belfast—where it enters the city center. To the north was the Shankill Road and to the south Sandy Row, both staunchly Loyalist Protestant working-class districts. The complex was part of the district known as the Lower Falls, an area of red brick rowhouses built during the 19th century to house workers in the linen, cotton, and other industries that blossomed in Ulster during

---

[1]The health section of the interview schedule did not include a question specifically about nerves. Instead, residents were asked to comment on health conditions in the community in general, and to identify and discuss health complaints suffered by members of the household. More than 70% of the households interviewed identified members who suffered from depression, bad nerves, insomnia, alcoholism, dependence on tranquilizers, or other psychological or emotional problems. These problems were discussed at length. In addition to the interviews, I had several dozen discussions with people about nerves in the informal situations characteristic of research based on participant observation.

the industrial revolution. It was in an advanced state of physical deterioration. The entire Lower Falls was designated for slum clearance and redevelopment, and was suffering from extreme redevelopment blight and social disruption as the old housing was slowly being knocked down and replaced with new rowhouses.

The Divis complex contained 850 flats, of which 775 were occupied at the time of the study with a total population of approximately 2,400 residents. It consisted of 14 seven- and eight-story-high blocks of flats, a 30-story tower block with a British army observation post on top (Divis Tower), a Catholic church, a primary school, and a community center. Most of the blocks had three vertical rows of flats, and they were linked at each of these levels, providing "continuous access" around the complex. Each flat had a living room, a kitchen, a bathroom and toilet, and from one to six bedrooms.

Divis Flats had a reputation for being the worst ghetto in Northern Ireland, and was frequently described as the worst ghetto in Western Europe. It was widely reputed to be a political hotbed, an IRA and INLA stronghold, and one of the UK's most violent housing estates. The complex had been the scene of some of the worst violence since the outbreak of the political "troubles" (as the war in Northern Ireland is euphemistically called) in August 1969. Economically and socially, the community was without doubt one of the most deprived areas in a province suffering an acute economic crisis, and it had become one of the most stigmatized communities in the province as well. Divis Flats exhibited some of the worst manifestations of Northern Ireland's considerable economic, housing, social, health, and political problems.

Scholars who have studied nerves have discovered that this experience is related to situations of marginal status, which include economic, social, and political stress deriving from powerlessness, disadvantage, and oppression (Davis & Guarnaccia, 1987). This was the case in Divis Flats, where economic, housing, social, and political stress each made their own contribution to the generation of nervous complaints.

Economic Conditions

Economic, housing, and social conditions in Divis Flats were similar to those found in other impoverished inner-city ghettos in Western Europe and America. The community was one of the hardest hit employment blackspots in Western Europe. As high as the unemployment rate in Northern Ireland was—at over 20%—it was more than three times higher in Divis Flats where, at the time of my research, 63% of the economically active adult population were unemployed. Those who were unemployed were dependent on welfare benefits, and because of low wages for unskilled and semiskilled workers even those who were employed were very often partially dependent on them as well. At the time of my research 51% of the households in the community were entirely dependent on welfare benefits, 41% were partly dependent on them, and only 8% were economically self-sufficient. As a result of the combination of high umemployment, low wages, and inadequate welfare benefits, 70% of Divis households had been forced into debt, particularly for rent and utility rates. In 1980, the Northern Ireland Housing Executive reported that the rent deficit in Divis was seven times the Northern Irish average (Northern Ireland Housing Executive, 1980).

Many of the residents of Divis Flats were caught in the classic "poverty trap" situation. Benefits levels are based on United Kingdom-wide averages, and did not make allowances for the fact that inflation and the cost of living were higher than these averages in Northern Ireland.[2] Benefits levels were set at the official "poverty line," and this meant that households in Northern Ireland that were entirely dependent on welfare benefits were living below the poverty line. This was further exacerbated by the application of the Payment for Debt Act. Operative only in Northern Ireland, this legislation allowed the government to deduct rent, rates, gas, and electricity arrears directly from welfare benefits.[3] This meant that many households in Divis that were expected to cope on benefits that were already below the poverty line were having arrears deducted from these benefits. The amount deducted for arrears often left barely enough to live on, and not enough to pay current bills. So the vicious cycle continued as new debts mounted as fast or faster than old debts were paid off (cf. Evason, 1978, 1980).

---

[2]Northern Ireland is one of the poorest and most deprived areas in Western Europe, and has the highest unemployment, lowest wages, highest rate of inflation, highest cost of living, highest rates of infant and maternal mortality, poorest health conditions, shortest life expectancy, and worst housing in the United Kingdom. More than a third of all households in Northern Ireland are living below the poverty line. (This is particularly true of households headed by women, less than 10% of which have resources placing them above the poverty line.) On almost every statistical scale of suffering, the working-class population of Northern Ireland emerges as the most deprived in the United Kingdom and often in the whole of Western Europe.

[3]In 1971 many Catholics participated in a civil disobedience campaign, a "rent and rates" strike, to protest against the use of internment without trial. The Payment for Debts Act was introduced to defeat this campaign. After the rent and rates strike ended, the act was kept on to "claw back" arrears and prevent that form of protest from being effective in the future.

Living Conditions

As with economic conditions, housing conditions in Divis Flat were similar to those found in high-rise public housing projects in other parts of the world. The problems people in Divis had with their flats at the time of my research were, as the saying goes, "many and varied," but the major ones can be briefly identified. The blocks were made of concrete and steel. Because of the "cold bridge" effect of concrete, the flats were fantastically expensive to heat. Because of poor insulation, inadequate ventilation, and cold concrete walls, condensation and dampness were a major problem. The results of condensation and dampness included mold and mildew, peeling wallpaper, and bubbling paint. The complex was provided with a totally inadequate waste disposal system that broke down continually. Garbage ended up scattered around the complex, and one result was a plague of rats. The effects on health of living in cold, damp, and unsanitary conditions—particularly among the elderly and children—are obvious. In the winter, water pipes froze and burst, flooding many flats. Other problems included cramped, overcrowded conditions, and dependence on elevators that were subject to frequent breakdowns and were easily (and repeatedly) vandalized. The difficulty involved in just climbing, let alone carrying groceries and babies in prams, up and down seven or eight floors restricted many people's mobility.

Social Conditions

Social conditions in Divis were as bad as economic and housing conditions. The residents were fragmented into isolated households and cliques. Many, particularly women, suffered from social isolation. Community solidarity, integration, and identity were weak—certainly much weaker than in the other traditional "urban village" communities of Belfast. The rowhouse urban village ghettos were socially tight-knit and well-integrated communities, the result of there being little geographical mobility among the residents, who generally lived their entire lives within the community. People were proud of their district, and there was a strong sense of community identity. But the tightknit social structure characteristic of the urban village ghettos was lost in the move from rowhouses to high-rise flats. There was a much higher degree of geographical mobility among Divis residents, and the community was not an urban village like the traditional rowhouse ghettos. Most people in Divis did not consider the complex to be their permanent home, and strong social relationships and extended social networks had not developed. Neither had community integration or a sense of shared identity. People often said they did not even known most of the people living on their own balcony even though they may have been neighbors for years. Many preferred to keep to themselves, and were almost completely isolated from other residents. Others associated only with a few relatives, their immediate neighbors, and/or a few close friends. In 1975 a Lower Falls Residents' Association newsletter was already expressing many peoples' concerns about social fragmentation in Divis when it asked, "Do you live in a community, or do you live in an area where rampant individualism is the order of the day?"

Social conditions in Divis were also partly related to the physical structure of the complex. The structure of the flats and the complex as a whole encouraged isolation and contributed to social fragmentation. People frequently compared their flats to prison cells. This was particularly true of women, who generally spent much more of their time inside their flats than did men and children.

Another aspect of social conditions in Divis Flats that had an impact on nervous complaints was the generalized breakdown of "law and order." Like ghetto communities the world over, people in Divis had problems with criminal behavior. Because the residents viewed the Royal Ulster Constabulary (RUC) as politically biased (pro-Unionist) and sectarian (97% Protestant), they had rejected them and there was no normal police presence in the complex. People said that there was no "law and order" in Divis, and they frequently described it as a "concrete jungle" where the only law was "the law of the jungle." They had problems with mugging, shops and flats being robbed, an occasional rape, joyriding in stolen cars, and vandalism. Responsibility for these activities was attributed to "hoods," who, residents frequently said in disgust, "ruled" Divis. At night, particularly on weekends, joyriders roared around the complex, sometimes crashing into walls and ground floor flats. Because anyone walking in the complex was at risk, joyriders were hard on everyone's nerves, but they were particularly hard on parents' nerves because they feared that their children might either be hit by stolen cars or get involved in joyriding themselves. The IRA and INLA played a role as "community police" and controlled criminal activity to some degree, but were not very effective, and the hoods and joyriders certainly created strain in the community.

Political Conditions

To appreciate political conditions in Divis Flats one has to bear in mind that the complex was one of the major battlegrounds of a war that, after more than 19 years of violence, represents one of the largest and most protracted conflicts experienced in the world since the end of World War II. In particular, in order to comprehend the relationship between the experience of nerves and the political environment in Divis, one needs to understand the nature of military repression—or Security Forces terror—in the Catholic ghettos. As Fairweather, McDonough, and McFadyean (1984, p. 15) have noted, along with the poverty of ghetto life, "The army patrols at will, raiding and wrecking homes and precious possessions, dragging children from their beds, abusing women, beating men and boys. It is almost impossible to find a working-class Catholic family who have not, at some point in the last few years, suffered directly at the hands of a brutal and brutalized army."

In Divis Flats the Security Forces were in many ways like an occupying army. Patrols of heavily armed soldiers and policemen, on foot and in armored vehicles, was a common sight day and night, and the complex was under constant surveillance from the army observation post on top of Divis Tower. The constant presence of troops and police patrolling the complex, stopping, searching, questioning, and sometimes abusing people, created tension and strain in the community. The residents viewed this as a daily experience of military repression and state terror, and it took a considerable toll on their nerves.

A full account of the violence that has occurred in Divis Flats is not possible here, but the major forms of political violence characteristic of the community can be briefly identified. Over the years, urban guerrilla warfare in the complex had primarily taken the form of IRA and INLA attacks on the Security Forces with gunfire and bombs. In these attacks guerrillas, soldiers, policemen, and innocent residents have been killed and injured. Another political reality Divis residents lived with was the threat of assassination by Loyalists. More than 600 innocent Catholics had been assassinated by Loyalist extremists in Northern Ireland, including several from Divis Flats. But the most common form of political violence in Divis was rioting. Probably more rioting had occurred in and around the complex than in any other locale in Northern Ireland. Again and again over the years, mobs of youths have hurled stones and petrol bombs at the Security Forces, who have responded with riot platoons, "snatch squads," baton charges, CS (tear) gas, and rubber and plastic bullets. On some occasions youths hijacked and burned dozens of vehicles and used them to barricade the complex and turn it into a "no go" area. Needless to say, the constant threat of gunfire, explosions, random assassination, and serious rioting was a strain on everyone's nerves.

People in Divis said they feared the Security Forces. They feared them because the personal behavior of individual soldiers and policemen was unpredictable, and because they had been harassed, intimidated, and abused by them. They believed and feared that they could be arrested at any time and subjected to harsh methods of interrogation, that they could be convicted and imprisoned on trumped-up charges on the word of any soldier or policeman, and that they could even be killed if they did not "keep their noses clean" politically. As one man put it, "The worst thing about the army and police, the most frightening thing, is that they literally get away with murder. They can beat people up, kill them, do anything they want, and they can just say they thought they had a gun or that they were rioting and they are automatically believed. They have complete power and there's no control over them. They are above the law."

Raids, patrols, and the use of plastic bullets had a particularly direct impact on people's nerves. Most of the flats had been raided and searched at least once, and some of them several times. Raids usually occurred in the middle of the night. The door would be kicked in and everyone dragged from their beds. Often considerable damage was done to the flat during the search. People were sometimes arrested or detained, and subjected to varying degrees of verbal and physical abuse.

People also had to live with the constant presence of patrols, and this was sometimes nerveracking. Whenever they walked through a patrol, they said, there was always an internal tension, a nagging apprehension at the back of their minds that for one reason or another they might not make it through this particular patrol without trouble. They knew that they might be stopped for an identity check, searched, and questioned, and they feared they might be arrested or subjected to verbal harassment or physical abuse.

Almost everyone in the community had some personal experience of Security Forces harassment or abuse. If they had not personally been the victim, someone in their family and/or some of their friends had been. Some common forms identified by Divis people included the following: beatings in alleys, stairwells, and other dark or isolated places, and other forms of physical abuse like unnecessary body searches; verbal abuse, such as threats, name calling, and the use of sectarian epithets (e.g., "fenian bastard" or "fenian whore"); being shot at with ballbearings fired from slingshots while walking on the streets at night; vandalism, such as breaking lights and windows with rifle butts and defacing political murals; writing political or sectarian graffiti on walls and people's doors; and motorized patrols picking up Catholics and "dumping" them in Loyalist districts at night.

Soldiers and policemen also caused a good deal of tension and "aggro" in Divis by taunting children. When they did this the children often threw stones at them—especially at the armored Landrovers—and this upset many people. Although these were generally small-scale near-daily occurrences that passed off without anything serious happening, they could have serious consequences. Soldiers and policemen might be injured, and children might be knocked down by Landrovers. These incidents might escalate, and petrol bombs and plastic bullets be exchanged. Whether these incidents stayed low key or escalated into minor riots, they were a constant strain on people's nerves, especially mothers' nerves.

Fifteen people, including seven school children, had been killed with rubber and plastic bullets in Northern Ireland, and hundreds more seriously injured, including loss of eyes, brain damage, and paralysis (Curtis, 1982). A great many people in Divis told me that they knew from experience that soldiers and policemen fired plastic bullets indiscriminately and with a near-total disregard for the regulations governing their use. For example, a 4-year-old was struck in the head with a plastic bullet in May 1981, and a woman told me about an incident she observed in which three 4-year-olds on the ground threw pebbles at some soldiers on a balcony above them and gave them the finger. She said they responded by firing two plastic bullets down at them. People in Divis Flats viewed the use of plastic bullets as an example of military repression and a form of state terror. Some of the bitterness they felt about the use of this weapon, especially against their children, was expressed by a man from Divis who said, "The penalty for rioting is, at most, six months, not death. The penalty for 10-year-olds throwing stones at armored cars should be a clip on the ear, not death. But we now have the situation where the penalty for being a Catholic and walking in your own street or even standing at your own window is death" (cited in Curtis, 1982, p. 35).

Finally, there was also the presence of the IRA and INLA. Critics of the IRA and INLA claim that they threaten, intimidate, and generally terrorize Catholics into tolerating their presence and not acting against them. However, I found no evidence that anyone in Divis had been intimidated or directly threatened by the guerrillas. No one I interviewed or spoke with said that they were afraid of the IRA or INLA or felt intimidated by them. The IRA and INLA were a strain on people's nerves, but not because of intimidation. They represented a threat to the residents' safety because they were at war with the Security Forces. The guerrillas' activities drew the unwanted and unpleasant attentions of the Security Forces down on the community, and there was always the possibility of accidents or mistakes, or of being caught in cross-fire or an explosion.

LIVING WITH IT ALL

Journalists and other observers frequently comment on how remarkably well the people of Northern Ireland have "adapted to abnormality" and become "acclimatized" to political violence. Usually this is phrased in terms of admiration, but sometimes it is not, as when it is sometimes claimed that they have become "hardened" by the violence and that it no longer bothers them to see people killed or injured. It is true that people in Divis Flats had developed a range of skills and a whole body of specialized knowledge that helped them to adapt to the political realities of their environment. But this did not mean that they had become "used to" political violence, that it did not bother them, or that it was not taking a heavy psychological and emotional toll on them. When the level of violence increased, for example, during the Republican hunger strike in 1981, many people suffered acutely from fear, anxiety, bad nerves, hysteria, and insomnia, and the use (or abuse) of alcohol and tranquilizers increased substantially. Most of the adults in the community used alcohol and/or prescription drugs to help them cope. But some drank too much or took too many tablets and had developed dependencies, and some failed to cope and became suicidal.

These subjective costs of living with political violence on a long-term basis have been relatively neglected by those who have done research in Northern Ireland. For example, while "bad nerves" is widely experienced in the Catholic ghettos and is publicly recognized as a common, even "normal" phenomenon, it has received little direct attention from researchers. Indirectly, scholars like Fraser (1973), who has studied the psychological effects of living in riot conditions; Heskin (1980), who has done a general psychological study of Northern Ireland; and Fairweather, McDonough, and McFadyean (1984), who have written about women's experiences, make an important contribution to the study of nerves in Northern Ireland, and my research generally supports what they have said in this regard.

The major factor that helped people in Divis Flats live with the violence was that it was episodic rather than constant. Although some act of political violence occurred somewhere in Northern Ireland almost every day, it did not occur every day, every week, or even every month in any particular district. Violence in Divis Flats, other than the everyday stoning of Security Forces vehicles, came and went. Nothing at all might happen for several months at a time, and then a single violent incident, for example, an IRA or INLA attack on the Security Forces or a riot, or a series of such incidents might occur over a period of a few days. Sometimes such "hot" periods might last for several months, like during the hunger strike in 1981. Some of the violence, such as that which occurs when Protestants march and burn bonfires in July and when Catholics do the same in August, was predictable. This allowed people to psychologically prepare themselves for trouble. When violence erupted Divis people were not able to just shrug it off, ignore it, and go about their business. They became agitated, anxious, and nervous, and suffered acute psychological and emotional distress. But they told themselves that it would not go on forever, and the belief that if they just hung in there long enough things would quiet down again helped them to cope with it.

More than 70% of the households I interviewed in Divis had members who suffered from depression, bad nerves, insomnia, alcoholism, dependence on tranquilizers, or other psychological or emotional problems. These problems were a result of the combination of economic, social, housing, and political conditions in the complex, and it is difficult or even impossible to isolate the impact of political conditions from the rest. But it was certainly the case that when violence flared up people drank more, took more tranquilizers and other prescription drugs, and increasing numbers of them complained about their nerves. The majority of people in Divis had adapted well to the situation psychologically, at least to the extent that psychiatrists had found little evidence of widespread mental or emotional disturbance, in the clinical sense, among them. However, this apparent "adaptedness" was at least partly maintained only by increased consumption of alcohol and tranquilizers (Heskin, 1980, p. 67).

The most common self-identified psychological problems were depression and bad nerves. It is fair to say that almost everyone in the community suffered from these two problems in varying degrees from time to time. People in Divis attributed depression and bad nerves to one or a combination of four factors: poverty, living conditions in the flats, social isolation, and political violence. Although I believe depression and bad nerves in Divis cannot really be considered in isolation, people did make a general distinction between their causes; they thought that depression primarily resulted from poverty, poor living conditions, and social isolation (generalized "ghetto conditions"), and that bad nerves primarily resulted from the political troubles.

Everyone in Divis suffered from some degree of depression, at least occasionally, and many psychological problems are by-products of depression. Several women had committed suicide in the complex, and there had been many attempted suicides. As stated, residents generally attributed this to poverty and the very bad living conditions in the flats, aggravated by social isolation. In the Northern Irish ghettos increases in neurotic illnesses have occurred primarily among women. Fraser (1973) suggested that this was because women often have the additional burden of major responsibility for children. Women in Divis also suffered more from social isolation than did men, and social isolation "is a potent factor in the precipitation of mental illness" (Fraser, 1973, p. 55). In Divis Flats, where social fragmentation and isolation were the norm (in contrast to the socially well-integrated "urban village" ghettos), this potent factor was very pronounced. Many residents turned to alcohol or prescription drugs to combat depression, but, as one man put it, "There's no cure for loneliness and like that."

Whereas depression was associated with generalized ghetto conditions, the most common self-identified psychological complaint associated with the political troubles was bad nerves, which people in Divis often referred to as "nervous debility." Commonly identified symptoms of this problem included nausea, inability to eat or sleep, feelings of anxiety and fear, hysteria, and paranoia. People said that when their nerves went bad they felt worried, excited, and agitated all the time, and that they reacted strongly to things, often with fear and panic. A more qualitative description of the experience of "nervous debility" was given by a man who described it as "a sort of feeling of impending doom and that there's no place to run or hide. You feel jumpy, and scared all the time that something is going to happen. You jump at noises and are agitated, and you can't sleep. It comes from living in these troubles."

Nervous debility sometimes also resulted in physical problems, such as ulcers, and a number of people in Divis suffered from nervous disability. They were unable to work because their nerves were shot, and this was recognized as a basis for receiving workers' disability benefits. For example, one man I interviewed had been unable to work for several years, ever since Loyalist extremists told him a bomb found on the bus he rode to work was meant for him.

The political troubles were not the only cause of nervous debility in Divis, but they were the primary cause or catalyst. As noted, this was indicated by the fact that it was when political violence (e.g., rioting) erupted that large numbers of people began to complain about their nerves. Some of the causes of nervous debility commonly identified by people included rioting, bombing, and shooting, and never knowing when these might happen; having family members shot or arrested, and worrying that this might happen or happen again; being raided by the Security Forces, worrying about this, and "never knowing when they might kick in your door some night"; and being assaulted, harassed, and intimidated by soldiers and policemen, and never knowing what to expect when stopped by them. Women also often attributed their bad nerves to being left alone and isolated in their flats when rioting and troubles were going on outside.

In his research, Fraser (1973) found that two kind of psychiatric ill health resulted from exposure to riot conditions in Belfast—acute but temporary mental and emotional disturbances, and more lasting and incapacitating psychiatric illnesses. The first kind of problems were generally normal anxiety reactions to stressful events, and closely corresponded to what Divis people meant by "bad nerves" or "nervous debility." Although these mental and emotional disturbances could be dramatic, they were generally short lived and resolved themselves when the violence declined or ended. Fraser (1973, p. 86) noted, "Acute anxiety is common during or after a stressful event, such as a riot or natural disaster. It can take bizarre and sometimes frightening forms—shaking, trembling fits, laughing for no apparent reason, uncontrollable weeping. This is not the same as a nervous breakdown or a mental illness; it is a normal reaction and rarely lasts for long." Most cases of "bad nerves" in Divis were normal stress reactions to "abnormally" stressful conditions. They were generally temporary and resolved themselves when the stress was alleviated. But sometimes mental breakdowns or mental illnesses did result.

Robert Liston (1977), a specialist on terrorism, has also noted that,

> Terrorism is now recognized as a cause for illness. Doctors in Northern Ireland report an increase in patients suffering from what they call the Belfast syndrome. The patients, usually women and children, cry and tremble uncontrollably. Often they can't remember their names or where they live. Sometimes they are unable to speak. Doctors usually prescribe tranquilizers and mild sedatives, but patients do not aways respond to such treatment. The Belfast syndrome is believed to be the result of living with constant terror, where the enemy is not easily identifiable and the violence is indiscriminate and arbitrary (p. 23).

Although this is generally true, and the "Belfast syndrome" corresponds to what people in Divis Flats referred to as nervous debility, the way Liston presents it is somewhat misleading. He fails to accurately identify the sources of the "constant terror," the enemy is easily identifiable, and the violence is not as indiscriminate or arbitrary as he implies. Nonetheless, Liston is correct to identify terror—the fear individuals have that they might, at almost any moment, become the victims of violence—as perhaps the most important catalyst, thought not the sole cause, of nervous debility.

Worrying About Children

People in Divis also identified the hoods, joyriders, and worrying about children as causes of bad nerves. Parents in Divis worried a great deal about their children. They worried that they might be injured or killed during rioting, shooting, or bombing. They worried that their children might be hit by joyriders or joyride themselves and be injured in accidents or shot by the Security Forces. They worried that their children might become involved in "hooding" activities and be punished (beaten up or kneecapped) by the IRA. They also feared that their children might be permanently unemployed, that they might become alcoholics, and that their future might be no better than the present, politically, economically, or socially. Finally, they worried about their children becoming involved in the IRA or INLA, though not because they considered this dishonorable or immoral. They worried about this because they knew that it meant a life on the run, with the probability of spending many years in prison and the possibility of violent death.

Fairweather et al., who have written what is perhaps the best book on women's experiences in Northern Ireland, note that mothers in the Catholic ghettos "live in a state of perpetual anxiety that one day it will be their child who is caught in the firing line, or their child who runs in front of a Saracen [armored car], or their child who is just a bit too cheeky to a soldier" (1984, p. 17). As one woman told them, "Every mother's frightened for her children. If they're late home from school they could be arrested, they could be trailed up an entry [by the Security Forces], you just don't know. You get so you're living off your nerves—I don't know a mother who doesn't" (1984, p. 17). They also noted that children as young as 5 years old have been "lifted" by the Security Forces:

> A Catholic woman from the Falls was quietly sitting having a cup of tea and a cigarette one day when a group of women came banging at her door. "Your Seamus is lifted," they said. At first Eileen didn't believe them, "My Seamus is only five years old," she said. The women insisted he was in the back of a Saracen being driven around the nearby park. Eileen rushed out to the Springfield Road barracks and after two hours her child, very bewildered and tear-stained, was returned to her (Fairweather et al, 1984, p. 17).

Another woman whose 13-year-old son was killed by a plastic bullet also expressed a Belfast mother's fears concerning her children: "The children here are destroyed, they've been turned into vandals, they steal cars and then go joyriding and the army shoots them dead for it. I used to bring my kids in when the army was in the streets and they used to complain, saying home was like a prison. But I was always afraid of any of them getting killed" (Fairweather et al., 1984, p. 25).

These were precisely the fears expressed by Divis mothers. Many of them also spoke of the frustration of being stuck in their flats all day with children. Bad nerves, as the joke ran, were "hereditary"—you got them from your children, from worrying about them when they were out playing and from having them underfoot when they were inside.

Women, Nerves, and Drugs

Because women in Divis Flats were more likely than men to suffer from bad nerves, the focus of the rest of this article is on their experience and gender differences. Many people in Divis used alcohol or prescription drugs to help them cope with depression, stress, and nervous debility. In general, I found that men usually preferred to drink, while women tended to cope by taking "tablets." This is not to say that women did not drink or that men did not take tablets, but there was a general division by gender, and it has been estimated that drug consumption rates for women in Northern Ireland are one-and-a-half to two times those for men (Fairweather et al., 1984).

In his research Fraser (1973) noted a substantial increase in tranquilizer prescription rates in riot-torn districts, and many of the symptoms of nervous debility experienced by people in Divis Flats were treated effectively with tranquilizers and other drugs. Many residents of both sexes and all ages, but primarily adult women, took drugs for their nerves, to combat depression, and to help them sleep. The most commonly used tranquilizer was Valium, which is widely prescribed for the symptomatic relief of, among other things, anxiety and insomnia. There is a danger of developing dependence on this drug, and that danger increases greatly if the user has a personal or family history of alcoholism. Alcoholism was a problem in Divis, and a good many women in the community had developed a dependency on Valium.[4] However, it was also true that some people, because they had seen relatives, friends, and neighbors become dependent on alcohol or drugs, had become sensitized to the danger of abuse and had reduced their consumption of these substances.

Fairweather et al. (1984, p. 35) say that women in the Catholic ghettos take tranquilizers "to forget, to escape, to dull the edge of panic, fear, and frustration, and theirs is a private hell." A young woman who worked in a doctor's surgery told them that:

---

[4]One of the few areas in which Northern Ireland does not lag behind the rest of the United Kingdom is in the production and consumption of drugs. Pharmaceutical production is the largest growth sector of American investment in Ireland. After only wages and salaries, expenditure on drugs is the largest expenditure in the National Health Service in Northern Ireland. More tranquilizers are consumed in Northern Ireland than anywhere else in the United Kingdom.

> I was a receptionist. We filled out prescriptions and the doctor signed them. There were so many women on Valium, tranquilizers and sleeping pills that you could have started the day just writing out 100 prescriptions for them. There was no desk for the receptionist and the waiting room was six foot square. Often there were 30 women there at once, all shouting for their prescriptions . . . some women were so desperate they'd go to a wake and take the Valium off the dead woman who didn't need them any more. They are addicted. It's funny really, they go on about young people and drugs, and yet they're hooked themselves. It's got a lot to do with the Troubles—a woman with 13 kids, the bother with sons at an age to join the IRA, the police and the army patrolling and searching. . . It's no wonder the women are living on their nerves. . . . The doctors I worked for were well worried, but what could they do? Women really need the tablets (1984, pp. 35–36).

Some women in Divis had been taking "tablets" consistently since the outbreak of the troubles in August 1969. Some took Valium and/or other drugs all the time, and many more took them only when violence flared up (e.g., when there was rioting). Many of the women I interviewed were not sure what drugs they were taking; they often knew them only by their brand names (e.g., Roches). Several women showed me shoeboxes full of prescription pill bottles. As one women said of Divis Flats, "You have to be a registered alcoholic or a drug addict to stand living here."

Fairweather et al. (1984, p. 15) noted that the number of women in mental asylums in Northern Ireland is 2.82 per thousand, compared with 1.90 per thousand in England, and comment that "it is hardly surprising" that many women living in the Catholic ghettos reach for "mother's little helper" (Valium and other tranquilizers) given the political situation, the poverty that undermines their lives, and the fact that they are often ultimately left alone to bear the responsibility for their children. The situation for many women was described by one women in this way: "You're constantly in deep depression. I've been on nerve tablets for three years. You take the kids out crying around you, but you've no money for fun or comfort. You feel like taking yourself out to the mountain and never coming back. . . . For women it's a hell of a life, left to cope on your own, living below the poverty line" (cited in Fairweather et al., 1984, p. 15).

In Divis Flats there were many single parent households. Women were alone for many reasons, domestic, economic, and political. Many were alone because they had left their husbands or their husbands had left them. Others were alone because their men had been killed or because they were on the run, in jail, or abroad looking for work. Even in households in which the men were present it was sometimes the case that the women were still left almost alone because the men spent little time in the flat and took little of the responsibility for helping raise the children. It appeared that women in Divis who had total or near total responsibility for children and were also socially isolated were also among the most vulnerable to nervous debility.

Of course, other women were vulnerable to nervous debility as well, for example, women who had family members who were directly involved in politics or were in jail. A Catholic mother with a son in Long Kesh prison described how she felt when she went to visit him: "I hate going up to the Kesh. I have to take nerve tablets. I never took them before in my life. I have to take two Roche 5; I take them so I won't break down in front of him because I would die of shame if I broke down and cried. It's not only for myself, it's for him. If I broke down maybe he would too. For days after I never leave my chair. I couldn't go to my bed at night and sleep. I could just sit here half the night crying to myself—he's like a dead son" (cited in Fairweather et al., 1984, p. 94). This woman's sister had also been shot dead in her presence by Loyalist assassins. She said, "My nerves are shattered, completely shattered. I'm having the burden of this house, the burden of my mother's house, and the worry of Peter [her son in Long Kesh]. How would you feel?" (1984, p. 95).

Other things could cause bad nerves as well. For example, a young ghetto woman described her experience of nerves to Fairweather et al. (1984):

> Before I ever had the intercourse, me da found out about the pill. He gave me a hiding and then he took me to the doctor to find out why I was on it. And the doctor says, "I cannae tell you." And me da says, "You'll tell me or I'll fucking wreck this office." I thought, Jesus, you're a fucking pig. I was tingling with nerves, shaking. And so the doctor told him, "Your daughter's on the pill for haemorrhages. And they're through *nerves.*" He was more or less throwing this at me da, to let him know what he was doing to me. Be me da didn't even blink, he just says, "I want to know if she's still a virgin. You get her up on that fucking table and find out." Well, I nearly fainted, from the shock and the fear. But the doctor was great, he just says "Mr. MacNamara, you've got nine daughters, and only one married, so that leaves eight. And I'm telling you, around the age of 14 every one of them's virginity breaks away *naturally.* And I'm not inspecting her, so you can go home and take your dirty mind with you." But me da still had to be thrown out. Then he gave me a hiding, because I was laughing. That was me nerves, too (pp. 143–144, italics in original).

Nervous complaints among the residents of Divis Flats derived from multiple causes: the political situation, poverty, poor housing conditions, social deprivation, domestic problems, or a combination of any of these. It is difficult if not impossible to isolate the relative impact of these factors individually, but it seems that generalized ghetto conditions in combination with political violence provided a powerful environment for the development of nervous complaints.

Physicians and Nerves

People in Divis with nervous complaints took them to their local general practitioner. Women in the Western world often complain that male doctors do not take some of their medical complaints seriously, especially more generalized complaints like "bad nerves." But women in Divis did not say that they had difficulty getting doctors to accept the validity of their nervous complaints. Evidently, doctors in Belfast accepted that the symptoms experienced and described by women were consistent with the environment in which they lived. General practitioners in Northern Ireland were well trained (though perhaps less well trained in handling psychological complaints than they are in handling purely physical ones), but in the Catholic ghettos local medical clinics were few and poorly staffed. Overworked doctors generally had little time to deal with women's complaints about psychological problems like nervous debility. They could do little to alleviate the causes of these problems, but they could help to relieve the symptoms by prescribing Valium and other drugs. In more serious cases, they sometimes also recommended psychological counseling.

At the beginning of the political troubles medical practitioners thought that the violence would only be temporary, and given that "bad nerves" are a normal stress reaction which generally resolves itself once the stress is alleviated, it was only natural that they would treat nervous complaints by prescribing Valium and other drugs. However, by the end of the 1970s, physicians recognized that a drug dependency problem had developed in the ghettos. I do not know for sure how they had responded to this. Several people said that they thought that physicians were trying their best to reduce reliance on drugs, and had become more careful in prescribing them. Whatever they had done, I could not see any evidence that fewer women were using drugs or were dependent on them than before, and none of the women I spoke with commented on there being any difficulty in getting or renewing prescriptions.

Two points should be made. First, in the absence of other resources to help people with nervous complaints, the residents of Divis Flats probably needed these drugs. Second, it is important to bear in mind that most of the people who took tablets for their nerves did not take them all of the time; they took them only when they needed them, such as when violence flared up, and did not have a dependency problem.

Children, Rioting, and Nerves

A focus on gender differences in the experience of nerves should not be allowed to obscure the experience of nerves among children. As noted, Divis Flats was one of the hardest hit riot areas in Northern Ireland, and people identified rioting as a major cause of "bad nerves." When rioting occurred, only a minority of people, usually children and teenagers, were actively involved. The majority of people generally stayed in their flats and avoided the scene of the disturbances. But they were aware that it was going on, and it often agitated and/or frightened them. If the rioting was serious and protracted, many began to complain about their nerves. Parents worried about their children, and some would go out and bring them in if they could locate them. However, rioting was, at least to some degree, socially condoned in Divis, openly by the youths and rioters themselves and at least tacitly by many adults.

Rioting occurred in Divis for two reasons: because it relieved the boredom in an area characterized by extreme economic and social deprivation, where recreational facilities and opportunities for children and teenagers were almost nonexistent, and because there were political reasons for it. Children and teenagers in Divis rioted because the danger involved made it tremendously exciting, because it was a chance to "get their own back" against the soldiers and policemen who harassed and abused them, and because they believed it was a meaningful and valuable form of political action. Generally, rioting was a spontaneous action in response to political events like the killing of innocent people by the Security Forces. It was a "natural" consequence of the political environment in the Catholic ghettos. In fact, to some degree rioting served as a "safety valve" for frustrated teenagers on the dole with no job opportunities, rising inflation, discrimination, and Security Forces repression.

Belfast is famous for its violent children, for its "hundreds of 'street guerrillas' in the 8–14 age group" (Darby & Morris, 1974, p. 83), and the children of Divis Flats had a reputation for being among the most violent in the city. The involvement of Divis children in political violence, particularly rioting, has been explained in many ways. Some say they are politically conscious, motivated, and already committed to Irish Nationalism; others say they are being manipulated by the IRA and INLA; and still others say that they are simply juvenile delinquents who do it for kicks. But rioting cannot be divorced from the political, social, and economic realities faced by young people living in the Catholic ghettos in Northern Ireland and blamed in a simplistic manner on immaturity, ignorance, psychopathology, parental neglect, or manipulation by evil men.

Near the end of July 1982, a 10-year-old boy told me how he was looking forward to rioting on August 9. He said, "I was born and bred in rioting," and that was no doubt true given that rioting had been a "normal" feature of life in Divis Flats since August 1969. Most of the children and teenagers in Divis had never known a time when rioting, shooting, bombing, assassination, kneecapping, arrests, and dawn raids were not a part of their environment. There had been heavily armed troops and policemen in their community all their lives, and they had never known a time when these were not viewed as "the enemy" and legitimate targets for attack. Not all the youngsters in Divis engaged in rioting and stoning the Security Forces. Many were frightened by such activities, and many had been taught by their parents to get off the streets and come home when trouble started. But a great many of the children in Divis were involved on a day-to-day basis in what is sometimes referred to as "street politics."

With regard to the role of parents in the involvement of their children in rioting and stoning the Security Forces, accusations of parental neglect abound. Although these activities were, at least tacitly, socially approved in Divis in response to particular political events, it was quite rare for parents to actively encourage their children to do these things. Parents in Divis expressed a great deal of concern about the dangers their children faced in such situations. They tried to get them to come home when trouble started, and they generally did their best to keep them off the streets when rioting was going on. But the streets were the only playgrounds these children had, and they had to let them out to play and go to school. They could not keep them locked up inside their flats for days and even weeks at a time. Fraser (1973, p. 118) recognized this when he noted that "most mothers in the ghetto areas, contrary to the impressions given in the Press, do make strenuous efforts to prevent their children from becoming involved in street rioting . . . [but] it is physically impossible to keep indoors a large family who are determined to go out." He concluded, "Short of locking children up, it is probably impossible to keep them away from the scene of a riot, once it has started" (1973, p. 47).

Psychiatrists in Belfast have done a good deal of research on the psychological effects of political violence on children. In general, they have found that, like adults, the majority of Northern Irish children have adapted well to the political violence. But, again like adults, the most vulnerable children are more likely to suffer serious and lasting mental and emotional problems requiring medical treatment. The most vulnerable children were those who were shy or timid, those with certain personality weaknesses, and particularly those who had one or both parents who were themselves psychologically disturbed by the violence (Fraser, 1973; Heskin, 1980).

Like ghetto children the world over, children in Divis Flats had a not undeserved reputation for being tough and resilient. Most of them had adapted remarkably well to the political violence that was a "normal" feature of their environment. But a substantial number of households I interviewed included children who suffered from apparent temporary or chronic psychological disturbances arising from traumatic experiences with political violence. Many Divis children suffered from stress reactions such as nervous debility, fear, anxiety, nightmares, difficulty eating and sleeping, bedwetting, hysteria, paranoia, withdrawal, trembling, crying fits, and fear of separation from parents. These were similar to the normal anxiety reactions experienced by adults, and they tended to disappear of their own accord shortly after the violence died down again (Fraser, 1973, pp. 60–61).

But a minority of the children who had been exposed to rioting, bombing, shooting, and other forms of political violence had developed severe psychological problems that persisted for long periods of time and required medical attention. A number of children had developed exaggerated fears of soldiers and policemen, and would run into their family's flat whenever they saw them nearby. They were often trembling and crying, and sometimes screaming; they hid behind their mothers or fathers, and would not leave the flat again for a considerable time. Other children exhibited just the opposite behavior. They reacted to soldiers and policemen in an exaggeratedly aggressive manner and "went wild" trying to attack them. Some very young children suffered from retarded emotional, intellectual, speech, and/or motor development, which their parents invariably attributed to living in the troubles. I also found that it was true that if the parents suffered from nervous debility or other more serious psychological problems, their children were more likely to have such problems as well. (This adds a tragic twist to the joke about bad nerves being "hereditary," that is, that parents get them from worrying about their children; vice versa, children are more likely to develop bad nerves if their parents have bad nerves.)

A number of children in Divis were also taking prescription drugs to help them cope with bad nerves and other problems. In most cases these were caused by living with political violence, but not always. For example, Fairweather et al. (1984, p. 36) report that, "It is not only adults who take 'mother's little helpers.' A nine-year-old who lives in the Divis

Flats in Belfast was prescribed Roche 5 after she woke up one morning with two rats gnawing her finger."

Fear of separation from parents was a very common problem experienced by children in Divis Flats, and a primary factor in precipitating nervous complaints among them. They feared that their parents and other family members might be killed or arrested, and if members of their family had been "lifted" before, these fears were often very pronounced. But this was not restricted to households in which family members had been killed, arrested, or imprisoned, or households in which family members were politically active. This was because Divis children believed that anyone could be arrested at any time and believed that many innocent people had been killed, arrested, interrogated, and imprisoned. I believe that the political situation in Divis Flats was more terrifying for young children than for anyone else, because to them these things did seem to be random, indiscriminate, and arbitrary.

DISCUSSION

The Causes of Nerves

In Divis Flats, nerves was not the vague, amorphous, hypochondriachal complaint or character flaw referred to in the turn-of-the-century literature. It was publicly recognized as a "natural" consequence for normal people living under abnormally stressful conditions. Nerves in Divis derived from multiple causes—the war, massive poverty, poor housing conditions, and social problems—and it is probably the combination of these factors that lay behind the very high incidence of nervous complaints among the residents. It is difficult if not impossible to isolate the relative impact of these factors individually, but it seems clear that generalized ghetto conditions in combination with political violence created a powerful environment for the development of nervous complaints. However, *terror*—the general fear that one might, at almost any moment, become a victim of violence—was perhaps the single most important cause or catalyst of nervous debility in Divis Flats.

In general, my research tends strongly to support Davis and Guarnaccia's (1987) conclusion that relationships of inequality and domination are "encoded in the complaint of nerves," and that nerves is related to situations of marginal status, which include powerlessness, economic disadvantage, social and political oppression, and strained economic and social resources. This explains, at least in general terms, why women in Divis Flats suffered more from nerves than did men; women were the most powerless, most dominated, and most disadvantaged residents of the ghettos. Along with the economic, social, and political disadvantages suffered by all of the residents of the Northern Irish ghettos, women had the additional disadvantages of living in a male-dominated society.

There was a complex relationship in Divis between social and political conditions on the one hand and their psychological effects—depression and bad nerves—on the other. Although one can, and Divis people did, make a generalization that depression resulted primarily from bad social conditions and bad nerves resulted primarily from bad political conditions, depression also resulted from political conditions and nervous complaints also resulted from social conditions. The combination of bad social and bad political conditions exacerbated the primary psychological effects of each, and these psychological effects exacerbated each other because people with nervous complaints were more vulnerable to depression and depressed people were more vulnerable to developing nervous complaints. Thus, social conditions aggravated nervous complaints caused primarily by political conditions, political conditions aggravated depression caused primarily by social conditions, and bad nerves and depression aggravated each other. Because there was a complex interaction between all of these things they cannot be considered in isolation from each other. This suggests that a holistic approach that looks at the total context of people's lives is perhaps best suited to studying the causes of nerves.

Gender and Nerves

Many researchers have argued that women are more likely than men to suffer from nerves because of special biological, social, and psychological stresses in their lives. Women in Divis Flats were more likely to suffer from nerves than men, and this was primarily because they more often had sole or primary responsibility for children and were more likely to suffer from social isolation. Both responsibility for children and social isolation appeared to be significant causal factors in the development of nervous complaints.[5]

The only other major difference between women and men with regard to "nerves" was a generalized difference in the primary methods of coping with this problem. While both men and women drank and took prescription drugs, men generally turned to drink and women were far

---

[5]These are, of course, generalizations. Men also bore responsibility for children and suffered from social isolation, and they were more likely than women to be the targets of Security Forces harassment and Loyalist assassins, which were significant causes of "bad nerves."

more likely to turn to drugs. An important point to note here is that drinking is perhaps in some ways more "therapeutic" in this respect than taking drugs. This is because drinking is generally a social activity whereas taking tablets is a solitary one. Getting out for a few drinks with friends helped counteract the adverse effects of social isolation. The effects of alcohol include a lessening of inhibitions and greater ease in talking about personal experiences, problems and feelings (e.g., nervous complaints), and this undoubtedly had some therapeutic effect. Tablets were taken alone in the privacy of the flat. No one got together with friends to pop a few Valium, so this did not counteract the effects of social isolation.

The symptoms of nerves in Divis corresponded closely with those described from other sociocultural settings, and there did not seem to be any significant difference between the symptoms described by men and women. Even though statistically more women than men suffered from bad nerves, nervous debility was not defined as a female complaint or experience. For example, I saw no evidence that men who experienced bad nerves were stigmatized or considered weak. Suffering from bad nerves was in no way socially stigmatized. Nervous debility was not viewed as a sign of emotional, psychological, or other form of "weakness." It was viewed sympathetically and considered understandable, normal, and natural given the political and social environment.

CONCLUSION: WOMEN IN DIVIS FLATS

Many of the women in Divis had taken to drink and tablets and some had become suicidal. This was because they were living out their lives under the combination of ghetto conditions and an urban guerrilla war, because the old type of community had broken down, and because they were often isolated, lonely, bored, depressed, and frustrated. Nonetheless, their lives went on as "normal," and as Fairweather et al. (1984) note,

> "Normal" life is full of problems and heartaches, joys and thrills, that have nothing to do with the war that flares on Belfast and Derry streets. People's capacity to live "ordinary" lives is amazing. Belfast people sit on one of history's oldest time-bombs, and do the things everyone in the Western world does. They eat ice cream, go to the pictures, drive cars, join trade unions, make love, fall out, make friends, go for walks, marry . . . but part of "normal" urban life is that very loneliness . . . which is the dreary, daily, slow poison of so many women's lives—women left wedded to their houses, women left while men are on the run, left by men who betray them, men in jail. Some fight the world, some

drink, some die a little every day of monotony, some enjoy their independence, some find new men, and some turn to Jesus, finding in "Him," in religion, the perfect panacea (pp. 326–327).

Not only did their lives go on as "normal," the war had even had some positive impact on their lives. As one women told Fairweather et al. (1984, p. 51), "Probably the only good thing to come out of this heart-breaking war is the great change in the role of women. With things so bad we had to be active, and with that we've found a whole new identity for ourselves. No longer was the woman just a piece of property: your man's missus, your children's mother. As we've come more and more to the forefront we've discovered our own strength, and power." But the war has also taken a heavy toll on them and they have paid a high price for the progress they have achieved. Even when the violence was only in the background and things were relatively "normal," they were often living close to the edge and any push—a riot, an explosion, a raid—threatened to tip them over into "nervous debility." They were, and still are today, literally "living on their nerves."

REFERENCES

Curtis, L. (1982). *They shoot children: The use of rubber and plastic bullets in the north of Ireland.* London: Information on Ireland.

Darby, J., & Morris, G. (1974). *Intimidation in housing.* Belfast: Northern Ireland Community Relations Commission.

Davis, D., & Guarnaccia, P. (1987). Health, culture and the nature of nerves. *Medical Anthropology, 11,* 1–7.

Evason, E. (1978). *Family poverty in Northern Ireland.* London: Child Poverty Action Group.

Evason, E. (1980). *Ends that won't meet.* London: Child Poverty Action Group.

Fairweather, E., McDonough, R., & McFadyean, M. (1984). *Only the rivers run free: Northern Ireland—the women's war.* London: Pluto Press.

Fraser, M. (1973). *Children in conflict.* New York: Basic Books.

Heskin, K. (1980). *Northern Ireland: A psychological analysis.* Dublin: Gill & Macmillan.

Liston, R. A. (1977). *Terrorism.* New York: Thomas Nelson.

Low, S. (1985). Culturally interpreted symptoms or culture-bound syndromes: A cross-cultural review of nerves. *Social Science and Medicine, 21,* 187–196.

Northern Ireland Housing Executive. (1980). *Divis Complex—present and future.* Belfast: Northern Ireland Housing Executive.

Sluka, J. A. (1989). *Hearts and minds, water and fish: Popular support for the IRA and INLA in a Northern Irish ghetto.* Greenwich: JAI Press.

Section III

THE UNITED STATES

EXPERIENCE OF NERVOUSNESS AND ANXIETY DISORDERS IN PUERTO RICAN WOMEN: PSYCHIATRIC AND ETHNOPSYCHOLOGICAL PERSPECTIVES

Joan D. Koss-Chioino, PhD
Department of Psychiatry, University of New Mexico
School of Medicine, Albuquerque, New Mexico

Analyses of case materials describe variations in the experiences of Puerto Rican women diagnosed as having an anxiety disorder, in treatment with mental health clinicians, physicians, or traditional healers. Their common complaints are examined as core symbolic elements in culturally patterned complexes of meanings focused around personal trauma, stressful life events, personal and social reactions, expectations about treatment, and the course of illness. Many of these women report themselves to be "nervous," to be "sick from nerves," or to have had an "*ataque de nervios.*" "Nervousness" is the base symbolic domain in Puerto Rico of what psychiatry labels "anxiety disorder," although it is also a common complaint of many disorders. What "nervousness" means to patients/clients and their clinicians or healers is examined within the frames of multilayered popular and biomedical interpretations. The special difficulties of women in Puerto Rico are highlighted, and psychiatric and ethnopsychological (Spiritist) models of etiology and treatment are compared.

"Nerves are almost always physical."
An *espiritista,* 1987

In a recent review of studies in culture and anxiety, Good and Kleinman (1985) observed that there are relatively few able to inform us about the full range of variations in the phenomenology of anxiety or the type of emotional distress classified as "anxiety disorders" by psychiatry. Among the questions these authors raise for future research the most interesting for clinicians are, "What is the relationship of different anxiety disorders to different styles of illness behavior and idioms of distress?" "Are there cross-cultural differences in the cognitive, affective, and communicative processes that contribute to the development and expression of anxiety disorders?" (Good & Kleinman, 1985, p. 323). My goal in writing this article is to contribute to the literature on cultural variations in the expression, course, and treatment of anxiety disorders, with a special focus on women. I record and analyze their and their clinicians' descriptions of experiences of suffering, identified by mental health professionals as due to "anxiety disorders" and by Spiritist healers as variations on spirit-caused distress that include the popular illness complaint (sometimes referred to as a syndrome) of *nervios* or "nervousness" (see Garrison, 1977; Koss, 1975, 1977). By comparing cases seen by mental health professionals and Spiritist healers (a widespread traditional healing system in Puerto Rico), I have the advantage of teasing out both popular and professional variations on the cultural construction of a Western medical nosologic category of emotional disorder. I also describe some of the ways in which Puerto Rican culture structures situations and stresses for women that render them vulnerable to both severe "nervousness" and "anxiety."

Material for this study was collected as part of the Therapist-Spiritist Project in Puerto Rico (see Koss, 1980, for a description of the project). Its goals were to foster a mutual understanding of biomedicine (particularly mental health/psychiatry) and of traditional healing among health professionals and Spiritist medium/healers. We carried out programs in three communities aimed at formalizing and structuring the interface between biomedical and popular healing systems in Puerto Rico and collected thousands of observations on how physicians, mental health workers, and Spiritist mediums worked with men and women who sought help with a variety of physical, emotional, and social problems. The case histories reported in this article were drawn from three opportunity samples: (a) recordings (video and audio) of all cases (990 women) seen over two 1-month periods by physicians, mental health professionals, and Spiritists who were core participants in the project's seminars; (b) cases jointly reviewed by various groups of healers and health professionals at project sessions (also tape recorded); and (c) cases collected by interviewing three new patients or clients of all core participants.

METHODOLOGY

My general approach to this paper is that of semantic network analysis following Good and Delvecchio-Good (1982), who define it as "based on an understanding of meaning as configurations of semantic fields which link key public symbols both to primary social values and to personal affects'' (p. 148). In a study reported elsewhere (Koss-Chioino, 1988), complaint profiles for six psychiatric higher rank categories, a ''deferred diagnosis'' category, and a nonpsychiatric (medical) category, were generated in a multivariate discriminant analysis of 770 cases of women seen by mental health professionals and physicians. The profiles are composed of frequent core complaints that are at the center of symbolic complexes made up of a number of personal/social meanings, stressful life events, interpersonal problems, somatic distress, failure in role expectations, and moral dilemmas (Good & Kleinman, 1985). Each complex significantly differs according to variations in a complaint profile typical of one type of experience of distress that corresponds to a psychiatric or medical category.

I describe the key symbolic domains reflected in cases of anxiety disorders of women who share common life events and stressful situations, such as the loss through death or abandonment of a loved person who gave them much-needed security, or marital dissolution.

Cases of Spiritist healers were also classified as anxiety disorders by discriminant analysis when the pattern of complaints would have led a mental health professional to diagnose that individual as suffering from that type of emotional distress. Both similar and distinctive complaints of Spiritist clients (as compared with therapist clients' profiles) are accounted for in the descriptions of symbolic complexes. The base symbolic complex in anxiety disorders is ''*nervios*/nervousness.'' This complex is also found in affective disorders (major depression and dysthymia) as well as other psychiatric diagnostic categories, though not to the same extent.

NERVES AND ANXIETY IN WOMEN

To say that there are many reasons why women in Puerto Rico are anxious is only to repeat the dreary litany of their marital and family problems, as well as point to deep feelings of abandonment and the fear that they cannot ''make it'' alone. As described elsewhere, both men and women find Puerto Rico a difficult society to negotiate. Women find their lives especially full of problems because they so often lack a sense of personal power. Surprisingly, many middle class women abrogate the potential power they acquire, via a good salary or prestige gained in professional life, to significant male others. Their spouses or partners much more often feel empowered to make decisions that can disregard these womens' achievements. The women described in this article who are patients or clients come largely from poorer social groups who lack education and opportunities to acquire personal power in whatever form. Their feelings of hopelessness over a personal future are often a realistic appraisal of the difficulties of trying to support themselves and their children without a partner's help. This unhappy realism exacerbates attitudes of dependence associated with being a woman and seems to arouse even a fear of independence.

Given the indeterminancy of Puerto Rico's political status and the continuing onslaught of cultural, social, and economic changes that typify its social life, it is no wonder that most Puerto Ricans have doubts and considerable difficulty applying themselves to future dreams or plans. Distress over social problems (such as teenage rebellion and substance abuse) aligns itself with the strains that poor, uneducated women already feel as a result of their predisposition to personal indeterminacy. The effect (and affect) of this dual source of stress is vividly illustrated by one of the Spiritist healers, Evangelina, who without prompting described herself as a "very nervous person," "very tense physically," and sometimes so "dizzy" that she "cannot walk." Possessed of a very sensitive, intelligent nature, but only a fifth grade education, she worked for years at routine and often menial jobs in a tobacco factory. Evangelina reports that she suffered a series of *ataques* during this period. But one day something snapped and she felt she could "never again roll another cigar," whatever happened. She suffered a prolonged illness that she describes as initiated by a crisis, an "*ataque de nervios*" (in her words), in which she felt her body weaken, and a "*momento fugaz*" (mental block). Evangelina succumbed to the crisis for almost 2 years, and was left without income or family members who cared about her. A childhood friend took care of her; she also began to develop as a medium.

Viewed from a psychiatric perspective, Evangelina suffers from "agoraphobia" (American Psychiatric Association [APA], 1987), initiated by "panic attacks." She describes her condition as chronic "nervousness" that keeps her from leaving the house except on special occasions.

Further details of Evangelina's story are given below. It is of considerable interest because she so well illustrates how one individual can simultaneously incorporate both patient and healer characteristics. "*Nervios*" (or *nerviosidad,* "nervousness"), the idiom of distress that she uses, is a very popular expression that identifies severe anxiety, but is also at the center of a network of associated complaints that incorporates references to somatic distress as well as interpersonal problems. The two terms, "nervousness" and "anxiety," as descriptions of experience of emotional distress, are not commensurate. "Anxiety" as "intensive apprehension, fearfulness, or terror associated with feelings of impending doom" (APA, 1987), implies a distressful inner state or emotion, that if severe can manifest in disordered behavior causing distress to both sufferer and others. In contrast, "*nervios*" or "nervousness" simultaneously implicates body structure, a chaotic emotional state, many somatic complaints, and especially a sense of loss of control over one's perception, behavior, and surroundings. As illustrated below, these idioms also connote feelings of bad treatment or rejection at the hands of family members, together with a sense of combined physical and social instability (see also Guarnaccia, de la Cancela, & Carillo, 1989; Guarnaccia & Farias, 1988). The remainder of this chapter explores the meanings nervousness has for women who complain of it and also the frequent core complaints that make up a network of meanings associated with the overlapping psychiatric concept of "anxiety" as disorder. As elsewhere (Koss-Chioino, 1988), I include descriptions of the ways each type of healer explains and diagnoses, locates the cause, and strategizes to treat illness centered either on severe anxiety or permutations of the condition of "nervousness."

THE NATURE OF NERVOUSNESS, INTRANQUILITY, AND *ATAQUES DE NERVIOS*

Perhaps through the popularization of early medical notions, some stemming from 16th and 17th century folk Spanish medicine, "nervousness" has become a general label for disordered emotions and behavior in Puerto Rico, as elsewhere. Without necessarily being associated with serious or chronic conditions of illness, "nerves" basically refers to temperament and to emotions that disturb and prevent "tranquility." However, compared with other societies such as Costa Rica (Low, 1981, 1985), the pattern of meanings connoted by the term "nerves" and the particular conditions it refers to (or accounts for) have some unique features.

Taken together, "intranquility," "nerves," and "nervousness" vie with sleep disturbances as the most frequent type of complaint presented to all of the healers and health professionals in the study described in this article; they are frequent complaints in all of the eight diagnostic categories. It must be noted that a few complaints of "*ansiedad*," "*agitamiento*" ("agitation"), and "*desasociego*" ("restlessness") are included within the "nerves" complaint category since they are closely related. However, a distinction is popularly made by Puerto Ricans between "intranquility," which most often occurs in relation to a distressing situation and commonly connotes a *state* of apprehension and fear, and "nervousness," which is seen as a *trait* with expected reactions of persons suffering from disturbed "nerves." (Spielberger, 1985, analyzes these differences.) Because of this difference "intranquility" as a complaint was assessed separately in the complaint profiles associated with each diagnostic category as well as considered separately in the descriptions of experiences of anxiety, nervousness, and other associated, distressful feelings.

Some researchers have described *nervios* as a popular term for an illness state (Garrison, 1977), such as when Puerto Ricans say they "suffer from nerves" (*padecer de los nervios*) or are "sick from nerves" (*enferma de los nervios*). Referred to in these ways the condition is not commonly considered a mental disorder. Moreover, "nerves" and "nervousness" are frequent complaints accompanying any type of physical distress brought to medical doctors. These same expressions are also popularly used to describe a person who would be diagnosed as chronically mentally ill by a mental health professional, in order to avoid the stigma of *locura* (craziness). The resultant confusion of distinguishing "craziness" from normality is compounded because persons who "suffer from nerves" are much more likely to have a sudden *ataque de nervios*. It is said that the inner heat commonly felt by the sufferer builds, and can be set off by an event or series of happenings perceived as stressful. The individual then succumbs to an episode of loss of consciousness initiated by sudden screams, followed by falling flat on the ground, twitching, flailing, and moaning. Such extreme behavior is accepted, and even expected for women at a viewing or funeral of a close relative, as a manifestation of extreme grief. I have seen *ataques* at viewings when the woman is supported by her relatives, given something pungent to smell, and sometimes held or held down to keep her from hurting herself. On one such occasion a distant male cousin of the deceased flung himself prone on the floor suffering an *ataque*. Whispered comments indicated that many felt that this was not appropriate, since his grief should not have overwhelmed him.

BACKGROUND STUDIES

Most who have researched and written about how mental disorder is culturally patterned in Puerto Rico have focused on the popularly named "*ataque de nervios*," labeled by some as the "Puerto Rican Syndrome" (Fernandez-Marina, 1961; Garrison, 1977; Mehlman, 1961; Rubio, Urdanetta, & Doyle, 1955). One might ask, why have so many differing psychodynamic interpretations and psychiatric labels been applied to this phenomenon? Psychiatrists early noted that *ataques* among male army recruits were associated with many different types of mental disorder, ranging from schizophrenia to an acute state of conversion. They felt that calling it a "syndrome" masked an understanding of the "real disease process" (Mehlman, 1961). However, other observers of *ataques* in psychiatric and other settings have viewed it as a "hysterical," dissociative phenomenon (Fernandez-Marina, 1961; Garrison,

1977). There is some agreement among the authors that *ataques* represent the "discharge of repressed or suppressed anger" (Garrison, 1977, p. 439) and that Puerto Ricans lack sufficient opportunities for discharging anxiety or aggressive impulses (Rothenberg, 1964). Most writers also agree that *ataques* are closely related to familial conflict and occur at times of extreme personal stress, such as accidents that befall oneself or a loved one. In my opinion, however, lumping together cases of men and women in studies of *ataques* obscures answers to the question of what *ataques* mean to those who experience them. The ways men and women relate to and express anger, for example, are very different.

The case material presented below is of three types: (a) cases of anxiety disorder presented to mental health professionals, (b) cases in which the complaints of "nervousness" and "intranquility" are presented to Spiritist healers (whether or not they meet criteria for "anxiety disorders"), and (c) organic problems presented to doctors in which women complain of "nervousness." Through an analysis of narratives about illness and emotional disorder I attempt to fathom the meanings of "nervousness" as (a) an expected aspect of the experience of distress in many women, (b) a popular label for illness, (c) a metaphoric way of connoting layers of experience of strain associated with interpersonal difficulties, and (d) a condition that can erupt into acute episodes of dissociative experience (the *ataques de nervios* and other *ataques*) in a few chronically nervous women. I also explore how "nervousness" as a complaint, as well as an experience, is related to the psychiatric diagnosis of anxiety disorder.

GENDER, NERVOUSNESS, AND ANXIETY DISORDERS

Is *nervios* more frequent in women than in men? Do women suffer more emotional distress than do men? Or, do women perceive their lives to be more stressful and more commonly express this in terms of "nerves"? The category of complaints called "nerves" in this study included the complaints "nervousness," "intranquility," "anxiety," "restlessness," "agitation," and "whiplashes (*latigos*) in the nerves." "Nerves" was presented to therapists (physicians and other mental health workers) by 31% of the women (245 women in the large sample analyzed quantitatively) and to Spiritist healers by 28% of the women (63 cases). Similarly, the complaint of "nerves" was presented by men to therapists by 33% of the large sample (218 cases) and to Spiritists by 30% (35 cases). It must be concluded that men who present their distress to therapists, physicians, or Spiritists manifest "nerves" as often as do women. However, it should also be noted that men present themselves less frequently to these health care givers. Since my data are not derived from strictly randomized samples, frequencies cannot be compared with a high degree of confidence. With this cautionary note in mind, it can be noted that in the largest of the three samples in this study, composed of 1,769 cases, women are overrepresented as patients by approximately 28% and as Spiritist clients by about 50% assuming that both men and women have equal opportunities to seek help from these providers. However, almost one-third of the men who do present to health care professionals or to Spiritist healers report they suffer some form of "nervousness."

When the prevalence of anxiety disorders is examined, as reported by Canino, Helzer, Rubio-Stipes, Bird, and Bruno (1987), women have significantly higher lifetime and 6-month rates for phobic disorders, particularly in the subcategories of simple phobia ("persistent fear of a circumscribed stimulus [object or situation] other than fear of having a panic attack or of humiliation . . . in certain social situations," APA, 1987, p. 243) and agoraphobia ("fear of being in places or situations from which escape might be difficult," APA, 1987, p. 241). However, men and women have about the same rates for panic and obsessive-compulsive disorders. As described below, via case material on women with anxiety disorders, their negative sense of self, augmented by restrictive social mores and situations devolving on women, partially explains the gender effect on being phobic.

It is of considerable interest that symptoms of panic disorder as defined by the Diagnostic and Statistical Manual of Mental Disorders (Third Edition Revised) (DSM-III-R; APA, 1987) (shortness of breath, dizziness, heart palpitations, trembling, sweating, choking, nausea or abdominal distress, depersonalization, numbness or tingling sensations, flushes or chills, chest pain, and fears of dying or going crazy) overlap with complaints most frequently associated with "nervousness." Guarnaccia, Canino, and Rubio-Stipes (1989) suggest parallels between the *ataque de nervios* and panic disorder. Although both of these ways of categorizing and labeling distress, the psychiatric and the popular, can be said to define the experiences of both men and women, I do not agree with these authors. In light of my data, their proposed culturally patterned symptoms of "panic" are representative of "nervousness" in general. But as these authors correctly point out, those who suffer from chronic "nervousness" are much more vulnerable to an *ataque*.

Examining data on persons labeled by mental health professionals, including physicians, as suffering from anxiety disorders, who also present the complaint of "nerves," there is almost no difference in frequency in men and women, even though there is a significant difference in the number of cases diagnosed (79 men and 108 women); 63% of the women diagnosed in the "anxiety disorder" category say they are "nervous" or suffer from "nerves." In contrast, 58% of the men diagnosed as having an anxiety disorder present with "nervousness." Thus examining both the careful epidemiological data presented by Canino and my own clinical data, it can be seen that although women suffer more from some states labeled "anxiety disorder" (specifically, phobias) anxious men are almost equally as "nervous," according to self-reported complaints in clinical settings. Moreover, more than twice as many men diagnosed as having a physical rather than a mental illness presented as "nervous," and more men (62%) compared with women (53%) diagnosed as "depressed" (dysthymic) say they are "nervous," even though women suffer dysthymia more than twice as often as men in Puerto Rico. In cases of schizophrenia the frequency is reversed: 55% of the women compared with 38% of the men said they were "nervous." The commonality of this type of expression of distress, and its pattern in relation to psychiatric and physical illness among men and women, supports my interpretation of "nervousness" as equivalent to a general notion of "stress" experienced as *in* the body. I discuss cultural permutations on this popular concept and attend to its meaning as "stress" in the concluding section.

Toward understanding comparisons between men and women who present as "nervous" or "intranquil," Canino et al. (1987) point to high rates of comorbidity between anxiety disorders and other psychiatric illnesses in Puerto Rico. Thus many "nervous" men may simultaneously suffer from several psychiatric disorders.

CORE COMPLAINTS OF PERSONS WITH ANXIETY DISORDERS

In the 770 cases of women seen by medical doctors and mental health therapists, "anxiety disorder" was the most frequent psychiatric diagnosis. There were 108 persons so diagnosed, 102 by therapists and 6 by medical doctors. As will be noted by those familiar with the American Psychiatric Association's diagnostic manuals, "panic disorder" did not appear in the 1968 version (DSM-II, APA, 1968) but was commonly diagnosed in Puerto Rico as "anxiety reaction with hysterical features" or was included under "generalized anxiety reaction." Obsessive-compulsive disorder was often diagnosed as a "personality disorder," and "phobia" does not appear in the diagnostic classifications. Descriptions of symptoms collected from patients or presented to the case discussion sessions of the Therapist–Spiritist Project certainly point to phobic behavior. Given this morass of change in diagnostic fashions I have chosen to lump all therapists' diagnoses into one higher rank category, "anxiety disorders," that subsumes variations in separately defined subcategories such as specific phobias. Variations will be mentioned in relation to individual cases when they seem significant.

Among the 220 reclassified Spiritist womens' cases there were 51 that had the complaint profile of "anxiety disorders," an even higher percentage than cases seen by mental health workers. Though they show considerable overlap, the two complaint profiles differ in interesting ways (Table 1).

"Sleep disturbances" (insomnia, sleep walking, nightmares, strange and "lying" dreams, sleep disturbances in general) in 46% of the cases is the most frequent single complaint of therapist patients. It is much less frequent in Spiritist clients (14%). In contrast, "mind" problems (mind is "blank," "dark," "molested," "in turmoil," "gone," "tired," "disturbed," "overloaded," "running on," "bewildered," or "stalled") in 43% of anxious women heads the complaint list of Spiritist clients. Individual complaints of "nervousness" and "intranquility" and "head problems/headaches" are presented as frequently by both therapist patients and Spiritist clients. However, therapist patients also frequently present with "crying jags," "hostility/anger/aggressiveness," "hallucinations," and "trembling." Instead of these frequent complaints, Spiritist clients commonly present "fatigue," "chest/heart problems," and "family problems." This last complaint is in accord with the very different approach of the mediums toward physical and mental illness; they usually focus equally on a client's social (external) and personal (internal) difficulties. In addition, clients at *centros* are more focused on their bodies (including "minds") as sites as which they experience disorder and malaise, in comparison with mental health clients.

"Mind" is popularly thought to have a definite physical dimension rather than being perceived primarily as a vehicle for psychic activity. Explanations for these differences in discourse about illness and distress are revealed in the narratives of illness experience below. They are arranged so as to illustrate the network of meanings in a culturally patterned category of illness typified by the expression of core complaints presented by persons diagnosed or diagnosable as having anxiety disorders. I shall illustrate how each complaint is a hub of a symbolic domain, each an overlapping subdomain of the personal experience of what psychiatry labels "anxiety" and "anxiety disorders" of various kinds. The parallel category for Spiritist healers seems to be a general condition of "nervousness," experienced within the body and caused by molesting spirits.

Table 1. Complaint Profiles of Patients Diagnosed as Having an Anxiety Disorder

Therapist patients (n = 108)	%	Spiritist patients (n = 51)	%
Sleep disturbances	46.0	"Mind disturbed, blank"	43.0
Intranquility	41.6	Headaches	39.0
Headaches/head problems	37.0	Intranquility	35.0
Nervousness	28.7	Nervousness	29.0
Crying jags	26.0	Fatigue	27.0
Hostility	24.0	Chest/heart problems	25.0
Hallucinations	15.7	Family problems	20.0
Trembling*	14.8	Sleep disturbances	14.0
Bad humor	9.0		

*Appears in only one or two diagnostic categories; low frequency in total sample.

DOMAIN OF INTRANQUILITY AND NERVOUSNESS

Although these complaints are also part of discourse and experience around depression, the particular ways "intranquility' and "*nervios*" appear in the presentations of those diagnosed as having an anxiety disorder are somewhat different. For example, Clara, diagnosed as having an "anxiety reaction with depressive features," (DSM-II, APA, 1968) reported that her "nerves went out of control" when her husband left her to go to the United States. The mental health worker did not identify Clara's episode as "an *ataque*" but it appears to have been what now might be classified in psychiatry as a "minor panic attack." It responded to a tranquilizer and once-a-month psychotherapy sessions. Clara's distress was the result of a long-term problem around relationships with men and phobic-like fears associated with abandonment.

Case 1: Clara

"My head hurts; I feel like I have a hole or emptiness; I am unable to sleep; my eyes are very irritated and tears pour out." This was Clara's description of how she felt the day the doctor referred her to the mental health center. Her sleep was disturbed by "strange" dreams in which she "lifted by her hair and sent to another world."

Thirty-five years of age with three daughters, Clara sheepishly says she is "separated." Her second husband left her only a few weeks ago.

Her only income is from food stamps since neither of her husbands send money "to feed their daughters." She maintains good relations with her siblings who try to help her, but one brother is also being treated at the mental health center. When asked about her family Clara says she was "an orphan at four years of age. My father left our home and my mother raised us alone." Her second husband's departure appeared to be more than Clara could bear; it was this third major abandonment in her life that seemed to her and her therapist to precipitate her "nerves [going] out of control." The image of a "hole" or "vacuum" seems fairly common as a complaint symbolizing rejection, and points to disturbance around feelings of abandonment by a man whom she needed to sustain and protect her. These feelings have long reigned in her consciousness. The dissociative quality of Clara's dreams fits within the reported experience of an "*ataque de nervios*" as well as being a symptom of a panic attack.

A description of another distressed woman's experience (recorded at a *centro* session where she sought help) illustrates Spiritist perspectives on what mental health professionals would label "phobic anxiety." Delia's two main complaints ("seen" by the healers, but confirmed by her) were "intranquility" and "nervousness," accompanied by "*susto*" (fear) and "pain in one leg."

Case 2: Delia

Four *videncias* were offered to Delia, a woman of 30 years, by three different mediums: First, "A spirit says that you are looking for a solution to material problems. You are involved in an accident and your leg is in a cast." Second, "You are nervous and frightened. There is a chain that you are trying to disentangle. There is something that comes from another existence that has you entangled in the chain." Third, "There is a spirit in your spiritual tableau that wants you to have an accident." Fourth, "You are very naive. I am frank. It is a *guia* (guide) that possesses me. But you come with a spirit who has been watching you for a very long time. The spirit makes you restless. He interferes with everything. You have to pray, meditate. Keep coming [here] and maybe you can be helped. You have to have more faith."

The suggestion to Delia is that she is fearful about accidents because she is "entangled" in an emotional morass brought on by a spirit. Moreover, her condition is "chronic" since the spirit has been around for a long time. This spirit evidence also contains the solution (treatment); that is, she should pray, and meditate on spiritual matters instead of being preoccupied by "material" fears. The spirits imply that the intranquility, anxiety, and fear can be countered or at least controlled by a spiritual attitude and practices that will put her in touch with spirits. The healers clearly distinguish Delia's feeling state as the problem and tend to take a preventive approach in the light of what they perceive to be her vulnerability.

An example of extreme but sudden nervousness, popularly labeled an "*ataque de nervios*" and diagnosed by a psychologist as "anxiety reaction with features of depression," is seen in Irene's story. From the perspective of current diagnostic fashion in psychiatry this would be labeled a "panic attack" but would not meet criteria for a panic disorder since it was not followed by at least two more attacks over a 3-week period. (See also the discussion by Guarnaccia, Canino, and Rubio-Stipes, 1989.)

Case 3: Irene

Irene, 43 years old and not yet married, returned to Puerto Rico for a vacation and dreamed the following:

> I was walking in a strange place in order to get home. I saw an iguana who became stuck to my left thigh. The iguana said, "You are not going to find anyone to get you out of this." I said, "Yes, I will find someone." I continued walking with the iguana stuck to me. I went into several houses and people laughed at me.

Two days later Irene began to feel "a current in my neck, and my arm (left) felt like it was going to fall off." She also felt depressed and very anxious at times. She consulted several physicians and underwent tests for hearing, heart, and thyroid problems. Two weeks later she suffered her first "anxiety attack" when she reached into the oven to take out a cake. She had "palpitations," felt "intense fear that she would die," and began to "tremble" and "sweat." When she got to the doctor's office he told her it was "emotional," an "anxiety attack," and prescribed a tranquilizer. Since that time she has suffered various attacks of anxiety as reported by the psychologist whom she saw at a mental health center in Puerto Rico. In Irene's words she sought this help because she was unable to "coordinate her thoughts and had almost no ability to concentrate."

Irene presented the events of her illness as if the dream precipitated them; it certainly had shaken and frightened her. Probing for an event that might explain this first sudden attack, her therapist could find nothing remarkable. Up until the time of the attack Irene had led a single life as a secretary and interpreter, and had taken on the responsibility of her mother and blind brother after her father left home. (He converted to the Pentecostal religion and the family refused to follow him.) A sister and brother were married and lived away from home but Irene had also helped to educate them. Despite her obvious devotion she expressed feelings of "uselessness" with regard to helping her blind brother and mother. She had had a boyfriend some years ago who left the island and returned married; he later (during her Puerto Rico vacation when she had the dream) dined with her and said that he was sorry he had not married her. She claimed not to care for him anymore and currently had another boyfriend whom she was planning to marry. But the therapist speculated that although Irene said she was content with her lot in life and reasonably happy, she was actually deeply hostile and resentful toward her brother and mother for limiting her opportunities to have her own life. She felt stuck in her obligation toward them.

Do the *ataques* offer a way that Irene can be angry without having to *act* angrily? Abad and Boyce (1979), following Garrison (1977) as mentioned above, suggested that an *ataque* is a "culturally learned and sanctioned symptom precipitated by unsuccessfully repressed anger or sexual tension" (p. 31). This could mean that "nervousness" and "intranquility" symbolize "trapped anger." One-fourth of the cases seen by mental health professionals complain of "hostility" (i.e., feeling "hostile," "angry," "hatred," or "desire to fight"). But perhaps this complaint is a trade-off for the one-fourth who have "crying jags," since many women cry when they are unable to express anger. In Irene's case, both her therapist and the study interviewer sensed that she exhibited a kind of bravado in the face of the heavy responsibilities she had carried for many years. It may be almost impossible to direct anger at persons who have always given your life meaning, since to do so would be tantamount to negating your own self-worth. Moreover, Irene was considering whether she was able to continue working, and so had found an indirect way to lighten the burden of her responsibilities toward her brother and mother, or, at the least, she could talk about doing so.

Rather than simply meaning "repressed anger," "nervousness" can be interpreted as describing the effort to suppress self-assertiveness in situations in which both inner personal values and outer social ones collude in thwarting its expression. I have elsewhere (Koss-Chioino, 1988) mentioned the prominent pattern of parents choosing a child to stay at home and care for them in their old age. Irene told her therapist that her third priority, following decisions about whether to continue working and how to deal with her worry over her brother, was to attend to "her own feelings."

Irene's psychotherapist brought her case to a case review session. On reviewing her treatment decisions the therapist commented that Irene was very desirous of "knowing herself," to "find something for herself." The therapist therefore used Gestalt therapy (Perls, Hefferline, &

Goodman, 1951), having Irene work with her own subpersonalities (including the submerged angry part) and also take the roles of other persons to explore how she had projected certain doubts and fears onto them. The therapist found it quite successful and commented that the use of this therapeutic modality was possible because Irene was "more sophisticated" than most other patients. The Spiritists' response to the discussion of Irene's case was to approve of Gestalt as an appropriate therapeutic modality for Irene, pointing out that it seemed similar to working spirits.

However, the mediums in their turn focused mainly on her iguana dream. They argued about whether the iguana was actually a spirit or only a distorted picture of one. But they all seemed to agree that the dream had a transformational meaning; it signified that Irene's balance in life had been disrupted and inner disorder had ensued, later to manifest as an *ataque*. Their interpretation of the iguana is quite similar to the kind of interpretation that an analytical psychologist might make, that is, that the iguana represents the "transcendant function" as described by Jung (1969; see also Koss, 1986). This means that a bridge between Irene's conscious feelings and material thrusting up from the unconscious had appeared (the iguana moves between land and water); she now was aware of the distress (e.g., anger, resentment, and loss) that surged within her. The *ataque* was viewed by the healers as an eruption of feelings her psyche and body were no longer able to contain once harmony had been lost.

HEADACHES, HEAD PROBLEMS, AND "MIND" DISTURBANCES

"Headache" (including the many kinds of head pain listed above) is the second most frequent complaint of those women diagnosed as suffering an anxiety disorder. Persons with severe headaches, sometimes accompanied by heart palpitations, commonly present first to medical doctors. Like Fela, whose case is described below, the "headaches" and other somatic symptoms are often associated with family and work problems and the sufferer feels trapped by a situation in which she perceives that losing her job threatens her very survival.

Case 4: Fela

Fela, 22 years old, married with two children, presented with "headaches, insomnia, poor appetite, palpitations, anxiety, and anguish" that she had suffered for seven months. The doctor ordered a series of laboratory tests, all of which came back negative. While waiting for the results she prescribed a tranquilizer and felt that she already knew Fela's condition was "emotional." Her first encounter with Fela was described as difficult because "she seemed very anxious, continually changing her position in the chair and wringing her hands." All vital signs seemed normal including low blood pressure (110/70) and a pulse rate of 68. She questioned Fela closely and got the following story:

> My husband is younger than I am and does not work. I work in a factory and pay my family's bills and care for my little sons (ages 1 and 3 years). I leave them with a neighbor each morning but sometimes I have to work overtime in order to earn enough money for our expenses; and I worry about them. Moreover, my husband brings me a series of problems. He drinks too much and stays out late at night. My mother died last year of breast cancer and my father always demands my attention. Although I try to please him it often seems impossible.

In discussing Fela's problems both the doctor and the Spiritist healers at the case review session recognized how her work could be a potent stressor within the knot of problems she was experiencing. Yet one medium pointed out that her somatic complaints were an attempt to compel her husband to feel guilty and take on some of the burden. She said, "Fela tries to use her illness to punish him." "This is very characteristic of the Puerto Rican woman, to act like a martyr." Yet the mediums and her doctor agreed that Fela's strong sense of responsibility toward her family actually kept her "from going crazy."

As described elsewhere (Koss-Chioino, 1988), "headaches" mean that the distress is so severe help must be sought; head pain commonly signals the need for health care and entrance into the sick role. It also indicates that the sufferer is overwhelmed with distressing circumstances perceived as beyond her power to change. These circumstances are usually interpersonal in nature; "head pain" often connotes disorientation with regard to significant others. Fela's distress seems to have been exacerbated by a feeling of lack of emotional support, especially from a mother who can be unfailing source of empathy and emotional security. Her probable current diagnosis would be "generalized anxiety disorder" on the basis of criteria such as "anxious mood continuous for over a month, worry, fear and anticipation of misfortune, as well as the physical sensations of palpitations and head pain (tension)" (DSM-III-R, APA, 1987). Her insomnia and crying jags point to a depressive component in her distress, related to grief over the loss of her mother.

Younger women (under 40) suffering from arthritis, hypertension, kidney infections, diabetes, and other illnesses also present to doctors with "headaches," as well as "stomach pains" (the latter often described as "nerves in the stomach"). Although their anxiety is not as debilitating as in those who meet criteria for an anxiety disorder, tranquilizers are frequently prescribed by physicians who identify their condition as due to "nerves." One woman complained that when Puerto Rican women go to clinics in the United States, they are treated like "crazy people" and their physical complaints dismissed as only due to "nerves." This may reflect non-Puerto Rican physicians' inability to interpret certain symptoms and attend to psychosocial problems underlying somatic expressions of distress.

"Nervousness" is also used by both patients and medical doctors in Puerto Rico to describe the condition and behavior of persons who suffer organic brain syndromes such as epilepsy, and it can be a descriptor for feelings and behavior that accompany physical (especially chronic) illness. It must be mentioned here that studies indicate that depression and anxiety are linked to many medical diseases such as mitral valve prolapse, angina, chronic obstructive lung disease, hyperthyroidism, anemia, embolism, cancer, and hypoglycemia (Shucket, 1983).

FATIGUE, WEAKNESS, AND CHEST PAINS

Approximately 25% of the women who come to Spiritist sessions, whose complaint profiles parallel those of mental health clients diagnosed with anxiety disorders, present with "fatigue" (including various forms of bodily weakness) and "chest/heart pains." These complaints may accompany panic disorder as part of a syndrome of extreme motor tension and autonomic hyperactivity; Canino et al. (1987) list chest pain as the second of five most common panic symptoms. Also included are palpitations, fear of dying or going crazy, choking, and sweating. Utilizing responses to the Diagnostic Interview Schedule study cited earlier (Canino et al., 1987) Guarnaccia, Canino, and Rubio-Stipes (1989) include "periods of weakness" and "chest pain" in an hypothesized scale of symptoms that characterize "*ataques*" and panic disorder. In the case of Linda described below, complaints of weakness in various parts of her body and a sensation of tightness in her chest are part of what Spiritist mediums "saw" of her experience of distress. Linda's "nervousness" seems to refer here to a kind of restless agitation, still another way in which *nervios* is expressed.

Case 5: Linda

A woman of 47 years, whose much older husband had just passed away, Linda's complaints (which the medium felt in her own body) were weakness in her arms, chest, and heart; hot and cold flushes; tightness in her chest and pain and palpitations in the nape of her neck; numbness in her body; and deep suffering and nervousness. Her problems were discussed as due to the fact that Linda's husband had died suddenly of a "heart attack" (*ataque cerebral* or thrombosis) and "did not say goodbye." The medium implied that the surprise of his death had unhinged Linda.

There were two *videncias* ("evidence") and a possession focused on Linda. One *videncia* described a "spirit mounted on a horse dressed in a white robe and hat, galloping, galloping. He comes and opens his hands as if he is going to give you something which is that you will become involved in the spiritual field so that this spirit can withdraw." A second *videncia* revealed that Linda had "married because she couldn't hold back even a little longer and wait for an opportunity to study. She could not stand the trials of living at home." The spirit possessing a medium said, "I am at the side of my companion. I appear to be material but I am not. They tell me that I am a spirit. But I want to tell you that I am at your side; I want to talk to you in an intimate way although it is through the medium of an outside brain. . . . I have to separate from you. My spirit is going to cleanse itself more each day in order to one day come and help you, but until then nothing will be able to help you because you have me stuck onto you."

The images and the spirits all describe the shock and helplessness that Linda feels because of the suddenness of her husband's death. They also point out that Linda is a person who feels unsupported and was overly dependent on her husband, to whom she is still strongly attached. The main direction of the spirits' interventions is the instruction that Linda should become a medium herself; her husband's spirit will "develop" and become her principal *guia*.

If we were to label Linda's state of extreme distress as an anxiety disorder it appears that Linda has had two or three panic attacks but is also anxious much of the time. The attacks appear to have been caused by her husband's death, but her "nervousness" is recognized as antedating that event. This is implied in the spirit evidence that she married an older man because she felt so insecure.

It appears also that Linda was experiencing an inner conflict of grief and anger over loss of the man she relied on to support her in her generally "nervous" state. The spirit of her husband speaks through the medium and clearly points out how "attached" he is to her. He implies that her complaints are those he himself suffered when he died. The commonality of experiencing the symptoms of a loved one who has died from a myocardial infarction has been discussed by Nemiah (1985), who describes how bereaved persons manifest chest pain, palpitations, tightness of the chest, difficulty with respiration, and subsequent numbness (due to hyperventilation). The mediums see that Linda must come to terms with her husband's spirit in order to be freed of the negative effects of his continued presence. They recommend that she tame his spirit through prayer as a route to involvement in spirit work. "Nervousness" as "symptomatic contagion" is still another dimension of a culturally patterned syndrome composed of both somatic distress and anxiety; in this case loss through death is a potent stressor that may even precipitate panic attacks. Cases such as Linda's may not become chronic and appear to be effectively helped by Spiritist treatment at least in the short term.

TREATMENT OF ANXIETY DISORDERS AND NERVES

The hierarchy of resort in seeking help in cases of "*ataque de nervios*" is illustrated in the case of Juanita.

Case 6: Juanita

Forty years old and the mother of three teenage children, Juanita suffered pains in her head, chest, waist, and the heels of her feet for 3 years. She was also "sick from nerves" and had insomnia. She then had an "*ataque de nervios* and of diabetes" and went to the local hospital emergency room. Her symptoms were not relieved and she was forced to stop working. She then sought help from a private physician, Dr. Reyes, in the metropolitan area and at the same time was being seen at the mental health center in her community. Even with these treatments, which consisted of control of her diabetic condition, tranquilizers (*pastillas de los nervios*), and supportive therapy, she could not find relief. It seemed that the doctors could only refer to problems with her husband (he had "abandoned" his family) and her children as causing her illness. Even more distressing to her, her children told her that she was "crazy."

In this sorry state Juanita responded to a friend's recommendation to see a Spiritist in their community, Doña Georgie. Juanita accompanied this woman to session, though with great trepidation since this was her first experience. She was the first to be called to the table and three *causa* spirits were lifted off of her. She returned the following week and the "work" continued; baths were prescribed. She told assembled mediums and other participants that she felt better, having slept well for the first time in years. She also received *despohos* (cleansing of negative spirit influences).

Doña Georgie said that another woman had come between Juanita and her husband and this woman had sent "bad thoughts" that penetrated Juanita's weakened defenses. These were countered by the *despohos* and prayers. Soon afterwards, Juanita's husband miraculously returned home and her daughter, who had bitterly fought with her father, made peace with him. Juanita then finally then got relief from her "nerves" and "physical pains."

It should be noted that the criterion of "help," for Juanita, was that she *felt* relieved, an experientially based assessment. Control over her diabetes was not even mentioned as an issue.

Successful Spiritist treatment of mild phobic behavior can be appreciated in the following brief case description.

Case 7: Laura

Twenty-eight years old, married 7 years, and the mother of four daughters, Laura and her physician husband had recently purchased a house in which a doctor had died. During these 2 months Laura frequently saw this man's ghost. She spent her days in a tense and frightened state, becoming especially upset as night drew near. To make matters worse Laura's husband began coming home late, saying that he had to take a female colleague home.

The medium whom Laura consulted talked to her about her dissatisfactions in life. It seems that Laura's husband wanted a son and Laura already felt tied down with too many children. She really wanted to pursue her studies, which were put aside when she married and became pregnant, yet she felt trapped by inner conflict over her own lack of self-determination. Should she follow her husband's needs or her own? The medium prescribed prayers and readings and told Laura that she was "developing faculties" to see into the spirit world. She also said that "someone was jealous" of Laura's marriage and so had caused the doctor's spirit to appear. But this *prueba* (test) was part of her "development." The medium then held several sessions at Laura's house as a kind of exorcism in which molesting spirits were instructed to leave Laura alone. Being told that someone envied her situation and that she had "special powers" appeared to satisfy Laura's need for greater self-expression, and her anxiety abated (at least for the moment).

It must be added that moderately severe cases of panic disorder, phobias, or generalized anxiety disorder, such as those of Irene and Fela, also are successfully treated by sensitive psychologists and even by psychologically minded doctors. Persons with severe anxiety disorders will eventually be seen by mental health professionals because they are unable to function normally. Treatments of anxiety disorders in the 108 cases of women, in order of frequency, were as follows: individual psychotherapy (61%), supportive therapy (22%), medication (unspecified type, 15%), group therapy (14%), and Mellaril (thioridazine, 13%). Explanations of the cause and course of these disorders are clearly different across the three healing systems, as illustrated in the case descriptions above.

PANIC DISORDER, AGORAPHOBIA, AND "DEVELOPMENT" IN SPIRITISM

I initially presented Evangelina, who has been a "nervous person" most of her life (her words). Here I shall present details on her early years and her much later initiation as a medium healer, which effected a kind of "cure" for her distress (as she perceived it). In this case, the folk concept of "nervousness" (or its equivalents) does describe her experience of an anxiety disorder, one initiated by a severe panic attack. The term "*ataque de nervios*" was used by Evangelina to describe a severe episode. Although this suggests a one-to-one equivalence of these terms (and categories), this is the exception rather than the rule. I repeat my postulate that "nervousness" is not directly equivalent to "anxiety" (defined as worry, tension) but does code an experience of severe strain and vulnerability experienced as within one's body.

Case 8: Evangelina

Evangelina was the 9th of 10 siblings born into a poor rural family. Their poverty seemed to have been so acute that she remembers seldom having a penny to buy a school lunch. She also recalls two terrible feelings about her family: They "rejected" her, and they taught her fear and disgust toward sex. She has stayed single but has a "profound resentment toward them because of it." Moreover, she attributes her timidity and fear of strangers in part to the isolated life her family led. She was forced to work at an early age after having only completed fifth grade, yet that was two grades more than her siblings completed.

As is the case of many Spiritists, Evangelina was socialized into a religious ambience. She took catechism classes and was a candidate for the "Daughters of Mary" society. When she was 10 years old for no apparent reason she began to have fainting spells. At 15 she gave catechism classes to neighboring children yet she would faint each time she went to church. Once when she felt very dizzy she had a vision of the priest as the devil, complete "with horns and tail." In addition, she suffered from bronchial asthma during the years when she was 9 to 14. The last time she had a fainting spell (when 18 years old) she was praying for someone who had died. She "felt an odd sensation in her feet" and lost her sight. "Something" had "bound up her chest"; she then fainted. This is a description of a "panic attack" according to DSM-III-R (APA, 1987) criteria of at least 4 symptoms of 12: dyspnea;

palpitations; chest pain or discomfort; choking or smothering sensations; dizziness, vertigo, or unsteady feelings; feelings of unreality; tingling in hands or feet; hot and cold flashes; sweating; faintness; trembling or shaking; and fear of dying, going crazy, or doing something uncontrolled during an attack.

At that time Evangelina said she had no knowledge about spirits attaching themselves to people; later she interpreted the attack as caused by the dead person's spirit having become attached to her. On another occasion (after she learned about Spiritism) she went again to pray for a deceased individual. This time she heard the dead person say, "Look down." When she did she saw a head on a plate. Later the spirit said, "This person will be next," and in 3 days the man died. As mentioned above, when Evangelina started work at a factory she suffered frequent "attacks." One day she felt suicidal, but prayed to God. She wanted to know if the devil was molesting her or if she was undergoing a test (*prueba,* a Spiritist belief) from God. That very night she became possessed and heard a *guia* speak. She described the spirit as an old woman, dressed in a skirt and jacket from "ancient times." Her name was Amalia and she earned her living as a laundress.

After this experience Evangelina began to attend Spiritist sessions in many places. She subsequently suffered other episodes of illness, one of which she called an "obsession" (an overwhelming by a spirit, and "craziness," such as delusions and trembling). (This seems to have been another panic attack.) It was then that her family "attacked her verbally" and "threw her out." She moved in with the woman friend who continues to care for her, and after intensive work at a Spiritist session the obsession left. One day Evangelina received a message from a *guia* named Miguel Angel who told her that she should form her own Spiritist study group. From that time forward (she was about 30 years old) she no longer suffered attacks but seems to worry that they could return.

Although this appeared to have been the end of the attacks, Evangelina gradually developed other problems: She became extremely anxious about leaving home and has difficulty accompanying her friend in her car. Dreams image the "inquisition pursuing her" while she is walking down a strange street. In another dream her friend tells her to wait in the car and leaves. Shortly afterwards men with guns enter the car and one points a pistol at her head. They rape her and her friend abandons her. In a third dream her friend leaves her in the car on the bank of a dry river. The friend disappears and more and more people keep appearing. Evangelina "feels lost, confused, and afraid."

All of the above experiences seem typical of agoraphobia as described in psychiatric manuals. Moreover, the friend with whom Evangelina lives appears to accept this state of affairs and even reinforces her fears by vocally worrying about her on the rare occasions when Evangelina leaves the house with someone else. Their relationship is "rationalized" by Spiritist belief; they say that the friend persecuted and abandoned Evangelina in a former existence and now her "test" is that she must protect and care for Evangelina in this one. Evangelina has never been seen by a mental health professional but had been treated by Spiritist mediums for the more severe panic attacks in early adulthood. She seems now to have adapted to her fears, coping with them through her friend who is patient to an extreme and accompanies her everywhere. They live a very homecentered life since they both stopped working more than 10 years ago and receive social security payments and fees for child care. About 10 years ago Evangelina established her own *centro* and does leave home regularly to preside over these sessions as well as very occasionally to attend others. Her agoraphobia appears to be rooted in early family experience fueled by pathologic fears around sex and death. She may have developed (or imitated) a "worrying" cognitive style during childhood as a result of the privations she and her parents experienced, her asthmatic condition, and her parents' very strict moral injunctions against sexual thoughts and behavior.

Researchers hypothesize that an "anxiety relevant cognitive style," composed of habitual catastrophizing, a focus on cues of danger while always screening out cues of safety, and obsessive holding onto intrusive, upsetting thoughts is etiologic to agoraphobia and other phobias (Beck, 1976). Superimposed on these cognitive distortions Evangelina may then have developed exaggerated appraisals of the degree of danger associated with her panic attacks (Ganellen, Matuzas, Uhlenhuth, Glasi, & Easton, 1986) leading to the expression of her present phobias.

The role of Spiritist treatment, first in relieving the panic attacks and later in alleviating her extreme fears through her "developing" as a medium is interesting to examine. As mentioned elsewhere (Koss-Chioino, 1988), Spiritism is almost unique among treatments for emotional distress in focusing directly upon death. It deals with the dead by providing ways in which the expected harmful effects of their spirits becoming attached to living beings can either be eliminated, controlled, or redirected into positive channels, such as when molesting spirits become *guias*. These practices apparently helped Evangelina recover from her out-of-control episodes (*ataques*) as her fears of death slowly subsided. However, other fears remain, as expressed in her current phobic behavior. One dimension of her worries might be described as extreme apprehension about moral transgressions around sexuality (and the death penalty for them). These seem to have lessened through her activities as a healer, since she does "good work," that is, according to the will of God. She seems also to have found a situation in which she can avoid sexual activity and still have a caring and protecting partner. Although the relationship is clearly personally satisfying, the women fall under the stigma of being suspected to be lesbians.

CONCLUSIONS

I have described herein women's experience of what have been diagnosed as "anxiety disorders" and similar disorders among clients of Spiritist mediums. "*Nervios*" and "nervousness" were also explored as a culturally patterned symptom presented by many women sufferers of anxiety disorders and also by others who present with both physical and emotional disorders. These popular terms are also sometimes used to refer to illness in persons who have not yet presented for treatment to mental health clinics or Spiritist *centros* or who do not accept the diagnoses of therapists, medical doctors, or healers. I have attempted to show that although there is much overlap in meaning, "nervousness" is not conceptually equivalent to "anxiety" as defined in psychiatry and psychology. It denotes instead a special type of stress concept, described below.

Puerto Rican mental health professionals are trained to use the psychiatric diagnostic manuals developed in the United States in much the same ways as their North American counterparts. However, their patients' most frequent complaints are somewhat different from symptoms listed as diagnostic criteria of various anxiety disorders. For example, therapists' patients present frequently with hostility, crying jags, and hallucinations, in addition to nervousness and intranquility. Since the complaint of "crying jags" is also frequent among depressed women, it may be that in therapists' diagnostic practices there is an overlap between affective disorder and anxiety disorder labeling. Elsewhere (Koss-Chioino, 1988) I characterized depressive states as falling much more on the agitated than the depressed side of the depression syndrome; it is frequently difficult to distinguish between them. Moreover, as in the experience of depression, some women suffering anxiety disorders also complain of hallucinations and delusions. Whether these complaints are associated with the depressed dimension of their disorder or with the common "intrusive thoughts" of most persons with phobias is difficult to tease out from these case studies. Since "visions" and sensations of spirits are fairly common expressions of distress among Puerto Ricans, it might be expected that they would accompany severe emotional disorder. (Abad and Boyce [1979] differentiated between "psychotic" and nonpsychotic hallucinations as I have done elsewhere [Koss, 1975; Koss-Chioino, 1988].)

Yet another complaint, "hostility," appears more frequently in persons diagnosed as suffering an anxiety disorder (about one-fourth) than in those diagnosed as dysthymic (about one-sixth). Here again angry and aggressive feelings are commonly released at highly stressful times among Puerto Ricans. This complaint seems to reflect the way women tightly suppress their negative feelings until a time when their emotions are so chaotic that they lose control over them. Even when they report angry or aggressive behavior a certain thinly veiled satisfaction appears that connotes a sense of "getting away with it." Yet anger and aggression in women most often stay at the verbal level and are rarely acted on except during psychotic episodes. However, in a few cases labeled *ataque de nervios* (or *obsesión* by the Spiritists) women did become physically violent against themselves or others. Whether these were panic attacks or "acute psychotic episodes" is difficult to determine.

Complaints of hostility, crying jags, and hallucinations are not common in psychiatric literature on anxiety disorders. They support the notion that culture makes a contribution both to the nature of anxiety disorders among women in Puerto Rico and to the construction of their illness behavior. Good and Kleinman (1985) comment that "anxiety disorders are not merely results of culturally influenced interpretations of an underlying disease; anxiety disorders are also disorders of the interpretive process" (p. 321). One's task doubles when analyzing cultural components of anxiety disorders, as these authors so clearly point out, because both disordered cognition and affect are integrally related to their genesis and course. Culture inevitably structures pathologies of interpreting and feeling, as well as supplying idioms of distress, illness concepts, categories, and models for responding to the inner experience of emotional chaos and disordered perception.

An analysis of spirit intervention in the 51 cases that parallel anxiety disorders seen by Spiritist healers revealed particular themes: Spirits warned sufferers about the following prospective difficulties: illness or operations, craziness, harm (undefined), family conflict, and marital breakup. Frequent images brought to the session by spirits (in possessed mediums) were smoke, black or rotten water, blackbirds, wheelchairs, crutches, and spider webs. Thus the harm Spiritist clients were being warned about seemed to echo their worse fears about suffering bodily harm, being abandoned, or becoming crazy. The images reflect these same concerns but add feelings of entrapment (the spider web), and also of puzzlement and confusion (smoke, black water, blackbirds). Moreover, spirit evidence reported by mediums to clients (*videncias*) focused around three themes: the sufferer felt trapped, she was being muffled by a spirit (it blinded or confused her), or she was in development (in which all of these feelings are common).

These metaphors express a quality of experience of inner disorder typical of what psychiatry labels as "anxiety disorders." But they also describe the ways fears are constructed as well as their content. Though there are other variations, the central fears highlight feelings around the body and the social self.

The way fear is expressed in both therapist and Spiritist cases (but especially the latter) is better explained by a concept of "worry" rather than of "anxiety" (Borkovec, 1985). "Worry" is defined as a "chain of negatively affect-laden, relatively uncontrollable thoughts and images," brought on by objects or events associated with fear Borkovec, 1985, p. 466). The chronic worrier tries to mentally solve the problem; the outcome is not only uncertain but contains primarily negative (harmful) possibilities. Moreover, highly distressed worriers seem unable to cope with the feared issue in an effective, action-oriented way. Spiritism seems to be an effective therapy for "worriers," because it both validates fears around negative outcomes *and* converts them into means to achieve a positive result. Thus Linda is told that the spirit of her dead husband, instead of continuing to inflict both physical and emotional pain, can become a supportive protector-guide. Similarly, the "bad thoughts" sent by the woman who wanted Juanita's husband, and caused her pain and "nerve sickness," could be taken off by a medium whose power countered that of the spirit sent to harm Juanita. (And once she was less "crazy" Juanita's husband seemed to feel more comfortable at home.)

Finally, I again take up the question of what *nervios* or "nervousness" means for Puerto Ricans. In the context of the eight cases described herein, "nervousness" is primarily reflective of bodily malaise. "Body," as I am using the term here, includes the head/brain/mind. This kind of inner distress almost completely disorganizes both thought and behavior, resulting in feelings of confusion, lack of control, and ultimately the fear and actualization of bodily harm. The idiom "nervousness" can be thought of as equivalent to the concept of "stress," except that it represents an internal experience, similar to what is popularly meant by the English expression, "I feel stressed." "Nervousness" for Puerto Rican women appears to be a cousin to the popular Mexican idiom of distress, "*asustado*" ("frightened"). Rubel, O'Nell, and Collado-Ardon (1984) showed *asustados* to have more disease signs and symptoms than matched controls, and higher rates of morbidity; their illnesses were also more life threatening. Like "fright" in Mexico, "nervousness" in Puerto Rico connotes vulnerability to illness of all kinds, whether physical, emotional, psychiatric, or spiritual.

REFERENCES

Abad, V., & Boyce, E. (1979). Issues in psychiatric evaluations of Puerto Ricans: A sociocultural perspective. *Journal of Operational Psychiatry, 10*(1), 28–39.

American Psychiatric Association. (1968). *Diagnostic and statistical manual of mental disorders (second edition).* Washington, DC: Author.

American Psychiatric Association. (1987). *Diagnostic and statistical manual of mental disorders (third edition revised).* Washington, DC: Author.

Beck, A. T. (1976). *Cognitive therapy and emotional disorders.* New York: International Universities Press.

Borkovec, T. D. (1985). The role of cognitive and somatic cues in anxiety and anxiety disorders: Worry and relation-induced anxiety. In A. H. Tuma & J. Maser (Eds.), *Anxiety and the anxiety disorders* (pp. 463–478). Hillsdale, NJ: Erlbaum.

Canino, G., Helzer, J., Rubio-Stipes, M., Bird, H., & Bruno, M. (1987, May). *The prevalence of anxiety disorders in Puerto Rico.* Paper presented at the meetings of the American Psychiatric Association, Chicago.

Fernandez-Marina, R. (1961). The Puerto Rican syndrome: Its dynamics and cultural determinants. *Psychiatry, 24,* 79–82.

Ganellen, R. J., Matuzas, W., Uhlenhuth, E. H., Glasi, R., & Easton, C. R. (1986). Panic disorder, agoraphobia and anxiety-relevant cognitive style. *Journal of Affective Disorders, 11,* 219–225.

Garrison, V. (1977). The "Puerto Rican syndrome." In V. Crapanzano & V. Garrison (Eds.), *Case studies in spirit possession* (pp. 383–449). New York: Wiley.

Good, B., & Delvecchio-Good, M. J. (1982). Toward a meaning-centered analysis of popular illness categories: "Fright illness" and "heart distress" in Iran. In A. J. Marsella & G. White (Eds.), *Cultural conceptions in mental health and therapy* (pp. 141–166). Dordrecht, Holland: D. Reidel.

Good, B., & Kleinman, A. (1985). Culture and anxiety: Cross-cultural evidence for the patterning of anxiety disorders. In A. H. Tuma & J. Maser (Eds.), *Anxiety and the anxiety disorders* (pp. 297–323). Hillsdale, NJ: Erlbaum.

Guarnaccia, P. J., de la Cancela, V., & Carrillo, E. (1989). The multiple meanings of *ataques de nervios. Medical Anthropology.*

Guarnaccia, P., & Farias, P. (1988). The social meanings of *nervios:* A case study of a Central American woman. *Social Science and Medicine, 26*(12), 1223–1231.

Guarnaccia, P. J., Rubio-Stipes, M., & Canino, G. (1989). *Ataques de nervios* in the Puerto Rico Diagnostic Interview Schedule: The impact of cultural categories in psychiatric epidemiology. *Culture, Medicine, and Psychiatry, 13*(3).

Jung, C. G. (1969). *Collected works* (Vol. 8, 2nd ed.). Princeton, NJ: Bollingen Press.

Koss, J. (1975). Therapeutic aspects of Puerto Rican cult practices. *Psychiatry, 38,* 160–171.

Koss, J. (1977). Social process, healing and self-defeat among Puerto Rico spiritists. *American Ethnologist, 4,* 453–469.

Koss, J. (1980). The therapist-spiritist training project in Puerto Rico: An experiment to relate the traditional healing system to the public health system. *Social Science and Medicine, 14,* 373–410.

Koss, J. (1986). Symbolic transformations in traditional healing ritual: A perspective from analytical psychology. *Journal of Analytical Psychology, 31,* 341–355.

Koss-Chioino, J. (1988). *Women as healers, women as patients* (Manuscript).

Low, S. (1981). The meaning of *nervios:* A sociocultural analysis of symptom presentation in San Jose, Costa Rica. *Culture, Medicine, and Psychiatry, 5*(1), 25–48.

Low, S. (1985). Culturally-interpreted symptoms or culture-bound syndromes. *Social Science and Medicine, 21,* 187–196.

Mehlman, R. D. (1961). The Puerto Rican syndrome. *American Journal of Psychiatry, 118,* 328–332.

Nemiah, J. C. (1985). Anxiety states (anxiety neuroses). In H. I. Kaplan, M. D. Benjamin, & J. Sadock (Eds.), *Comprehensive textbook of psychiatry/IV* (Vol. 1, pp. 883–894). Baltimore, MD: Williams & Wilkins.

Perls, F. S., Hefferline, R. F., Goodman, P. (1951). *Gestalt therapy.* New York: Julian Press.

Rahe, R. (1987, June 27). Depression, stress and immunity. *Lancet,* pp. 1467–1468.

Rothenberg, A. (1964). Puerto Rico and aggression. *American Journal of Psychiatry, 121,* 962–970.

Rubel, A., O'Nell, C. W., & Collado-Ardon, R. (1984). *Susto: A folk illness.* Berkeley: University of California Press.

Rubio, M., Urdanetta, M., & Doyle, J. L. (1955). Psychopathologic reaction patterns in the Antilles command. *U. S. Armed Forces Medical Journal, 6,* 1767–1772.

Shucket, H. A. (1983). Anxiety related to medical disease. *Journal of Clinical Psychiatry, 44*(11), 31–36.

Spielberger, C. D. (1985). Anxiety, cognition and affect: A state–trait perspective. In A. H. Tuma & J. Maser (Eds.), *Anxiety and the anxiety disorders* (pp. 171–182). Hillsdale, NJ: Erlbaum.

NERVIOS AND DYSPHORIA IN MEXICAN AMERICAN WIDOWS

Margarita Kay, PhD, and Carmen Portillo, MS
College of Nursing, University of Arizona, Tucson, Arizona

One hundred widows participating in experimental research entitled *Efficacy of Support Groups for Mexican American Widows* were studied to learn how they express the loss of their husbands. Mourning practices, acknowledged symptoms of dysphoria, and somatic reactions were studied to learn if the syndrome of *nervios* subsumes their reaction to bereavement. In addition, their responses to instruments designed to measure depression, the Spanish version of the Beck Depression Inventory and the Center for Epidemiologic Studies Depression Scale, were examined for correlation with *nervios* and relationships to Mexican American acculturation. *Nervios* seems to be a manifestation of dysphoria rather than a specific syndrome for these women.

The grief felt by a recently bereaved widow is expressed in various ways. In this article we report how Mexican American widows in the 1st year of their bereavement respond culturally to the loss of their husbands. How do these widows experience and communicate their sadness, grief, and despair (Good, Good, & Moradi, 1985)? Does the dysphoria of widows differ from the depression of a fundamentally trouble person? Clues come from language, from the network of words and

In the *Coping and Health Among Older Urban Widows* (1RO1 AGO 3810-03) study, Bette Ide was principal investigator. Members of the research team included Cynthia Tobias, Martha Fimbres, Margarita Kay, Janice Monk, and Jill de Zapien.

The project reported in this article is supported by Grant 1RO1 MH41978 to the Southwestern Institute for Research on Women and the College of Nursing, University of Arizona, from the National Institute of Mental Health. They are not responsible for our findings.

Margarita Kay, Principal Investigator; Merle Mishel, Co-Investigator; and Carmen Portillo, Research Associate acknowledge the following contributions from the research team: Jill Guernsey de Zapien, Carmen Altamirano Wilson, and Ma. Eugenia Fernandez assisted in the translation of the symptom scales and in data collection; Ma. Sandra Gonzalez Marshall coded the data; and Marianne Yoder and Ma. Eugenia Fernandez managed the data. We also thank Delia Carbajal, Irma Marmion, and Olga Durazo, interviewers.

meanings (Good & Good, 1982) that Mexican Americans use to describe how they feel. In particular, illnesses or symptoms labeled in English as *nerves* and *nervousness,* called in Spanish *nervios, problemas con los nervios,* and, in serious cases, *ataque de nervios* might answer these questions. We studied the widows' mourning practices, symptoms of dysphoria, and somatic reactions to learn if the syndrome of *nervios* subsumed their reaction to bereavement.

In this article issues of *nervios* in Mexican American widowhood are discussed as follows. First presented are the contexts of two research projects on Mexican American widows, the first of which yielded a pilot for the second, an experimental study of an intervention called *Efficacy of Support Groups for Mexican American Widows.* Next, the cultural characteristics of the widows who lived the grief and provided the words are examined. Their traditional mourning practices are described.

After presenting the circumstances of the Mexican American widows, we follow with a discussion of the problem: how to study *nervios* and depression as emotions of these women. The probing of emotions is a study "still in its infancy" (Wikan, 1988, p. 459). We wanted to know if the dysphoria of widows is a passing feeling or a kind of depression. To do this, we needed to concentrate on the widows' "idioms of distress" (Nichter, 1981, p. 379). Ethnosemantics, the study of words and their distinguishing features (Frake, 1961; Kay, 1979), is one method for learning how a specific people label emotions, their *emic* concepts. However, ethnosemantics is limited (Good & Good, 1982) because it does not provide for equivalence across cultures. The meaning of words must be interpreted in the context of the culture. Further, the widows are not homogeneous but present different degrees of linguistic acculturation of Spanish and English. Many speak *norteño* Spanish, a lexicon used in northwestern Mexico and southwestern United States. Therefore, to measure emotional and somatic reactions to bereavement emically, we had to develop symptom scales in *norteño.* In addition, we needed to relate cultural symptoms to an *etic,* biomedical category, depression. We looked for tools used in other studies that appeared to have cultural sensitivity. In this article we present summaries of responses to the symptom scales we developed and compare these with results from tools standardized to measure depression. We conclude with case examples from the study.

The Research Studies

Data came from two research projects. The first, *Coping and Health Among Older Urban Widows,* was a longitudinal study of how Anglo and Mexican American widows coped with bereavement, and how their coping styles related to their physical and emotional health. The widows were asked if they experienced certain symptoms in order to evaluate the relationship between their bereavement and their health. One symptom frequently claimed by subjects was *problemas con los nervios,* nervousness.

The *Coping and Health* research served as a basis for a second research project, *Efficacy of Support Groups for Mexican American Widows.* In this longitudinal study recent Mexican American widows are randomly recruited for experimental or control conditions. The purpose of this project is to test an intervention designed to help Mexican American widows resolve their grief and adapt to a new role. The intervention uses the support group concept, modifying the procedures and content for the specific culture it serves. Individuals in the experimental group participate in professionally facilitated support groups. The control subjects rely only on their naturally occurring support. Our final sample should reach 150; the first 100 are discussed in this writing.

The Widows

The widows recruited for this study are Mexican Americans living in Tucson, Arizon. Tucson is a metropolitan area with a population of more than 500,000, with probably no more than 25% of Mexican descent. The widows range from five generations removed from Mexico to Mexican by birth. The women may be monolingual in Spanish or English or bilingual. Typically they are working class with an income and educational level below their Anglo counterparts (Kay, 1977, 1980; Kay et al., 1988).

The stereotypic role of the Mexican American woman is culturally prescribed throughout her life, with activities limited to those of wife and mother. She rarely relates to the outside world. She marries at a young age, often to a man some years older than herself. Husband and wife live their lives segregated by gender roles. Sometimes their lives are quite separate, with the two living apart, even when not formally divorced. In any case, the women live in matrifocal households, maintaining responsibility for cooking, laundry, and domestic decisions for husband and children. The husband might be a womanizer, alcoholic, or violent, but the woman continues with her duty. Even if divorced, she may care for him when he is ill. After the man dies, his widow loses the role of wife, but not of mother. Her ritual *obligación* to her husband continues for up to a year, but her cultural duty never ends with children, even her adult children and grandchildren. When she is widowed, her life continues to be centered on her family, subordinating her own needs. In return, she is now supposed to be accorded respect and care. It is expected that she would be assisted in her grief by her natural support system, that is, her family: conjugal, affinal, and ritual kin.

Traditional mourning practices (*luto*) keep the widow in her home, almost secluded except for church and necessary errands. Other culturally specific actions include wearing black dress from 3 months to 1 year; having a rosary (*rosario*) recited and a wake (*velorio*) at the mortuary on the evening preceding the burial; having a rosary conducted in the home on the nine consecutive evenings that follow the funeral (*novenario*); requesting weekly masses; and visiting the grave on a daily or a weekly basis or on anniversaries, when the grave is swept and decorated with flowers, typically marigolds. With this background of expected behavior, we look at the effect of cultural practices on their dysphoria. Do women who follow these practices complain of *nervios* or other forms of dysphoria more or less than the women who do not? In other words, are the cultural practices protective or promoting of *nervios* or other manifestations of grief? How does *nervios* relate to depression? "The prototype for adult depression is grief, the almost universal depressive response to the loss of a loved one through death" (Klerman, 1989, p. 11). Kleinman and Good (1985) asked, "Is unresolved grief over the loss of spouse . . . the same disease as depression of a more fundamentally troubled person?" (p. 2).

MEASURING SYMPTOMS OF *NERVIOS* AND DEPRESSION

To evaluate the support group intervention designed to help the widows resolve bereavement, we looked at the various tools that have been used to measure mood, reduction of stress, anxiety, mastery, and depression. However, few of the existing instruments had ever been used, and fewer yet had been validated with Mexican American women, let alone widows. We assumed the existence of dysphoria, but were also aware of "differences in cultural idioms for articulating distress" (Good, Good, & Moravi, 1985, p. 419).

The problem was the development of an instrument to label dysphoria in *norteño.* Although it has been demonstrated that there is a direct bearing on the effect of inadequate translation of language on responses to health surveys (Berkanovic, 1980), we had no symptom list that we were confident had been well translated in the language of our participants. Thus we had to consider the words for emotional symptoms in the context of Mexican American widows' bereavement.

We found that no instrument standardized on Anglo Americans can simply be translated into Spanish. Moreover, the Spanish of Mexican Americans differs in subtle but significant ways from the Spanish of other American Hispanic groups. Some of the words that are emotional expressions of dysphoria for other Hispanic groups proved not to be familiar in daily use to the Mexican American population of Tucson, *norteños* or northwestern Mexicans. Examples of these included *melancolico* (sad), *descorazonado* (discouraged), and *satisfaga* (satisfied), words that appeared in one instrument we tested. Thus instruments validated for Puerto Ricans or Cubans were not always usable. We also found generational differences in illness concepts and their labels. Such factors had to be considered in constructing a symptom health list, which we needed for the study, especially specific symptoms associated with bereavement-depression-anxiety.

We went back to the symptom list used in the first study, *Coping and Health.* This scale had been used to measure changes in health status, albeit rather crudely. It mixed chronic diseases with symptoms that might be somatic expressions of dysphoria, imprecise for populations that are reputed to somaticize depression (Jenkins, 1988; Rosen, Kleinman, & Katon, 1982), and it included emotional symptoms. Because the scale had been designed to measure symptoms in three ethnic groups, *etic* (outside of a particular culture) categories had been used in order to have comparable data. Compromises were made in the choice of questions in order to accommodate cultural differences among Anglo, Mexican American, and American Indian participants. The symptom scale was in English, translated into Spanish. However, the symptom scale did not always encode emic data, i.e. culture-specific concepts, even though the English words were translated by using back translation techniques (Brislin, 1980).

Shweder (1985) states that "A people's lexicon for emotions is a rather poor index of their emotional functioning" (p. 184). Lutz and White (1986) state, "The emphasis upon socially constructed meaning in anthropological views of language leads investigators to doubt the validity of single words or sentences as invariant representations of knowledge or experience" (p. 414). Moreover, the difficulty of creating a scale with culture-specific meanings is compounded when dealing with people of various degrees of acculturation and language use. Such is the case with the population that we are studying. All these factors had to be considered in constructing a symptom list.

Vega, Kolody, and Valle (1986) and Golding and Karno (1988) have found differences in symptoms related to intracultural variation. For the *Efficacy of Support Group* research, we used the index of Cuellar, Harris, and Jasso (1980) to assess the widows' level of acculturation. We found that language preference was the most salient indicator of acculturation. Forty percent of the study population spoke little English, 47% considered themselves bilingual, and 13% were most comfortable in English. However, there was a considerable amount of code switching between Spanish and English during the interviews, all of which were conducted by bilingual women. Few of the American-educated women could read Spanish, even those who preferred Spanish.

With all this in mind, we constructed three symptom scales. The first listed chronic diseases that the widows had suffered before widowhood. The second was physical symptoms that tend to be classified as psychosomatic and were experienced after bereavement. The third listed symptoms or words used for dysphoria. Final form for testing came after the scales were given to 12 bilingual widows recruited from the *Coping and Health* project. Table 1 presents the list of symptoms of dysphoria in Spanish and in English.

To accommodate the different degrees of bilingualism, we offered the symptom lists in both Spanish and English. Note that a few Spanish terms appear in the English list. A different semantic space is occupied by at least some of the English and Spanish terms. Furthermore, some of the English terms were not understood by the widows who were interviewed in English. We simply could not gloss satisfactorily *tirisia,* although the components of meaning are similar to the English "separation sorrow." *Arrimada* (beholden) is a concept that the widows understood better in Spanish than in its English translation. *Trastornada* translates as "disturbed" and *desequilibrada* as "unbalanced," but the Spanish words have connotations different from those of the English.

Some words, particularly the cognates, were tricky. One Spanish word for "worry" is *mortificación.* It does not translate as "embarrassment," as one might guess from the English cognate. *Preocupación* can be glossed as "preoccupation" but the widows used the word to signify a less severe form of worry than *mortificación.* We were prepared for this difference. However, *nervios* was not necessarily the same as the gloss that we chose for the term "acute nervousness" to the Mexican American widows who were interviewed in English.

SOMATIC SYMPTOMS

As noted by Jenkins (1988), symptoms commonly associated with nerves include physiological responses such as trembling, headache, sleeping disorders, eating disorders, dizziness, and stomach ailments, as well as dysphoric emotions such as fear, worry, anxiety, and anger. Nations, Camino, and Walker (1988), dealing with an Anglo population, found that the term "nerves" is an ethnomedical illness involving somatic, psychological (or emotional), and social distress. Their informants described the acute attack in psychosomatic terms, as "a wave of tension which breaks over the patient in a fit of body shaking and quivering, stomach pains and nausea, headaches, heart tremors, shortness of

Table 1. Symptoms of Dysphoria

English	Spanish
Fear	*Miedo*
Fright	*Susto*
Worry	*Mortificación*
—	*Preocupación*
Anguish	*Congoja*
Anger/rage	*Coraje*
Acute nervousness	*Nervios*
Separation sorrow/*tirisia*	*Tirisia*
Nightmares	*Pesadillas*
Loneliness	*Soledad*
Depression	*Depresión*
Sadness	*Tristeza*
Remorse	*Remordimiento*
Disoriented	*Desorientada*
Feel like you don't want to do anything	*Sin ganas de hacer nada*
Without energy	*Sin ánimo*
Feeling empty	*Se siente vacla*
Confused	*Confundida*
Trastornada	*Trastornada*
Desequilibrada	*Desequilibrada*
Bad mood	*De mal humor*
Being in the way of other people	*Siente que es un estorbo*
Siente que está arrimada	*Siente que está arrimada*

breath, chest pains, dizziness, trembling in the extremities, blurred vision and hot flashes; it then calms into a state of lethargy, sadness, tension, insomnia and feelings of weariness, of weight pressing on the chest, arms and head, and of obsessive worrying'' (p. 1248). We, too, asked about these symptoms generally considered to be psychosomatic. Does the grieving widow somaticize her emotions? We constructed a somatic symptom list, as shown in Table 2.

To provide data for cross-cultural study of depression, we are using instruments that have been employed with some degree of success with Mexican Americans. These include a Spanish version of the Beck Depression Inventory (BDI; Lopez & Serrano, 1975) that we adapted further and the Center for Epidemiologic Studies Depression Scale (CES-D; Radloff, 1977). We compare results from our symptom scales with these standardized tests. There are no norms for Mexican American widows for the BDI (W. A. Vega, personal communication, May 12,

Table 2. Somatic Symptoms

Spanish	English
Dolor del corazón	Heart trouble
Aire en el corazón	*Aire en el corazón*
Agruras, Acedías	Heartburn
Atarantamiento o atarantada	Dizziness
Mareos	Nausea
Falta de aliento	Shortness of breath
Problemas de la piel	Rash
Tos	Cough
Debilidad	Weakness
Decaimiento	*Decaimiento*
Dolor de cabeza	Headache
Cansancio	Tiredness
Estreñimiento	Constipation
Dolor de espalda o cintura	Backache
Dolor de cerebro o del cuello	Stiff neck
Gases	Gas pains
Sin energía	No energy
Agotamiento	Exhaustion
Siente frio	Feel cold
Siente calor	Feel hot
Le dan calores	Feel hot flashes
Temblores	Tremors

1988). Several studies using the CES-D have reported that the highest age-specific rates of psychological symptoms are found in middle-life Hispanic women (Vega, Valle, Kolody, & Hough, 1987).

Relationship of *Nervios* to Other Variables

Forty-five percent of the subjects said that they suffered from *nervios.* We cross-tabulated *nervios* with variables including age, language preference, and observance of *luto* (the length of time wearing dark clothing). None was statistically significant as tested by chi-square. None of these predicted *nervios.* Closest to significance ($p < .11$) was acculturation as measured by the Acculturation Rating Scale for Mexican Americans (ARSMA; Cuellar, Harris, & Jasso, 1980), suggesting that the bicultural widow was less troubled by *nervios.* Thirty percent of the sample was bicultural and only 8% of these had *nervios.* Vega, Warheit, Buhl-Auth, and Meinhardt (1984) found the prevalence of depressive symptoms for Mexican American English-speaking samples much lower than that reported by Spanish-speaking Mexican Americans and suggested that differences in educational levels appear to be accounting for many of the variations in depressive symptoms.

We were eager to know if *nervios* predicted depression as measured by standardized scales. First we tried to correlate *nervios* with scores in the BDI. In this inventory, a score higher than 16 is considered to be diagnostic of depression. Eleven percent of the sample scored at 17 or above, but only 4% of these complained of *nervios*. The CES-D fared somewhat better. Using a score of higher than 23 to be diagnostic of depression, *nervios* was related to the CES-D, but not at a statistically significant level.

Next we looked at the results of the various measures of health status. First we considered chronic diseases suffered prior to widowhood. *Nervios* was statistically not related to arthritis, hypertension, or diabetes, or to respiratory, teeth, heart, uterine, menstrual, or urinary problems. It related only to previous gall bladder disease and to a category of various other problems not in the list.

Following the chronic disease history, the women were asked about somatic symptoms that might be related to bereavement. From the somatic symptom list shown in Table 2, we cross-tabulated complaints of a somatic symptom by women who said they had *nervios* and those who did not. Frequencies are shown in Table 3.

Although there are considerable differences in the frequencies of somatic symptoms between the group with *nervios* and the group without, few are statistically significant. We see that the somatic symptoms reported by the women suffering from *nervios* were statistically significant only for tiredness, rash, and tremors.

DYSPHORIC SYMPTOM RESPONSE

The widows were asked to respond to the 23 dysphoric symptoms listed in Table 1. In the first interview each was asked, "Do any of these words describe what you have felt since the death of your husband?" If the answer was "yes," the participant was asked to give an example of a time when she experienced that symptom. In the second interview, the widows were asked, "Since the last interview, have you experienced any of the following? If 'yes' what do you do about it?"

Of the first 100 widows interviewed, 99% responded affirmatively to "*tristeza*" (sadness). The widows often said that they became sad when "they would think of him," "*casi todo el tiempo*" ("almost all the time"), "at night mostly," "*en ratitos cuando estoy comiendo*" ("at times when I am eating"), "on weekends," and "on special occasions." To relieve their sadness, the women in general would try to occupy

Table 3. Percentages of Somatic Symptoms by *Nervios*

Symptom	*Nervios* (n = 45)	No *Nervios* (n = 55)
Heart problems	33	42
Aire in the heart	33	26
Heartburn	42	31
Dizzy	44	36
Nausea	37	27
Shortness of breath	33	33
Rash	37*	15
Cough	26	22
Weak	44	26
Decaida	57	60
Headache	53	49
Tired	84*	64
Constipation	24	31
Backache	55	44
Stiff neck	51	46
Gas	48	33
No energy	66	58
Exhaustion	62	44
Feels cold	48*	20
Feels hot	40	26
Feels hot flashes	40	27
Tremors	35*	16

*$p < .05$.

themselves with some form of activity such as gardening, reading, talking to family members or friends, watching the "*novelas*" (soap operas), or "saying the rosary."

"*Soledad*" (loneliness) was reported by 87% of these widows. It appeared primarily to be associated with the memory of their husbands. For example, loneliness was described as "used to him being home, doing things for him," "when I come home from work and on weekends," "in the evenings," "when I see his things, his clothes in the closet," "at the time when he would come home to eat," and "especially in the mornings and the evenings." Loneliness for some of these women was a state of being, as two widows described it, "loneliness twenty-four hours a day" and "all the time." As a way of dealing with their perceived loneliness, they would generally attempt to distract themselves by becoming involved with family and friends, read, sew, clean, or "pray to God." One widow reported a self-resignation to the loneliness. The two widows who described loneliness as part of their state of being reported keeping their loneliness to themselves, perhaps indicating a self-prescribed destiny.

The third symptom most frequently responded to was worry, as "*mortificación*" (75%) or as "*preocupación*" (75%). The more severe form, *mortificación*, was said to occur when thinking about "the future—can't live on what I have," "any little thing," "about the children and grandchildren." Another widow said, "*mortificación de todo que me cae a mi*" ("I worry about everything that happens to me"). Worry for these widows involved finances, the future, children, and just the state of being for some.

Preocupación was cited by the widows as frequently, but not identically. Since the symptom scale could not always capture the emic concept, responds to "worried" as expressed by *preocupada* were similar to the other form of "worried". *Preocupación* also dealt with the future, family, and finances. A 35-year-old widow stated, "*Casi siempre me desespero por no poder darles a los buquitos*" ("Almost always I am desperate not being able to give to the kids"). Another widow stated, "Dealing with all the bills." As with the previous symptoms, worrying can be part of the overall situation or a state of being for some of these widows. The statement of a 40-year-old widow illustrates this permanence: "*soy múy preocupada,*" not "*estoy*." In Spanish, "to be" has two forms: the *soy* form signifies a permanent condition, whereas the *estoy* means a temporary state. In order to alleviate their worry, most of the women commented on becoming involved in activities or simply trying not to think about it. Treatment for a number of these women (15%) involved modifying their behavior by "trying to put it out of mind." One widow reported the use of a prescribed medication. No one reported the use of home remedies for this particular symptom.

The Spanish term *depresión* also had an interesting significance. Lower than anticipated, 67% of the widows responded to the symptom *depresión.* The majority of the widows stated that a feeling of depression was experienced at a particular time of the day, remembering their husbands, or because of the adjustment they were having to make. Only three said that depression for them was "all part of it" with no specific resolution. Again, the widows engaged in activities as part of their way of dealing with this symptom. Two widows cited using a herbal remedy for their *depresión.*

The symptom *nervios* was identified fewer times (45%) than any of the symptoms mentioned above. (*Ataque de nervios,* which they translated as "nervous breakdown," was denied by all.) One widow described herself as "*muy nerviosa, es lo mismo de una desesperación* ("very nervous which is the same as despair"). Still another said "closer to the death"; "*Siento coraje y nervios con todas las cosas que tengo que hacer para arreglar mis negocios. Yo nunca tenía que hacer nada de eso*" ("I feel angry and nervous with everything I have to do to arrange my affairs. I never had to do any of this"); "*poquito al dormir*" ("a little when I go to sleep"); and "*cuando se hace tarde en la noche y cuando viene a la mente como murió*" ("when it gets late at night and when I think of how he died"). Interestingly, a few of the widows commented on *nervios* as part of their overall being: "I've always been nervous" or "*soy nerviosa y no hago nada*" ("I am nervous and I do not do anything"). *Nervios* for most of the widows was not specifically treated, but accepted as part of the situation or themselves. Two widows reported using a prescribed medication; none reported using a home remedy. In the *Coping and Health* study, many widows reported using herbal remedies, particularly *té de azahar* (orange blossom tea).

Fewer than 50% of the widows said that they experienced the other dysphoric symptoms on the scale. *Tirisia,* one of the symptoms without a direct translation, was identified by 38%. Twenty-two widows identified feeling trapped or beholden, expressed as *se siente que esta arrimada.*

For the entire population, the dysphoric symptoms were cross-tabulated with *nervios,* as was done with the somatic symptoms. (All widows identified "sadness.") *Nervios* was significantly related to fear, *mortificación,* anger, *tirisia,* loneliness, disoriented, feeling empty, confused, and being in the way. Symptom percentages are shown in Table 4.

CASE REPORTS

The statistical considerations are one thing. How do they translate to the widows themselves? Reports of six widows were selected to illustrate the women's expression of grief by the words they have employed and their scores on the scales. In addition, their bereavement practices and levels of acculturation shall be discussed.

Alicia. Alicia, a 76-year-old woman who has lived all her life in Tucson, was born in Sonora, Mexico, and emigrated at a young age. Her education in the United States went through the third grade. Alicia speaks both English and Spanish, but communicates primarily in Spanish. A mother of two children who has never worked outside of her house, she reports having been in poor health as an adult. She suffers from a chronic problem of arthritis. Alicia's husband worked as a migrant worker in the cotton fields all his life, until he developed cancer of the stomach, which incapacitated him for a number of years.

After the death of her husband, Alicia followed *luto,* the traditional

Table 4. Symptoms of Dysphoria by *Nervios*

Symptom	% With *Nervios* (n = 45)	% Without *Nervios* (n = 55)
Fear	66*	36
Fright	37	24
Mortificación	86*	67
Worry	88	75
Anguish	60*	44
Anger	51*	44
Tirisia	48*	29
Nightmares	31	20
Loneliness	95*	80
Depression	75	58
Remorse	73	27
Disoriented	53*	16
Feel like doing nothing	75	58
Without energy	71	53
Feeling empty	86*	60
Confused	51*	27
Trastornada	82	6
Desequilibrada	40	11
Bad mood	42	47
Being in the way	40*	15
Arrimada	20	7

*$p < .05$.

bereavement practice. She wore black clothing through the entire 1st year and had a *velorio* for him at the time he was buried. Alicia lacks the spiritual and family support that are strengths of the Mexican American culture. This is illustrated in her ARSMA score of 53.

On the somatic symptom scale, Alicia scored 15. She identified dizziness, heartburn, and weakness, saying "*no como todo el dia*" ("I don't eat the whole day long"). She also cited headache, tiredness, no energy, and exhaustion. Her dysphoric symptom score was 16. Alicia lives with her children and does feel *que está arrimada* (trapped, beholden): "*No soy la que mando—no es igual*" ("I am not the one that gives the orders—it is not the same"). In addition, she cited sadness, worry, loneliness (she stated, "*Me mantengo en mi cuarto sola*" ["I stay in my room by myself"]), and worried. She did report *nervios* ("*si, muy nerviosa*"). When questioned about *depresión,* she did not recognize the word and was not able to identify with it.

Alicia's score of 21 on the BDI and 26 on the CES-D concur with the reported symptoms. Despite the fact that Alicia did not recognize *depresión,* it is evident from the scores that she is experiencing the symptomatology. In fact, *depresión* and depression do not occupy the same semantic space.

Marta. Marta, a 58-year-old bilingual native Tucsonian, completed the graduate equivalency diploma, and has taken several courses at a junior college. A mother of five children, Marta worked outside of the home for 15 years as a teacher aide. She and her husband had been married for 30 years when he became ill as a result of heart failure. Marta's husband had been ill for 11 months before he passed away. She reported her own health as being very good.

Marta's *luto* practices were not as traditional as Alicia's. She stated, "He never wanted me to wear black." Since the death of her husband, she has had special masses for him and participates in local church activities, such as having the statue of the Virgin Mary visit her home for a week at a time. The somatic symptom score for Marta was 5. She reported feeling *decaimiento* "right after he died," tiredness, stiff neck, no energy, and exhaustion. She said, "Right after he died, I would try to keep so busy that I would become exhausted." Her score for dysphoric symptoms was 10. Marta reported the symptom sadness: "I feel like crying missing things we did together." Some of the other symptoms mentioned were worry, loneliness, fear, *tirisia,* and *nervios,* citing, "sometimes I can't sleep at night."

Although Marta cited only a few symptoms, the reported scores from the scales do not concur with the symptomatology. The BDI score was 2, and the CES-D score 27. This may indicate that the number of symptoms are not as significant as the particular symptoms identified.

Marta's ARSMA score of 57 is similar to Alicia's 53, indicating that both are bicultural. Both adhere to a number of the traditional cultural practices that may be beneficial during this process of adjustment. Marta, however, is culturally more flexible. This helps her function in a dual world and may account for her far lower score on the BDI.

Alicia and Marta had symptoms of dysphoria that corresponded with the CES-D. Four case studies are now presented to exemplify the incongruencies that exist between the actual acknowledgment of the dysphoric and somatic symptoms and the scale scores. The choices are based on the frequencies of the symptoms and the scores of the BDI and the CES-D. Also a point of interest was the score from the ARSMA.

Maria. Maria, a 75-year-old widow, was born in Mexico but has lived in Tucson since she was a young girl. She went through the fourth grade, learning to read and write only in Spanish. As a housewife and mother, Maria raised seven children. Maria's husband supported the family working as a plasterer. His death occurred quite suddenly after 49 years of marriage.

On behalf of her husband, Maria had a *velorio* (wake), a *novenario* (saying of the rosary), and more than one special mass. She also visits the cemetery every week and says a rosary for him. Although Maria seems to be unacculturated and traditional as indicated by the ARSMA (her score was 25) and by her other religious mourning practices, she does not wear the dark *luto* clothing.

Maria describes her health as being "*malo*" (bad). As an adult she has had high blood pressure, diabetes, urinary tract infections, and headaches, as well as gall bladder surgery. Her summed somatic symptom score was 13. Since the death of her husband, Maria has experienced additional symptoms, for example, not being able to breathe at times and dizzy spells.

The summed dysphoric score was 8. She indicated depression and sadness, "something that does not go away." When asked about loneliness as part of the dysphoric symptom interview, she asked, "What is it?" Maria's total of eight symptoms is not particularly high, but perhaps lower than would be expected given her score of 22 on the BDI, well above the cut off point, and 23 for the CES-D. While Vega et al. (1986) stated that the CES-D is particularly sensitive to situational stress, the question here becomes, Why is Maria not expressing her stress level equally in the symptom scales as it is being measured by the standardized scales?

Unlike Marta, Maria experienced a number of the symptoms described by Jenkins (1988) that are associated with nerves, such as headaches, stomach ailments, dizziness, and worry. The additional difference between Maria and Alicia was their acculturation scores, suggesting that the more acculturated are the less troubled with symptomatology related to *nervios*.

Lupita. Lupita is a 71-year-old Mexican American widow. Born and raised in Tucson, Lupita went through the seventh grade, learning to read and write in Spanish and English. Her interview was conducted in English, but she would frequently switch languages. Lupita's 18-year work experience included work in a factory and as a kitchen aide in the school cafeteria. Her only child, a son, was from her first marriage. She and her late husband had been married for less than 5 years. (Two months before he died, he became ill from complications of anemia.) Lupita made the traditional religious arrangements for her husband, a rosary the day before the burial, a *novenario,* and a special mass. She wore dark clothing for less than 4 months, because, she said, "The priest said I didn't need to anymore."

During childhood, Lupita suffered from chronic tonsilitis, and as an adult she has had thyroid problems and knee replacement surgery, from arthritic damage. Her somatic symptom score was 15, including heart trouble, ("I get a strange pain") and shortness of breath ("*Me siento como no puedo respirar*"; "I feel like I can't breathe"). Additional symptoms that she cited were dizziness, nausea, feel hot, *decaimiento,* constipation, backache, exhaustion, and weakness, stating "*Es muy natural cuando uno pierde a alguien*" ("It is very natural when one loses someone"). The dysphoric symptom score was similarly high, 14. Symptoms that she marked were fear, worry, *mortificación,* anguish, anger, loneliness, depression, sadness, feeling like she didn't want to do anything, without energy, feeling empty, confused, and being in the way of other people. Although Lupita did not mark nervous, she claimed the particular symptoms we have identified as part of the semantic network of *nervios.* Unlike the previous two cases, Lupita's scores were higher for the symptom scales than the measurement scales. A score of 3 was calculated for the BDI and a score of 9 for the CES-D.

Dolores. Dolores, a 63-year-old bilingual widow who identifies herself as American, was born in a small mining town. Her educational background included high school and a few college courses. Mother of four children and housewife, Dolores worked outside the home for 26 years as a secretary and bookkeeper. She was married for 36 years to "a fine carpenter."

A sudden heart attack was the cause of her husband's death. Two months prior, he was given a complete physical examination and was told "he would live to a 100." Although Dolores's acculturation score was 63, which would indicate that she was highly acculturated to American society, she exercised the traditional mourning customs of *luto*. In addition, she had a wake, a *novenario* in her home, and special masses said in his name. She has not visited the cemetery since his death because "I find it very hard—can't go." Her children and immediate family were close at hand following her husband's death, but she is currently living alone.

Dolores herself suffered a heart attack 7 years before her husband's death. She claims good heath as a child and still claims good health as an adult, despite her heart attack. Since her husband died, she denied having experienced any somatic symptoms and claims only five psychological symptoms. She admits "anger with God," feeling loneliness, sadness, "empty all the time" and "feeling like everything seemed so useless." She added, "I feel so vulnerable—he was so loving and took care of me. I felt so secure—it was like someone pulled the rug from under me." The symptom *nervios* was denied. Although her symptom scales scores were essentially negative, her CES-D score was 26 and the BDI was 6.

Olga. Olga is a 63-year-old widow who was married for more than 46 years and had 10 children. Although she was born in rural southern Arizona, she has lived most of her life in Tucson. Olga's education took her through eighth grade, where she learned to read and write in both Spanish and English. The interview was conducted in Spanish, but often code switching took place. Her parents and grandparents were born in Mexico, thus making her a first-generation Mexican American. She identifies herself as "*Mexicana*." Olga never worked outside of her home. Her husband worked as a miner and then in the post office.

After the death of her husband, Olga made the traditional arrangements: a *velorio,* a *novenario,* and a number of special masses. In addition, she wore the traditional black clothing for *luto,* having given all her other clothes away. Olga is unmistakably Mexican in her traditions, daily habits, and values. Since the death of her husband, her children and her sister call her on a daily basis.

Twenty years ago Olga developed diabetes and she has become insulin dependent. In addition, she suffers from hypertension and experienced several mini strokes 4 years ago. The summed somatic score was 12. Olga recalls experiencing heart pain "*en el momento que el murió*" ("at the moment he died"), bitter taste, nausea ("I was vomiting every morning"), skin problems ("*unas ampollas en la cabeza de los nervios*", "blisters on my scalp from nerves"), cough, *decaimiento,* headache, feeling cold, and tremors. The dysphoric symptom score was 15. Olga cited the following symptoms: fear, fright, *mortificación, preocupación,* and nightmares. "I would feel pressure when I had this desperate feeling—*quisiera salir corriendo* ["I felt like getting out and running"]" she said. *Tirisia,* she said, would remain with her for the rest of her life. Other symptoms were *nervios,* loneliness, *depresión,* sadness, without wanting to do anything, without energy, and feeling empty.

The BDI and the CES-D scores correspond to Olga's symptomatology, at 16 and 38, respectively. Here was a widow who identified *nervios* and who measured depressed on the standardized scales.

As can be seen in the six case studies, *nervios* is not distinguished primarily by somatic symptoms, but in conjunction with certain dysphoric symptoms that are related to the semantic network of *nervios* within the Mexican American culture. The themes of loss or sudden loss, loneliness, sadness, headaches, stomach ailments, and overall general weakness were present. In all cases, the process of adjusting to the loss of their husbands was severe enough to make them susceptible to experience a form of *nervios,* although it was not necessarily so labeled. Rather than evaluating the symptoms, *nervios* needs to be evaluated from a psychosocial and cultural perspective.

These cases demonstrate some of the important aspects of the semantic network. The process of bereavement; the feeling of being tired, fearful, and lonely; the sensation of tremors; the constant state of worry (*mortificación*); and the sense of feeling empty can pose as a threat to one's well-being, both physically and mentally. For example, widows who have traditionally adhered to a stereotypical role may not adjust or know how to adjust to a change in role, and are thus susceptible to *nervios* or other manifestations of their dysphoria. A widow who does not have a strong support system may often become more debilitated or experience symptoms related to *nervios,* as in the case of Lupita.

Nervios is manifested in various ways. Most widows claimed somatic symptoms, but not to the degree of some other populations, for example, those studied by Nations et al. (1988), in whom *nervios* seemed to be manifested primarily by somatization. There was only one case (Dolores) in which physical symptoms were denied, but *nervios* would not be ruled out in this case because she had a high CES-D score. But for these Mexican American widows, *nervios* is expressed in feelings of dysphoria, with different words to label the loss. The relationship between worry and *nervios* is almost inseparable. Worry was one of the most often documented symptoms by the widows.

The symptomatologies of the English term depression and the Spanish term *nervios* overlap in definition of categories. Although the widows describe the hallmark symptoms of depression—sadness, feeling like not wanting to do anything, without energy, and tiredness these same descriptions may be used for *nervios.* However, *nervios* may or may not be cited. In the questionnaire used in the first study on widows, *Coping and Health Among Urban Widows,* there were only eight items that measured emotional responses to widowhood. Many of the widows in that study claimed *nervios.* In this study, we separated this syndrome into 23 dysphoric symptoms.

Nervios is not a discrete category, but it can be seen that *nervios* occupies the same semantic space of other psychological and physical symptoms. The framework for *nervios* serves to interpret or make sense of an otherwise misdiagnosed psychiatric syndrome or mislabeled somatization. Moreover, *nervios* for the Mexican American widow needs to be analyzed in a social and cultural context, rather than by symptoms in isolation.

CONCLUSION

We return to the questions posed at the beginning of this article. First, how do the widows experience and communicate their sadness, grief, and despair? They follow culturally prescribed mourning rituals, depending somewhat on their levels of acculturation to the dominant Anglo society. The least acculturated women wear *luto* (dark clothing) and restrict their social activities for an entire year; others truncate the rituals. Their grief is reflected in some of the same somatic and emotional symptoms that appear in cultures of other Western societies. But the widows label their feelings in a rich, highly differentiated vocabulary of sorrow.

Is the dysphoria of widows a different depression from that of a fundamentally troubled person? From the widows' responses to the emotional and somatic measures of dysphoria, we believe that this is so. There was too little correspondence between scores on the emic scales developed for this research and those on the etic (the BDI and the CES-D) instruments standardized to measure depression.

Finally, is there a syndrome of *nervios* specific to bereaved widows? The word *nervios* was but one symptom, acknowledged by fewer than half of the widows. Those with *nervios* noted that the emotional symptoms of loneliness, severe worry, feeling empty, fear, confused, disorientation, and feeling in the way of others to a much higher (and statistically significant) degree than did those widows who did not complain of *nervios*. Somatic symptoms of feeling tired, cold, tremors, or rash were greater (to a statistically significant degree) in widows suffering from *nervios* than in those who did not admit to *nervios*. However, we cannot say that there is a specific syndrome of *nervios* for these women. All of the widows acknowledged some of the symptoms. *Nervios* did not always differentiate between the widows who scored high on the emic symptom scales or the standardized instruments. It is possible that at the completion of our study, when the scales and instruments have been administered five times to 150 subjects, in 750 interviews, we may have more definitive quantitative findings. However, the challenge continues to lie in emic research, to learn culturally specific manifestations of the widows' bereavement.

REFERENCES

Berkanovic, E. (1980). The effect of inadequate language translation on Hispanics' responses to health surveys. *American Journal of Public Health, 70,* 1273–1276.

Brislin, R. W. (1980). Analysis of oral and written materials. In H. C. Triandis & J. Berry (Eds.), *Handbook of cross-cultural psychology* (pp. 389–444). Boston: Allyn & Bacon.

Cuellar, I., Harris, L. C., & Jasso, R. (1980). An acculturation scale for Mexican-American normal and clinical populations. *Hispanic Journal of Behavioral Sciences, 2,* 199–217.

Frake, C. O. (1961). The diagnosis of disease among the Subanun of Mindanao. *American Anthropologist, 63,* 112–132.

Golding, J. M., & Karno, M. (1988). Gender differences in depressive symptoms among Mexican Americans and non-Hispanic whites. *Hispanic Journal of Behavioral Sciences, 10,* 1–19.

Good, B. J., & Good, M. (1982). Toward a meaning-centered analysis of popular illness categories: "Fright-Illness" and "Heart Distress" in Iran. In A. J. Marsella & G. White (Eds.), *Cultural conceptions of mental health and therapy* (pp. 141–166). Boston: Reidel.

Good, F. J., Good, M. D., & Moradi, R. (1985). The interpretation of Iranian depressive illness and dysphoric affect. In A. Kleinman & B. Good (Eds.), *Culture and depression* (pp. 369–428). Berkeley: University of California Press.

Jenkins, J. H. (1988). Conceptions of schizophrenia as a problem of nerves: A cross-cultural comparison of Mexican Americans and Anglo Americans. *Social Science and Medicine, 26,* 1233–1243.

Kay, M. (1977). Health and illness in a Mexican American barrio. In E. H. Spicer (Ed.), *Ethnic medicine in the southwest* (pp. 99–166). Tucson: University of Arizona Press.

Kay, M. (1979). Lexemic change and semantic shift in disease names. *Culture, Medicine, and Psychiatry, 3,* 73–94.

Kay, M. (1980). Mexican, Mexican American and Chicana birth. In M. Melville (Ed.), *Twice a minority: Mexican American women* (pp. 52–65). St. Louis: C. V. Mosby.

Kay, M., Tobias, C., Ide, B., Zapien, J., Monk, J., Bluestein, M., & Fernandez, M. E. (1988). The health and symptom care of widows. *Journal of Cross Cultural Gerontology, 3,* 197–208.

Kleinman, A., & Good, B. (1985). Introduction. In A. Kleinman & B. Good (Eds.), *Culture and depression* (pp. 1–33). Berkeley: University of California Press.

Klerman, G. L. (1987). The nature of depression. Mood, symptom, disorder. In A. J. Marsella, R. M. A. Hirschfeld, & M. M. Katz (Eds.), *The measurement of depression* (pp. 3–19). New York: Guilford Press.

Lopez, V. C., & Serrano, E. U. (1975). Adaptación Catellana de la escala de evaluación conductal para la deprecion de Beck [Spanish translation of the Beck Depression Inventory]. Revista de Psiquiatria y Psicologia Medecina de Europa y America Latina, 12(4), 217–236.

Lutz, C., & White, G. M. (1986). The anthropology of emotions. *Annual Review of Anthropology, 15,* 405–436.

Nations, M. K., Camino, L. A., & Walker, F. B. (1988). Nerves: Folk idiom for anxiety and depression? *Social Science and Medicine, 26,* 1245–1259.

Nichter, M. (1981). Idioms of distress. *Culture, Medicine, and Psychiatry, 5,* 379–408.

Radloff, L. S. (1977). The CES-D scale: A self-report depression scale for research in the general population. *Applied Psychological Measurement, 1,* 385–401.

Rosen, G., Kleinman, A., & Katon, W. (1982). Somatization in family practice: A biopsychosocial approach. *Journal of Family Practice, 14,* 493–502.

Shweder, R. A. (1985). Menstrual pollution, soul loss, and the comparative study of emotions. In A. Kleinman & B. Good (Eds.), *Culture and depression* (pp. 182–215). Berkeley: University of California Press.

Vega, W. A., Kolody, B., & Valle, J. R. (1986). The relationship of marital status, confidant support and depression among Mexican immigrant women. *Journal of Marriage and Family, 48,* 597–605.

Vega, W. A., Valle, R., Kolody, B., & Hough, R., (1987). The Hispanic social network preventive intervention study: A community-based randomized trial. In R. Muñoz (Ed.), *Depression prevention: Research directions* (pp. 217–231). New York: Hemisphere.

Vega, W., Warheit, G., Buhl-Auth, J., & Meinhardt, K. (1984). The prevelance of depressive symptoms among Mexican Americans and Anglos. *American Journal of Epidemiology, 120,* 592–607.

Wikan, U. (1988). Bereavement and loss in two Muslim communities: Egypt and Bali compared. *Social Science and Medicine, 27,* 451–456.

NERVES, WORRIATION, AND BLACK WOMEN: A COMMUNITY STUDY IN THE AMERICAN SOUTH

Linda A. Camino, PhD
International Counseling Center, Washington, D.C.

The experience of nerves among women in a low-income Black neighborhood was examined. Research conducted in the neighborhood revealed nerves as a formal classification of folk illness linked with life stress, yet in-depth interviews with a purposeful sample of 24 residents showed that a greater manifestation of nerves among women contributes to tendencies among family members to ignore the severity of its symptoms and to equate experiences of nerves with life conditions deemed inevitable for women. Lack of support for nerves among female sufferers was also evident among friends and physicians.

These findings are analyzed against a background of gender-specific concepts of nerves and "worriation" operating in the neighborhood. Residents aver that women's "naturally" weaker constitutions and a moral imperative to worry places them at greater risk for nerves. Implications for clinical care of low-income Black women with nerves are discussed, and specific recommendations for culturally appropriate interventions are outlined.

Anthropological investigations of popular, folk, and ethnomedical illness have tended recently to interpret the sufferer's experience as "idioms of distress" (Parsons, 1984). The major assumption of the approach is that illness means something besides immediate physical disorder, and communicates messages about distress in psychological, social, and cultural spheres. Thus, illness serves as a repository of condensed meanings that individuals can exploit in order to relay messages about their experiences and situations. Because of the culturally determined basis for such meanings, studies in this genre frequently demonstrate the miscommunication that results when a patient suffering from

For their helpful comments and suggestions, I am grateful to Loudell Snow, Edith L. B. Turner, Roy Wagner, Dona Davis, and Setha Low. Speical thanks go to the late Victor Turner for his early encouragement of this project, and to R. Shepherd Zeldin for help in completion of the final manuscript.

an ethnomedical syndrome seeks treatment and hence tries to convey the experience to a clinician who holds another culturally determined (biomedical) set of meanings for the complaint. The implication is that the meaning of ethnomedical complaints and syndromes is mutually comprehended by patients and their affiliates within community settings.

In this paper I challenge this underlying assumption about the communicative power of folk illness as idioms of distress. I do so through analysis of the syndrome *nerves* as it is experienced by low-income Black women. A review of the cross-cultural research on nerves reveals some noteworthy trends. First, nerves constitutes an illness syndrome that carries substantial symptomatology (Barlett & Low, 1980; Jenkins, 1988; Low, 1981, 1985; Nations, Camino, & Walker, 1988). Second, complaints of nerves serve as idioms of distress that communicate powerful messages about physiological, social, and emotional distress of its sufferers (Davis, 1984; Guarnaccia & Farias, 1988; Low, 1981; Nations et al., 1988). Third, the frequency of nerves is documented to be higher among women than men, no matter what the cultural group (see Low, 1985; Finkler, 1985). And fourth, it is noted that women are believed by laypersons and professionals alike to be at greater risk for nerves (Cayleff, 1988; Davis & Whittin, 1988; Maybry, 1964). This assemblage of findings would seem to indicate that nerves as a meaningful expression of distress by women would be acknowledged, accepted, and comprehended by family and friends, if not by clinicians.

It shall be shown in this article, however, that the greater manifestation of nerves among a group of Black women in the United States, in fact, contributes to tendencies to ignore the severity of its symptoms and thereby causes nerves to be recognized among women not so much as an illness, or even an idiom of distress, but as an inevitable condition of life. As shall be demonstrated, the symptoms of nerves tend to be accepted by relatives of the female sufferer as indicative of normal feminine behavior or physiological processes.

In addition, the information in this article serves to enrich the ethnography of nerves by offering a description of its occurrence among a group of Black Americans, a cultural group overlooked in analyses of nerves. Although nerves has been recognized as a common folk complaint in various studies of the ethnomedical system of Blacks (Hill, 1988; Hill & Mathews, 1981; Mathews, 1987; Snow, 1977), the literature reveals little attempt to investigate the semantics of the experience of nerves or the ramifications of the distress it indicates.

As such, the research provided here takes an exploratory rather than experimental approach and is organized into a research report format. First, the methodology is described, followed by a depiction of the community setting. Next, concepts of nerves and "worriation," and how these are perceived to vary according to gender by community residents are discussed. Subsequent sections relate the actual experiences of nerve sufferers and the recognition and support they receive from family, friends, and physicians. These findings are then discussed in light of sociocultural influences operating in the community as well as results from other studies. In the final sections clinical implications of low-income Black women presenting with nerves are reviewed and recommendations for appropriate health care interventions made.

Research Methods

The present research formed part of a larger ethnographic study of Prosperity Heights neighborhood (a pseudonym), concentrating on ethnomedical beliefs and practices and conducted over an 18-month period. Overall, the study relied on anthropologic methods of full-time residence in the community, participant observation of daily life, open-ended interviews (formal as well as informal), and the administration of standardized instruments. The specific investigation of nerves was based on a similar composite of methodologies and was initiated after a year's residence in the neighborhood. It took a year of consistent interactions with residents, in a variety of settings, before they were comfortable enough to discuss their own experiences with nerves.

Formal interviews were planned in advance and followed a modified version of a schedule developed by Kleinman, Eisenberg, and Good (1978) to elicit explanatory models of illness from anyone who complained of nerves. Interviews were either tape recorded (with the permission of the interviewee) and transcribed verbatim, or responses were hand recorded verbatim. These interviews lasted between 1 and 3 hr. Informal interviews were also conducted whenever and wherever possible, for example, in residents' homes and yards or on the job (e.g., accompanying several people in their custodial duties or in my car while on errands with residents). Notes were taken during these interviews, and again, verbatim responses were recorded whenever possible. When it was not possible to take notes directly, content summaries were written up as soon as possible. These data were reviewed and analyzed by frequency of response or statements as well as by content.

Research Setting

Prosperity Heights neighborhood, located in a large (40,000 inhabitants) Piedmont city in the American south, is home to approximately 140 adults, 85% of whom are Black. The neighborhood is a well-bounded enclave in the city and possesses a business district in addition to its residential area. Three Black churches are also located within its boundaries. Thus, activities in the neighborhood draw other Blacks from the surrounding environs and are not limited solely to the residential population.

The beginnings of Prosperity Heights are traced to settlements that sprang up on either side of a well-known Indian trail used to link the state's mountainous region with its tidewater area, and its Black heritage is traced from the Reconstruction era when significant numbers of Blacks moved into the area. Most of the present residential section was erected, though, at the turn of the century and was considered to constitute the most affluent area in which Blacks could dwell. From that time until the 1960s unskilled labor for men and domestic work for women represented the major forms of employment.

Economic shifts in the 1950s and federal spending for urban renewal in the 1960s effected several changes in the character of the neighborhood. Businesses declined, and an entire major Black business district located adjacent to Prosperity Heights was razed for urban renewal. Reverberations from these activities were felt in the neighborhood and resulted in the decline of businesses, physical deterioration of buildings, and changes in the residential structure during the last decade. The city received a grant to redevelop Prosperity Heights, but most of the new businesses foundered and community action associations were disbanded owing to increased frustration with business failures, antagonisms between well-established and newer rental residents, and growing apathy. Presently, the majority of residents are either employed in a variety of "blue" and "pink"-collar jobs or derive their income from social security benefits.

CONCEPTS OF NERVES AND WORRIATION

In a literal and anatomical sense, nerves are understood to constitute a part of human physiology that in conjunction with bones, muscle, and skin keep the body intact. They are likened to "strings" or "wires" that "hold you together," and it is believed that anatomical nerves can vary with the physical constitution of individuals. Thus, because women and children are thought to be of weaker physical substance than men, their nerves are defined as weaker and thinner. Because the bodies of women and children are "softer and spongier" than men's, it is held that their nerves do not provide as much support for their constitutions as do men's. Nerves are susceptible to damage when a force outside the body impinges upon them, causing them to become "broken," "frazzled," "torn," "shot," "wore out," or "wrung out."

Although the force can be a physical one, such as an extreme of temperature or climate exposure, nerves are more often damaged by social, psychological, and emotional stressors that usually work their deleterious effects consistently and insidiously. Consequently, although children may possess weak nerves, it is thought that their nerves remain for the most part uninjured simply because they have been exposed to stressors for a shorter time than adults. Exceptions do exist, however. Those children who are faced with an abundance of life stress (such as the case of one little girl whose parents both died of drug overdoses and who lived in a variety of foster homes) can have afflicted nerves, and sometimes parents can suffer from nerves so badly that they are believed to pass on enfeebled nerves to their offspring through biological inheritance.

Problems with nerves are inextricably linked with "worriation," and worriation is omnipresent in Prosperity Heights. In a neighborhood where most people are employed in low-paying, hourly wage jobs (such as fast-food cooking and construction, which are typically classified as high stress and low control) and experience changes in residence patterns that bear upon the breakup of extended families, it is not surprising that people worry about finances, on-the-job racism, and troubled family relations.

In the words of residents:

> If you don't got enough money, life be running you ragged trying to get it to pay this bill and that bill. Then tomorrow the next one comes to and back you are to finding the money to send it.

> Black people got life harder than Whites. There's more pressure on a job because the boss be looking all the time at you and the minute you make one little mistake, bang, you are out.

> All these changes [in the neighborhood] seem like they're affecting the family most, breaking them up 'cause people don't know what to do anymore.

The synergistic effects of these stressors cause residents to feel that Blacks are at higher risk than Whites for worriation. It is commonly held that Blacks have to work harder and longer and receive less pay for their jobs than do Whites. People believe that White city officials overlook their neighborhood for physical or economic improvements because of prejudice. The urban renewal effort is referred to as "urban removal" because of the relocation of nearby residents. One direct result of excessive worriation is a higher incidence of disease and illness. As one woman puts it,

> Worriation can cause you to become sick. Can take your mind. Some people worry theirselves down to nothing, and one way worriation is sure to come out is in sickness. Why do you think people say "he's *worried* hisself sick"?

The view that worriation can result in various illnesses is shared among other urban Black groups (Jackson, 1981; Jackson, Neighbors, & Gurin, 1986; Snow, 1973).

For all that worriation is a pervasive theme in Prosperity Heights, it assumes particular characterizations that are distinguished along gender lines. Concepts of gender roles follow traditional guidelines that are promulgated in the Bible or other religiously oriented texts. The institution of the family is highly respected, and the ideal of family life (no matter what the actual configuration is) posits the man as protector and provider for women and children; women are believed to take a more nurturing role, to be focused on the home and family.

Consequently, men's worriation clusters around (in descending priority) the issues of wages, on-the-job discrimination, material provision for children and/or wives, the emotional welfare of their families, and keeping extramarital romantic/sexual liaisons discreet. In contrast, a woman's primary role is that of mother. Women who remain childless are viewed as somewhat marginal and with a certain amount of sympathy. The role of wife is also considered important for women, and together the duties and responsibilities of mothers and wives constitute the defining edge of female experience. Thus, whether women are formally employed or not, and whether or not they face the attendant stresses of discrimination, low wages, and low-control jobs, the locus of women's worriation is family members, their care, and the upkeep of the household:

> Black man is the head of family but the woman, she's the worrying head. My mama, she worried about the least little thing that gone wrong with any of us. I raised up my own kids—spent my life doing it. All that worry's wrung out my nerves.

The feminist movement has had little impact on the division of labor in Prosperity Heights households. Women are still held responsible for the affective life of the family as well as for cooking meals and performing housework. These are the "natural" inclinations of women, just as the "natural" tendency for men is to be "in the streets."

A comparison between men's and women's issues for worriation thus yields not only a difference in structure, but also one associated with moral substance. The worriation priorities of men may or may not involve close personal attachments, yet the core of women's worriation always contains an explicitly affective element and one that is always supposed to be directed to family members.

Worriation works its effects primarily on anatomical nerves. Men predominantly agree that their thicker and stronger nerves serve to better protect them from impairment. Extending the biologic explanation to women, men also concur that women experience damaged nerves more frequently not only because they have weaker and thinner nerves, but also because of their gender-specific physiologies. That is, menstruation, pregnancy, and childbirth act to render women "weak-nerved":

> That's just women's nature, with women having kids and all. And monthlies. Wears out the nerves.

While women generally agree about their weaker constitution, they contend their higher frequency of nerves is *really* due to the fact that they have more worriation in their lives than do men:

> Men get by in life so easy, honey—they just don't seem to worry that much about life. They don't have to look after as many people. They just go about their life, always having some woman doing for them—cooking, cleaning, fussing about them.

> Women get it more because they got more in life. Men, anyways Black men, don't pay no mind to worries in life. They all got some woman to do the worrying for them.

The syndrome labeled *nerves* is one of the illnesses believed to result from excessive worriation. Jumpy and shaky feeling on the general inside of the body or in specific locations such as the stomach or heart or chest, trembling hands, frequent urination, "edginess," "fussiness," tight throat, "wobbly knees," headaches, gas on the stomach, blurred vision, seeing black dots in front of one's eyes, crying and "carrying on," obsessive talking, "wooziness on the brain," yelling, rashes, itching feet or hands, and hollering or screaming make up the symptomatology of nerves.

Although nerves is prevalent, people with nerves do not openly talk about their experiences, labeled as such. There are two related reasons for this. In Prosperity Heights, as in other Black communities, there exists a solid boundary between kin and fictive-kin (ingroup) and nonkin (outgroup) affiliations (Kochman, 1981; Stack, 1974). Individuals and kinbased groups, it is maintained, should possess an integrity, implying that any evidence of vulnerability invites an attack that weakens such integrity and sets the stage for illness. Too much knowledge about one's life by an outgroup member renders an individual susceptible to the deleterious effects of gossip. Carried to an extreme, gossip is believed to actually injure a victim's health. In fact, gossip is attributed as one of the primary causes of conjuration illness in which one's mind can be "captured" and controlled by another person. Gossip, like worriation, damages the nerves. Thus, a claim of "nerves" is tantamount to a proclamation that one is already weakened and is ripe for exploitation, or an announcement that one has been conjured. In the views of residents, therefore, only a very "stupid" or very "messed up" person would complain publicly of nerves.

Yet, people, especially women, *do* complain of nerves, albeit in guarded and masked ways. As we shall see, nerves is communicated to others who are "safe"—family members, ministers, God, and sometimes to clinicians. However, certain confidants of the female nerves sufferer do not accept the complaint of nerves as an illness or disorder, but instead attempt to conventionalize it into a part of the woman's regular experience.

Strategies used by patients to communicate the experience of nerves to outgroup members are to emphasize worriation, while never mentioning "nerves," or to amplify particular symptoms. The next sections report how nerves as an illness is experienced and how it is communicated.

THE EXPERIENCE OF NERVES VICTIMS

In-depth interviews were conducted with 24 persons who reported having a "bout" or spell of nerves. Nineteen of these were women; 5 were men. The highest education level was 12th grade; the lowest, 3rd grade. The women described themselves as housewives and/or reported occupations such as custodial housekeepers, restaurant cooks, store clerks, or cashiers. The men worked at construction or custodial jobs and one was on social security disability. All of the women had children; 16 were married. Two of the men were married with children; 3 were single and childless.

Woman and men reported the same general symptoms (as listed above); where their experiences of nerves diverged were in attribution, support, and treatment. Four of the men stated that they felt their nerves were caused by excessive drinking, and although they mentioned worriation as a contributing cause, only one man thought that his nerves were directly caused by his worriation about finances. Only this man sought social support; the remaining 4 did not. It is noteworthy that 3 of the men (and one of the women) later came to view their nerves as a major symptom of conjuration.

Women, on the other hand, primarily attributed their nerves to worriation resulting from family discord, often coupled with job stress.

They told of husbands who were unable to meet their responsibilities, of parents and husbands who needed some manner of care or attention (physical or emotional), and of children who were disobedient, had problems in school, or were disrespectful. Those who were employed outside the home related stories concerning the unreasonable demands of supervisors and the lack of cooperation among co-workers. A few the women held that they were "born for" nerves, indicating that they had either inherited a predisposition for nerves or experienced too much worry throughout their childhoods that had "worn down" their nerves. A few also thought that their nerves derived from their feminine physiology, but they saw neither inheritance nor physiology as sufficient causes; these were always discussed in tandem with family discord or job pressures.

The case of Mary B., age 27, is fairly characteristic of the quality of the experience and the texture of its difficulties. The onset of Mrs. B.'s nerves was, she believed, traceable to the time before her marriage, for that is the point at which all her responsibilities began. Prior to her marriage, Mary and her child had been living with her parents, which had proven to be a strain, because her mother was dying of cancer. Mrs. B. reported that her father "had desires" to help care for his wife but as the disease progressed, he had opted out of his responsibilities, claiming that Mary knew better how to handle the technical side of care, as well as how to respond to the mother's emotional demands. Mary had tried to enlist the help of her sister who lived across town, but was told not to expect much help because she had her own family to "do for." At this time, Mary was juggling continuous care for her mother, a job waiting on tables, and self-study to pass the high school equivalency examination.

At age 19, Mary met Joe, and they married and moved into a tiny rented house. Even after they moved, Mary's father declined major responsibility for his wife's care. Mary and her sister began arguing about their expected obligations toward their parents. Joe was laid off his job, and he and Mary argued about finances. At this point, Mary reported that she began to feel "shaky all over the inside" of her body. She had frequent headaches, her knees were "wobbly" so that it became difficult for her to stand or walk. She experienced "wooziness in the brain," which she elaborated as an inability to concentrate on her tasks at hand. She cried frequently at "any little old thing" and often experienced sudden nocturnal wakenings, feeling her chest pounding.

Mary B. and other women's attempts to relate their nerves to someone else were met with responses that tended to controvert, overlook, or minimize the experiences. The next sections elaborate and describe the quality of such responses.

Recognition and Support From Family and Friends

Support was determined in the interview protocol by asking whether the patients had talked about their nerves with anyone else; probes such as family members, preachers, pastors, ministers, friends, or healers were used to encourage responses. In addition, patients were asked "What did he or she tell you?" or "What did she or he do for you?" An attempt was also made to assess the extent to which parents said they had perceived sympathetic comment, encouragement to talk freely about themselves, or advice.

Only one man had sought support, and that was from his pastor. The man was told to "stay off alcohol" and was given various Bible passages to read. He was also told that ministers at the church (Baptist) would pray for him. In striking contrast, most of the women felt they had received little or no support from the relatives or ministers they had sought out. Although the comments and advice of affiliates did not completely deny the experiences of nerves, they did tend to controvert them into commentaries about the existential condition of women. Patients indicated that affiliates did see the described stressors, but saw no true cause for concern. There were three ways in which affiliates did this: They explained the symptoms as part of feminine physiology, they explained them as a natural part of life, or they explained them as part of the role of women. Some examples serve to illustrate these tendencies.

Nerves redefined as aspects of feminine physiological processes was common. One 23-year-old woman with an infant who complained of nerves so bad that she was sometimes afraid of losing control and throwing her baby on the floor was told by her mother: "You got baby blues. It'll pass." Another woman, age 36, with a recent history of amenorrhea ("not coming on") was told that it was her "messed up monthlies" that were causing her nerves and that it was "nothing to worry about" since a return to regular cycles would mean a return to normal nerves.

Nerves was also explained away by confidants as a natural part of the hardship of life. A 24-year-old woman with three children who reported dizziness, forgetfulness, and crying spells was told by her mother, "You young people nowadays expect life to be like a dream. When I was coming up we knew that life was tough. That's just the way life is. You can't have everything." Another woman, age 40, had excessive feelings of anger and worry about her 14-year-old daughter, who was often in trouble at school for absenteeism and fighting with other students, and consulted her pastor, who told her the girl had demons. As the pastor explained, demons were part of everyday life "just sitting there waiting to strike you and get you," and it was the mother's responsibility to help see that the girl found her way back to the "protection of the blood of Jesus Christ."

The third way in which nerves was minimized was to view it as part of the role prescribed for women. A 45-year-old housewife who related the stresses of having five children to care for, who "just think I'm there to wait on them," was told by her husband (who was on worker's disability), "Well, what do you expect? You are a mother with five kids. No one ever said having kids was easy." Another woman told of an alcoholic, abusive, and often-times absent husband—"He gets upset when any of the kids makes any noise. He drinks and when he gets upset he starts beating on anyone in his way. Then one day he gets dressed up so fine and he goes trotting off and that's it. I think he's running numbers. I worry he's going to jail. I wake up in the middle of the night and keep expecting to find people that's looking for him busted down the door." This woman was told by her sister and cousin, "that's the way men are and that's how women have to be doing for them. You either waiting *on* them or waiting *for* them."

Only one woman reported a sympathetic husband who would talk with her, try to calm her down, and had advised her to go see a doctor. A few women related that they talked to God about their nerves in prayer and knew that "he would be there" for them. Most of the women were inclined to conceal nerves from friends. Only one woman said she had attempted to talk about her nerves with a female friend. The reasons given for this reluctance were a sense of shame and an overwhelming need to protect themselves from the "talk" of others. "It just couldn't look right for me or for my family," explained one woman who experienced such bad nerve attacks that she would get into her car, close the door, and "scream and holler. I couldn't tell my friends the things I'm tell you. People get something on you and they make you pay for it. You say you got nerves and they act like you belong in State [a local inpatient mental health facility] or something."

Nearly three quarters of the woman, though, did in one sense attempt to communicate with other women who had children about general problems in worrying for them. However, they rarely mentioned the extent or severity of their physical or emotional symptoms, their fears of physically harming their children, or the labeling of the experience of "nerves." Consequently, discussions with other wives and/or mothers tended to be restricted to objective problems rather than subjective feelings. As one woman put it,

> Yeah, my girlfriends come over during the day and we watch the stories [soap operas] together and some brings their kids. They gets to running around and I say "Yeah that's the way kids is. Worry their elders

crazy," and they say "yeah." We just sort of talk like that, know what I'm saying?

Thus, it was the symptoms, as well as aggressive and angry feelings of the women, that they tried to conceal from friends, rather than their problems and worry as such. At the same time that women felt they received little support, or useful advice, for their nerves from family and preachers, nearly one-third were advised to seek medical assistance, most often by their husbands. Even so, this advice could be construed as unsupportive or as outright rejection. A few of the women who were told by their husbands to go to see a doctor related, "That's the easy thing to say 'Go and see the doctor. Don't bother me' " or "He just says that and goes right on looking at the TV," or "What he think, the doctor is God? Doctor isn't going to change none of this stuff around here."

Recognition and Support From Physicians

Although only about one-third of the women were advised to consult a physician for their nerves, 15, in fact, had visited a physician. Retrospective interviews with these patients were conducted to investigate how patients had actually presented to their doctors and whether or not the doctor recognized their nerves. The majority (10) of patients reported that they had presented with one of their symptoms, not with nerves directly. The general reason given for this trend was that nerves is an unsuitable complaint to present to a doctor (e.g., "Doctors do not understand nerves"; "My doctor don't have the time for me to explain it to him"; and "Doctors are only interested in physical symptoms so that's what I tell him").

Physicians presented with physical complaints, therefore, tended to recommend specific treatments; for example, one patient was told to take an antacid for her "jittery stomach," one was given a prescription cream for her rash, and one was given a series of laboratory tests for her headaches, blurred vision, and "falling out" spells (which the doctor may have construed as fainting; see Lefley, 1979, for an explanation of the difference). The 5 patients who did present with "nerves" reported that their physicians responded by either prescribing medication or by telling them not to worry and to try to find someone with whom they could talk. None of these methods was judged as adequate:

> I went up to primary and the doctor gave me some little yellow pills. They made me sleep all day. I didn't want to do anything, housework never got done. With nerves I don't want to do what I got to do but at least I'm awake and I know I'm alive.

> I told them up at the hospital about my nerves. They told me to let my problems out—to talk to other people. Onliest thing is there is no one to talk to.

> I told my doctors—doctor gave me pills all the time and said to stop worrying. He says that but he never tells me how.

These women spoke, moreover, of wanting to elaborate on their nerves during the office visit but feeling as if the doctor wanted to hasten the course of the interview to an end after only a few moments. Entering and leaving the room abruptly, speaking quickly and looking more at the chart than at the patient, and sending aides or nurses into the examination room to complete the consultation were also listed as evidence of physician disinterest.

DISCUSSION

The most striking finding of this study is the perceived lack of social support and validation of nerves among female sufferers, a phenomenon made all the more startling when considered against a background of a diverse and severe symptomatology, and the consequent seriousness of nerves experiences for the patients. This feature demands explanation especially in light of the evidence from previous sociocultural studies of nerves noting the culturally sanctioned right of the nerves sufferer to expect, if not outright claim, at least some attention, assistance, or comfort from their peers (Davis, 1984; Low, 1981; Nations et al., 1988). As we have seen in Prosperity Heights, however, women who complain of nerves to family members are likely to be met with response that seek to controvert nerves into aspects of normal feminine role behavior or physiological processes. Women fear labeling their experiences as nerves to persons outside of the family because they run the risk of rendering themselves and their families vulnerable to detrimental gossip. What does this mean for the communicative power of nerves as an idiom of distress in the community as well as in the clinic?

There are several forces at work in the community that contribute to the tendency to ignore, overlook, or even refute nerves among women. We have seen that the belief that women have a "normal imperative" to worry, joined with the expectation that women are naturally more emotional and prone to demonstrate it, as well as the belief that women are naturally of weaker constitution with thinner nerves and "spongier" bodies conspire to make the complaint of nerves appear unremarkable. In addition, the association of nerves with the more serious affliction of conjuration, an illness carrying substantial stigma, serves to restrict direct communication about nerves outside of families. Thus, Prosperity Heights contains a substantial sociocultural framework that reinforces lack of direct support for nerves among women. Granting the importance of the role that such beliefs and expectations play in the manifestation and interpretation of nerves, it cannot be concluded however that they entirely account for all of the dynamics at work that reinforce the lack of recognition and support for nerves as an idiom of distress.

It is likely that negotiation for the sick role (Mechanic, 1978) also influences nonsympathetic responses to women's nerves. Although no attempt was made to systematically interview those persons whom nerves patients listed as their confidants, a number of allusions were made in general discussions of illness about people who commonly try to feign illness or magnify symptoms in order to "get you to do for them," or in other words, to manipulate you into assuming their tasks and responsibilities. As was demonstrated by the case of Mary B., a female relative is usually the prime candidate to fulfill duties left by an ailing woman. Such expectations for women in other Black communities are noted by Jackson (1981), but also for women in general (Eichler & Parron, 1986) as well as those from lower socioeconomic status (Miele, Johnson, & St. Peter, 1976).

On the other hand, the husbands of nerves patients may have tended to overlook or minimize the complaints as a result of a slightly different factor associated with sick role behavior. Women with nerves in Prosperity Heights are able to perform their daily activities, albeit in much diminished ways. Because men in Prosperity Heights are socialized to be less involved with the emotional lives of other people, it is possible that they saw no cause for concern as long as a basic level of household functioning was maintained. The work of several researchers (Alexander, 1982; Angrist, Lefton, Dinitz, & Pasamanick, 1968; Apple, 1960) attests that disruption of daily activities or inability to perform tasks represents a major criterion whereby illness is defined and recognized.

The third major feature acting to reduce the probability that nerves constitutes cause for serious concern lies in the nature of the symptomatology. A review of nerves symptoms demonstrates a composite of signs that are readily apparent to an observer (e.g., crying, obsessive talking, hollering, screaming, and trembling hands), those that are directly manifested to patients themselves (e.g., jumpy and shaky feelings in the stomach, heart, or chest; tight throat; and "wooziness in the brain"), and those that might be apparent to a keen observer but more likely missed altogether (e.g., frequent urination, rashes, "fussiness," and "edginess").

People in Prosperity Heights consider that crying, talkativeness, edginess, and fussiness are part of women's greater arsenal of emotional expression; hence, these symptoms themselves may be perceived as manifestations of normal feminine behavior and consequently they warrant no extra attention. Some symptoms, such as trembling hands and obsessive talking, are associated with the effects of alcohol; others, such as frequent urination, rashes, and sensations in the stomach, heart, chest, and throat, can be construed as symptomatic of other ailments. Hence, people may only typically perceive some of the signs of nerves in a patient, and they may misassociate them with other conditions. There is, therefore, great potential for nerves communicated through symptomatic idioms to remain undetected or misinterpreted.

Implications for Health Care

Most of the women who consulted a physician for nerves felt that they needed to present with one or more symptoms having a somatic valence. Prosperity Heights women are given to understand that physical complaints equal legitimate complaints in clinical settings. Unfortunately, the socialization of physicians and other clinicians continues to emphasize somatic distress and diagnostic workups while minimizing detection of psychological and emotional problems associated with vague somatic complaints (Lazarus, 1985; Walker, Novack, Brynes, & Keiser, 1982). Emotional distress, even if detected, is still regarded, for the most part, as not meriting special attention (Johnson, 1985; Lipowski, 1986).

In addition, prejudice surrounding the presentation of ambiguous complaints by low-income Black patients lingers, in that patients with ambiguous illnesses such as nerves are often considered to be attempting to garner secondary gain out of clinical visit (Satcher, 1973). The phenomenon is not limited to Blacks, but also extends to other minority or low-income groups (Luborski & Penick, 1973; Mannon, 1976). On their part, Prosperity Heights women agree that doctors do not really comprehend nerves or do not have enough time to listen to their experiences. These sentiments have been echoed in other specific studies of nerves (Davis, 1984; Nations at al., 1988) and in studies of treatment seeking among Blacks (see Jackson, 1981, for a review).

Given that there is a large body of literature depicting the strength of ties with family and friends in Black communities (e.g., Gwaltney, 1980; Martineau, 1977; Myers, 1982; Stack, 1974), clinical personnel may simply assume that all Black patients have access to a wide support network for their problems and, by extension, that the inability of a Black patient to access formal health resources may not constitute a dire situation. Jackson et al. (1986) challenged this assumption in a national study of help seeking among Blacks for psychologic problems and found that emotional problems were less frequently taken to affiliates than were interpersonal problems, the effects of tragedy, or economic problems. Data from Prosperity Heights also demonstrate this assumption to be erroneous when applied to women with nerves; the women did not even find active support from their ministers. Their problems are obviously made more serious if they can find social support neither in their communities nor among their physicians.

In light of these facts, the persistence the women demonstrated in pursuing assistance for their nerves is remarkable. It is evident that they feel their experiences with nerves to be significant and meaningful. It is also evident that patients feel their physicians do not listen to them, do not have time for them, or do not give adequate treatment for nerves. It is likely that these feeling underlie patients' tendencies to present their nerves in somatic guise.

Against this in-depth investigation of women and nerves in a low-income Black community, four major recommendations emerge for health care interventions and planning. Essentially, clinicians need to possess an awareness that low-income Black women tend to communicate indirectly about their nerves by focusing on particular symptoms, which themselves are of an ambiguous nature. It should be kept in mind, moreover, that nonassertiveness in the clinical interview by some Blacks in considered respectful or a means by which to assess a physician's competence to "read" illness (Jackson, 1981). In addition, the very nature of emotional distress itself tends to contribute to lack of confidence and assertiveness so that a patient may not contribute forcefully to the interview.

These awarenesses concerning the response patterns of low-income Black women toward physicians lead to a second recommendation—specifically, that it is advisable for the practitioner to take an active role during the interview. Especially when presented with any of the symptoms listed above, clinicians should initiate direct questions such as "Do you suffer from nerves?" and "Could it be your nerves acting up?". Such questions may minimize the possibility for misdiagnosis, extraneous laboratory workups, unnecessary medication prescriptions, and non-compliance, not to mention frustration in themselves and their patients. Once such questions have been asked, clinicians would do well to listen empathetically to the experiences a woman with nerves may have to relate. Studies demonstrate that Black patients simply want their practitioners to actively listen and to talk to them (Davis, 1966; Jackson et al., 1986; Krug, 1974), as do most other patients (Good & Good, 1982).

A third recommendation is that although health care professionals may or may not choose to prescribe medications, it is important that supportive therapy be offered as an integral part of the overall treatment. The authors of one classic study have noted, for example, that while medication can quickly improve mood for affective disorders, social readjustment of patients lagged far behind (Weissman & Paykel, 1974). Other studies demonstrate that social support for women acts to significantly buffer the deleterious effects of stressful life events (Brown & Harris, 1978; Kessler & McLeod, 1985). Social readjustment for nerves victims is particularly difficult given the responses and lack of support offered by affiliates; a professional could aim to support a victim in her struggle. Further, social dynamics strongly suggest that the supportive therapy reflect an individual rather than group-centered approach, given that low-income Black women are highly sensitive to self-disclosure outside of their families.

Finally, it is suggested that the clinician ensure that he or she distinguish women's vulnerability to stress by virtue of their social status and role expectations (Kessler & McLeod, 1985) from inclinations to view emotional distress as following "naturally" from women's tendencies toward greater emotional expression. As we have seen in Prosperity Heights, certain lay theories postulate women's "natural" moodiness and greater "emotional expression" as responsible for their nerves, and they ultimately serve to diminish opportunities for successful treatment since they mask recognition of serious distress. The work of Briscoe (1978) and Broverman, Broverman, Clark, Rosenkrantz, and Vogal (1970), as well as a recent report on diagnosis of women with mental disorders (Public Health Service, 1985) reminds us, however, that such "naive theories" may also be present in the medical community.

SUMMARY

Nerves among women in Prosperity Heights, as in other cultural settings, signifies substantial physiological, interpersonal, and emotional distress. But it also tells of a quality of distress that is particular to low-income Black women in the American South. As an idiom, it speaks of women's status in a variety of ways. Through its link with beliefs about the "naturally" weaker state of women's anatomical nerves; through its association with worriation, telling about women's role expectations for primary involvement with husbands, children, and other relatives; and through women's lack of support for complaining of nerves, an episode of the illness is equated with conditions deemed inevitable for women. Perhaps most of all, then, the data reported here raise a fundamentally ironic question: Who listens to and understands nerves as an idiom of distress?

REFERENCES

Alexander, L. (1982). Illness maintenance and the new American sick role. In N. J. Chrisman & T. W. Maretzki (Eds.), *Clinically applied anthropology* (pp. 351–368). Boston: Reidel.

Angrist, S., Lefton, M., Dinitz, S., & Pasamanick, B. (1968). *Women after treatment: A study of former mental patients and their normal neighbors.* New York: Appleton-Century-Crofts.

Apple, D. (1960). How laymen define illness. *Journal of Health and Human Behavior, 1*, 219–225.

Barlett, P. F., & Low, S. M. (1980). Nervios in rural Costa Rica. *Medical Anthropology: Cross-Cultural Studies in Health and Illness Quarterly, 4,* 523–559.

Briscoe, M. E. (1978). Sex differences in perception of illness and expressed life satisfaction. *Psychological Medicine, 8,* 339–345.

Broverman, I., Broverman, D., Clarkson, F., Rosenkrantz, P., & Vogal, S. (1970). Sex role stereotypes and clinical judgments of mental health. *Journal of Counseling and Clinical Psychology, 34,* 1–7.

Brown, G. W., & Harris, T. (1978). *The social origins of depression.* New York: Free Press.

Cayleff, S. E. (1988). Prisoners of their own feebleness: Women, nerves and Western medicine. *Social Science and Medicine, 26,* 1199–1208.

Davis, D. L. (1984). Medical misinformation: Communication between outport Newfoundland women and their physicians. *Social Science and Medicine, 18,* 273–278.

Davis, D. L., & Whitten, R. G. (1988). Medical and popular traditions of nerves. *Social Science and Medicine, 26,* 1209–1221.

Davis, M. S. (1966). Variations in patients' compliance with doctors' orders: Analysis of congruence between survey responses and results of empirical investigations. *Journal of Medical Education, 41,* 1037–1048.

Eichler, A., & Parron, D. L. (1986). *Women's mental health: Agenda for research.* Rockville, MD: National Institute of Mental Health, Public Health Service.

Finkler, K. J. (1985). *Spiritualist healers in Mexico: Successes and failures of alternative therapeutics.* South Hadley, MA: Bergin and Garvey.

Good, M. J.., & Good, B. (1982). Patients requests in primary care clinics. In N. J. Chrisman & T. W. Maretzki (Eds.), *Clinically applied anthropology* (pp. 275–296). Boston: Reidel.

Guarnaccia, P. J., & Farias, P., (1988). The social meaning of nervios: A case study of a central American woman. *Social Science and Medicine, 26,* 1223–1231.

Gwaltney, J. L. (1980). *Drylongso: A self-portrait of Black Americans.* New York: Vintage Books.

Hill, C. E. (1988). *Community and health systems in the rural American South.* Boulder, CO: Westview Press.

Hill, C. E., & Mathews, H. (1981). Traditional health beliefs and practices among southern rural Blacks: A complement to biomedicine. In M. Black & J. Shelton (Eds.), *Social Science Perspectives in the South* (pp. 307–322). New York: Gordon and Breach.

Jackson, J. J. (1981). Urban Black Americans. In A. Harwood (Ed.), *Ethnicity and medical care* (pp. 37–129). Cambridge: Harvard University Press.

Jackson, J. S., Neighbors, H. W., & Gurin, G. (1986). Findings from a national survey of Black mental health: Implications for practice in minority communities. In M. R. Miranda & H. H. L. Kitano (Eds.), *Mental health research and practice in minority communities* (pp. 91–116). Rockville, MD: National Institute of Mental Health, Public Health Service.

Jenkins, J. H. (1988). Conceptions of schizophrenia as a problem of nerves: A cross-cultural comparison of Mexican-Americans and Anglo-Americans. *Social Science and Medicine, 26,* 1223–1243.

Johnson, T. M. (1985). Consultation–liaison psychiatry: Medicine as patient, marginality as practice. In R. A. Hahn & A. D. Gaines (Eds.), *Physicians of Western medicine* (pp. 269–292). Boston: Reidel.

Kessler, R. C., & McLeod, J. D. (1985). Social support and mental health in community samples. In S. Cohen & S. L. Syme (Eds.), *Social support and health* (pp. 219–240). Orland, FL: Academic Press.

Kleinman, A. M., Eisenberg, L., & Good, B. (1978). Culture, illness, and care: Clinical lessons from anthropological and cross cultural research. *Annals of Internal Medicine, 88,* 257–288.

Kochman, T. (1981). *Black and White styles in conflict.* Chicago: University of Chicago Press.

Krug, E. F. (1974). Folk medical beliefs. *Annals of Internal Medicine, 81,* 705–706.

Lazarus, R. S. (1985). The trivialization of distress. In J. C. Rosen & L. J. Solomon (Eds.), *Prevention in health psychology* (pp. 279–298). Hanover: University Press of New England.

Lefley, H. P. (1979). Prevalence of potential falling-out cases among the Black, Latin, and non-Latin White populations of the city of Miami. *Social Science and Medicine, 13,* 113–114.

Lipowski, Z. J. (1986). Consultation-liaison psychiatry in the first half century. *General Hospital Psychiatry, 8,* 305–315.

Low, S. M. (1981), The meaning of nervios: A sociocultural analysis of symptom presentation in San Jose, Costa Rica. *Culture, Medicine, and Psychiatry, 5,* 25–47.

Low, S. M. (1985). Culturally interpreted symptoms of culture-bound syndromes: A cross-cultural review of nerves. *Social Science and Medicine, 21,* 187–196.

Luborski, I. J., & Penick, S. (1973). Onset conditions for psychosomatic symptoms. *Psychosomatic Medicine, 35,* 187–204.

Mannon, J. (1976). Defining and treating 'problem patients' in a hospital emergency room. *Medical Care, 14,* 1004–1013.

Martineau, W. (1977). Informal social ties among urban Black Americans. *Journal of Black Studies, 8,* 83–104.

Mathews, H. F. (1987). Rootwork: Description of an ethnomedical system in the American South. *Southern Medical Journal, 80,* 885–891.

Maybry, J. H. (1964). Lay concepts of etiology. *Journal of Chronic Diseases, 17,* 371–386.

Mechanic, D. (1978). *Medical sociology.* New York: Free Press.

Miele, R. L., Johnson, D. R., & St. Peter, L. (1976). Marital role, education, and mental disorder among women: Test of an interaction hypothesis. *Journal of Health Social Behavior, 17,* 295–301.

Myers, J. F. (1982). Stress, ethnicity and social class: A model for research with Black populations. In E. Jones & S. Korchin (Eds.), *Minority mental health* (pp. 15–45). New York: Holt, Rinehart, & Winston.

Nations, M. K., Camino, L. A., & Walker, F. B. (1988). "Nerves": Folk idiom for anxiety and depression? *Social Science and Medicine, 26,* 1245–1259.

Parsons, C. D. F. (1984). Idioms of distress. *Culture, Medicine, and Psychiatry, 8,* 71–93.

Public Health Service. (1985). *Women's health: Vol. 2. Report of the Public Health Service Task Force on Women's Health Issues* (DHHS Pub. No. [PHS] 85-50206). Washington, DC: U.S. Department of Health and Human Services.

Satcher, D. (1973). Does race interfere with the doctor-patient relationship? *Journal of the American Medical Association, 223,* 1498–1499.

Snow, L. F. (1973). I was born exactly with the gift: An interview with a voodoo practitioner. *Journal of American Folklore, 86,* 272–280.

Snow, L. F. (1977). Popular medicine in a Black neighborhood. In E. H. Spicer (Ed.), *Ethnic medicine in the Southwest* (pp. 19–95). Tucson: University of Arizona Press.

Stack, C. B. (1974). *All our kin: Strategies for survival in a Black community.* New York: Harper and Row.

Walker, F. B., Novack, D. H., Brynes, G., & Keiser, D. L. (1982). Recognition of anxiety and depression by residents in a general medical clinic. *Journal of Medical Education, 57,* 195–197.

Weissman, M. M., & Paykel, E. S. (1974). *The depressed woman: A study of social relationships.* Chicago: University of Chicago Press.

INDEX